THE HIDDEN DANGERS OF THE RAINBOW
THE NEW AGE MOVEMENT AND
OUR COMING AGE OF BARBARISM

The Hidden Dangers
of the Rainbow

*The New Age Movement and
Our Coming Age of Barbarism*

Constance E. Cumbey

HUNTINGTON HOUSE, INC.
P.O. BOX 53788
LAFAYETTE, LA 70505
(318) 237-7049

Revised edition.

ISBN Number 0-910311-03-X
Library of Congress Catalog Card 83-080044

Excerpts from *The Aquarian Conspiracy: Personal and Social Transformation in the 1980's,* copyright © 1980 by Marilyn Ferguson, published by J.P. Tarcher, Inc. (To order direct from publisher send $15 plus $1.25 postage and handling to 9110 Sunset Boulevard, Los Angeles, California 90069.) Used by permission.

A series of cassette tapes with Constance Cumbey entitled *The Hidden Dangers of the Rainbow: The New Age Movement* is available from Huntington House, Inc.

Front cover design by Jan Hendricks of East/West Video Productions, Inc. Video tapes of Constance Cumbey discussing the New Age Movement are available by writing Video Bible Library, Inc., P.O. Box 17515, Portland, Oregon 97217. The video tapes are also entitled *The Hidden Dangers of the Rainbow.*

The front cover graphically depicts various symbols of the New Age Movement.

THE RAINBOW

Although the rainbow seems to be only a colored arc of light refracted through raindrops, to both Christians and New Agers it has a deep meaning.

According to the Bible, the rainbow is symbolic of God's everlasting covenant that he would never again destroy the earth by a flood.

However, the New Age Movement uses rainbows to signify their building of the Rainbow Bridge (antahkarana) between man and Lucifer who, they say, is the over-soul.

New Agers place small rainbow decals on their automobiles and book stores as a signal to others in the Movement. Some people, of course, use the rainbow as a decoration, unaware of the growing popular acceptance of its occult meaning and the hidden dangers.

"It is the contention of this writer that for the first time in history there is a viable movement — the New Age Movement — that truly meets all the scriptural requirements for the antichrist and the political movement that will bring him on the world scene.

"It is further the position of the writer that this most likely is the great apostasy or 'falling away' spoken of by the Apostle Paul and that the antichrist's appearance could be a very real event in our immediate future."

— Constance E. Cumbey

"And after these things I saw another angel come down from heaven, having great power; and the earth was lightened with his glory.

"And he cried mightily with a strong voice, saying, Babylon the great is fallen, is fallen, and is become the habitation of devils, and the hold of every foul spirit, and a cage of every unclean and hateful bird.

"For all nations have drunk of the wine of the wrath of her fornication, and the kings of the earth have committed fornication with her, and the merchants of the earth are waxed rich through the abundance of her delicacies.

"And I heard another voice from heaven, saying, Come out of her, my people, that ye be not partakers of her sins, and that ye receive not of her plagues.

"For her sins have reached unto heaven, and God hath remembered her iniquities" (Revelation 18:1-5, KJV).

Contents

Preface

Millions around the globe awoke to a great surprise on April 25, 1982. They opened their newspapers only to be greeted with full-page display ads brazenly proclaiming, "THE CHRIST IS NOW HERE."

From Rome to Jerusalem, from Kuwait to Karachi and from New York to Los Angeles — in more than 20 major cities — newspaper readers blinked in shocked disbelief as they tried to digest this particular piece of "news" along with their breakfast.

The $500,000-plus ad campaign featured the following copy:

THE WORLD HAS HAD ENOUGH . . .
OF HUNGER, INJUSTICE, WAR.

IN ANSWER TO OUR CALL FOR HELP,
AS WORLD TEACHER FOR ALL HUMANITY,

THE CHRIST IS NOW HERE.

HOW WILL WE RECOGNIZE HIM?

Look for a modern man concerned with modern problems — political, economic, and social. Since July, 1977, the Christ has been emerging as a spokesman for a group or community in a well-known modern country. He is not a religious leader, but an educator in the broadest sense of the word — pointing the way out of our present crisis. We will recognize Him by His extraordinary spiritual potency, the universality of His viewpoint, and His love for all humanity. He comes not to judge but to aid and inspire.

WHO IS THE CHRIST?

Throughout history, humanity's evolution has been guided by a group of enlightened men, the Masters of Wisdom. They have remained largely in the remote desert and mountain places of earth, working mainly through their disciples who live openly in the world. This message of the Christ's reappearance has been given primarily by such a disciple trained for his task for over 20 years. At the center of this "Spiritual Hierarchy" stands the World Teacher, LORD MAITREYA, known by Christians as the CHRIST. And as Christians await the Second Coming, so the Jews await the MESSIAH, the Buddhists the FIFTH BUDDHA, the Moslems the IMAM MAHDI, and the Hindus await KRISHNA. These are all names for one individual. His presence in the world guarantees there will be no third World War.

WHAT IS HE SAYING?

"My task will be to show you how to live together peacefully as brothers. This is simpler than you imagine, My friends, for it requires only the acceptance of sharing.

"How can you be content with the modes within which you now live: when millions starve and die in squalor; when the rich parade their wealth before the poor; when each man is his neighbor's enemy; when no man trusts his brother?

"Allow me to show you the way forward into a simpler life where no man lacks; where no two days are alike; where the Joy of Brotherhood manifests through all men.

"Take your brother's need as the measure for your action and solve the problems of the world."

WHEN WILL WE SEE HIM?

He has not as yet declared His true status, and His location is known to only a very few disciples. One of these has announced that soon the Christ will acknowledge His identity and within the next two months will speak to humanity through a worldwide television and radio broadcast. His message will be heard inwardly, telepathically, by all people in their own language. From that time, with His help, we will build a new world.

WITHOUT SHARING THERE CAN BE NO JUSTICE;
WITHOUT JUSTICE THERE CAN BE NO PEACE;
WITHOUT PEACE THERE CAN BE NO FUTURE.

The ads went on to list four information centers strategically scattered about the globe: Amsterdam, London, New York City and North Hollywood, California.

For myself, unfortunately, these ads came as no surprise. In fact they and the vast network of organizations behind them — known collectively as the New Age Movement — had been the source of a near obsession with me for all of the previous year. They should have come as little surprise to most of the Christian community either — had the all-too-numerous clues been observed.

The Age of Aquarius was at last arriving and it meant nothing pretty as far as the Judeo/Christian world was concerned. And that world well needed to be concerned. For sadly, apathy was the order of the day — an apathy that if not soon shaken would result in the New Agers' long-awaited "New World Order."

Hiding behind an aura of undeserved respectability, the New Age Movement has managed to actively recruit many unsuspecting Jews and Christians to work for their own destruction.

"THE CHRIST IS NOW HERE" ad campaign was preceded by an incredibly sophisticated public relations cam-

paign including a worldwide speaking tour by one Benjamin
Creme — an aging English esotericist who happened to be a
disciple of several occult pioneers including Helena Petrovna
Blavatsky and Alice A. Bailey. Touring the globe since 1975,
Creme had managed to win the support of influentials rang-
ing from U.N. officials through Methodist Ministers; from
Belgian nuns through Elizabeth Kubler-Ross; from the
Hunger Project through holistic health leaders; and from
mind-control trainers and trainees through astrologers.
Clearly he was not out there on his own. The man's audacity
was justified by his broad base of support.

Creme's front organization was the Tara Center — based
in New York, Los Angeles, Amsterdam and London. Spin-off
"transmission groups" were left behind in every city where
Creme lectured. Even if Tara Center had been the only
organization backing the so-called Christ, it might have been
a legitimate source of concern. But Tara was not the only
such organization. Also involved were religious leaders, including many Unity and Unitarian leaders, educators,
cooperating New Age networking groups who turn their
members out to submit themselves to Creme's bizarre hypnotic powers, occultists of every shade and description,
political activists, opportunists, and those who had a sincere
and genuine concern for the world's poor and labored under
the mistaken impression that they were lending their support
to a remedy for the world's numerous wrongs. They were unsuspecting that they were supporting a movement that
parallels Nazism in every grotesque detail, including a
teaching that a "blood taint" rested on those of Jewish extraction and another being that of a planned new "super-race."

Many did not know that this movement planned the
eventual extermination and replacement of these very peoples they labored to help with a "new root race" and even the
violent extermination of themselves should they persist in orthodox religious beliefs. And many, for certain, did not
know that they were actively involved in the very same
movement that was proud to claim Jim Jones as its own prior

to his Guyana murder/suicide fiasco.

And you may further be certain that many of these sincere but deluded people did not know that they were actively participating in a movement which gives Lucifer the status of a divinity and plans mass planetary Luciferic "initiations" for those wishing to enter this "New Age" alive.

Yet despite the naivete in a movement which traffics in ignorance and despair they *were* involved. They are often sucked in by good intentions and held in by sophisticated forms of mass hypnosis and mind control. Those participating in Creme's lecture audiences as well as thousands upon thousands of New Age activities designed to program participants to unquestioningly accept this new "Christ," were unwitting and unsuspecting victims in the largest, best financed con job this world has ever seen.

I did not discover the New Age Movement after learning of Tara Center and Benjamin Creme. Rather I discovered Creme while in the midst of an extensive researching of the intricate but huge New Age Movement — a movement that includes many thousands of organizations networking throughout every corner of our globe with the intent of bringing about a New World Order — an order that writes God out of the picture and deifies Lucifer. I am also not talking about what I found reading between the lines — although some of that should desirably be done, as well. I am talking about what the leaders of this movement have set forth in cold print.

The danger to both Jews and Christians should not be underestimated. Benjamin Creme's announcement of "Maitreya the Christ" is the culmination of over 100 years of meticulous planning and labor by those seeking this "Age of Aquarius." They have garnered the support of some of the most powerful and influential individuals in the world. It is a fact that they will not and cannot be successful until God is ready for prophetic fulfillment. However, if God is ready, are you?

This book sets forth a small portion of my research find-

ings. What will be difficult to fully convey is the sense of
mounting horror I found while piecing this multitude of data
together. It appears to culminate in a scheme both fulfilling
the prophetic requirements for the antichrist as set forth in
the Bible, and also matching Nazism down to use of swastikas. Frightening the material is. However, what should be
kept in mind by the believer is the much more potent power
generously bestowed upon us by our Lord — the latter rains
which were to be even more abundant than the former.

As Isaiah said, looking towards our own latter days:

> "The wilderness and the solitary place shall be glad for
> them; and the desert shall rejoice, and blossom as the rose.

> "It shall blossom abundantly, and rejoice even with joy
> and singing: the glory of Lebanon shall be given unto it,
> the excellency of Carmel and Sharon, they shall see the
> glory of the Lord, and the excellency of our God.

> *"Strengthen ye the weak hands, and confirm the feeble
> knees.*

> "Say to them that are of a fearful heart, Be strong, fear
> not: behold, your God will come with vengeance, even
> God with a recompence; he will come and save you"
> (Isaiah 35:1-4, KJV).

The purpose of this book is to inform the unsuspecting of
the events that may lie immediately ahead and of the persons
and organizations helping to manipulate them. More importantly, it is about "strengthening the weak hands and
confirming the feeble knees," with the help of God, so that
we "might be counted worthy" to stand the things that must
come upon the earth if all is to be fulfilled as written.

CHAPTER 1

Maitreya: The New Age Messiah

Who is Lord Maitreya? Is he the antichrist? Is he already in the world today? Is he an ordinary man who is demonically possessed?

Only the insiders of the New Age Movement hierarchy know his true identity.

Maitreya is living somewhere. He eats. He sleeps. He paces the floor. He studies world conditions. He knows his time is soon.

What do we know about Maitreya?

The full-page newspaper ads give us some clues. According to Tara Center, sponsor of the ads:

• He is a world teacher for all humanity.

• He is a modern man concerned with modern problems — political, economic and social.

• Since July of 1977 he has been emerging as a spokesman for a group or community in a well-known modern country.

• He has extraordinary spiritual power.

• His location is known only to a very few of his disciples.

• He will soon announce his identity.

• He will communicate to all humanity through a worldwide radio and television broadcast.

• He plans to build a new world.

Exactly what does the name "Maitreya" mean?

Maitreya is supposed to be the fifth reincarnation of Buddha. The world's Buddhists are already expecting Lord Maitreya to return to earth. So, the name was a very shrewd choice.

In order to appeal to Christians, New Agers say Maitreya is the Christ. For Moslems he is the Iman Mahdi. For Hindus he is Krishna.

Maitreya's followers are now in the last stage of the New Age scheme to take the world for Lucifer.

Lucis Trust — formerly Lucifer Trust — ran ads in the *Reader's Digest*, which displayed The Great Invocation to Maitreya.

The Great Invocation refers to The Plan. It says, "Let Light and Love and Power restore The Plan on Earth."

What is The Plan?

It includes the installation of a New World "Messiah," the implementation of a new world government and new world religion under Maitreya.

They have numerous political, social and economic goals, including the following:

• A universal credit card system.
• A world food authority which would control the world's food supply.
• A universal tax.
• A universal draft.

But there is more to The Plan — they intend to utterly root out people who believe the Bible and worship God and to completely stamp out Christianity.

They have stated that they plan to outlaw all present religious practices and symbols of orthodox Jews and Christians. The Movement is working quickly and efficiently to execute its scheme to take control of the world for Maitreya.

New Agers have threatened violence and even extermination of Jews, Christians and Moslems who fail to cooperate with Maitreya and his new religion.

The Tara Centers are part of international networks involving tens of thousands of different organizations behind the New Age Movement and its false Christ. Creme describes it as being worldwide.

During an interview with Jack Kisling of the *Denver Post*, Creme discussed Maitreya. Kisling gives this account:

"Benjamin Creme . . . told me . . . that not only has The

Christ been back on earth since July of 1977, but that some-
time in the next eight or nine weeks he will reveal himself in a
worldwide 'day of declaration,' at which time the millennium
will have dawned. . . . He explained that by The Christ he
means not Jesus Christ, but the Master of Wisdom of whom
Jesus and such other spiritual leaders as Mohammed, Brahma
and Krishna are disciples. . . . Asked what will happen after
the great galvanic day, Creme said progress will be slow but
steady. World needs and world resources will be reassessed
and redistributed and the groundwork for a single global
religion will be started and probably flower fully within 20
years.

" 'Won't the advent of a single world religion annoy the
hierarchies of all the current orthodox religions?' I asked.

" 'More than that,' he said with a smile. 'They will be
shocked. I daresay they will be among the last to accept the
Christ.' "

But, according to Kisling, Creme said confidently, "It will
come, anyway, because it must. We will begin to live,' he
said . . . 'as potential gods.' "

The Club of Rome is another very prominent New Age
organization. It has drawn up the blueprints for a new world
order.

How could this ever happen? What conditions must
emerge to pave the way for a world takeover by the antichrist, or Lord Maitreya or anyone else?

Interestingly enough, in *The Aquarian Conspiracy*,
Marilyn Ferguson comes flat out and makes an admission
that the purpose of the LSD circulation in this country was to
get people open, to get their channels open so they would
have what she called a "religious experience." But this is
nothing more than possession.

Another New Age leader is David Spangler who is right at
the top of Planetary Citizens which is the Secretariat for
Planetary Initiative.

Spangler says that in order to enter the New Age we must

take a Luciferic initiation. He says we're heading into a vast planetary initiation, a mass initiation of people.

They intend to give us our mark or number in that Luciferic initiation ceremony.

No wonder God told us if we take the mark, we go to hell — no "ifs," "ands," or "buts" about it. It is literally a choice between God and Lucifer.

You will have to pledge loyalty to Lucifer or Maitreya to get a permit to do business in the New Age.

We also note another distinguishing characteristic of the New Age Movement — the 666.

Within the Movement there is extensive usage of the numerals 666. I have noticed the 666 in various books by David Spangler. One example is a little booklet called *Love Is* by The New Troubadours and published by the Findhorn Foundation. There are numerous triple six formations worked into the pictures in the book.

New Agers consider the 666 a sacred number.

Those who so freely use the numbers 666 honestly believe they are sending signals to outer space, or to what they call the superior intelligences which they believe inhabit our planet. They are asking those superior intelligences to come in and bring a new advanced civilization.

They believe that the more times and the more places that the numerals 666 are used the quicker that new civilization will come.

The Bible teaches that Satan will try to deceive the very elect of God.

When Maitreya goes public yet another imposter will come forward saying, "I am the Master Jesus."

This Master Jesus will say: "Now all you Christians and all you church members, you come forward and worship Lord Maitreya."

Actually, the New Age Movement correlates many of its aims with Bible prophecy. A letter from an organization called "Mission of Maitreya" from Albuquerque, New Mexico, contains the following statement:

"The word Maitreya has always been associated with messiah, who will come to unify the world and synthesize all religions under one banner. This expectation is now fulfilled. Known to Christians and Jews as the Messiah, Buddhists and Hindus as Maitreya and Moslems as Mahdi or Mohammed. Maitreya is called by all these names. The names Maitreya, Messiah and Mohammed are given to him; he did not call himself by these names, so besides other prophecies, the prophecy that 'many shall come in my name' would be fulfilled."

They say that all the prophecies Jesus made concerning those that would come in his name are now fulfilled. Jesus said, "For many shall come in my name, saying, I am Christ; and shall deceive many" (Matthew 24:5).

Although the full-page newspaper ads said Maitreya would soon appear, he has not done so yet.

This worries me. For it could cause many Christians to develop a false sense of confidence over the fact that he has not yet appeared.

The average false Christ — and there have been many — is not bashful. He comes out, collects his followers, his accolades, and especially the money. Then, he lives like a king.

The real antichrist cannot appear until the Lord permits it. And I believe the Lord will not let it happen until his people are fully warned.

Everyone will know when Jesus comes to earth again. It will be as clear as a flash of lightning in the sky.

I believe the New Agers will attempt to give the impression to Christians that the emergence of Maitreya is actually the return of Christ.

Revelation 13:13-15 is an interesting prophecy. It says:

"And he doeth great wonders, so that he maketh fire come down from heaven on the earth in the sight of men,

"And deceiveth them that dwell on the earth by the means of those miracles which he had power to do in the

sight of the beast; saying to them that dwell on the earth,
that they should make an image to the beast, which had
the wound by the sword, and did live.

"And he had power to give life unto the image of the
beast, that the image of the beast should both speak, and
cause that as many as would not worship the image of the
beast should be killed."

That prophecy puzzled me until I studied the New Age
Movement in depth. I have learned that the Movement has
devoted a great deal of research and attention to the use of
holographic images. These are three-dimensional images
created in space by use of laser beams.

David Spangler said in a meeting in Southfield, Michigan,
February 1, 1982, that laser beam projectors had been in-
stalled for use on top of the Cathedral of St. John the Divine,
Episcopal, in New York City.

I talked to lighting experts to see what laser beam projectors are capable of and I was told they can be beamed onto
telecommunication satellites.

The New Agers have several of these at their disposal.
When the lasers bounce from the satellite back to earth, the
light rays can be bent in such a manner as to appear that
flames are coming from the sky. These satellites can also be
used to project a three-dimensional holographic image
viewable by up to one-third of the earth's population.

There is even technology to make the image speak in the
language of the areas to which it is beamed. Of course, we
also know that lasers can be used as weapons.

New Agers deify Lucifer and that is the worship of devils.

Through transmissions to Benjamin Creme, Maitreya has
claimed that Jesus is one of his disciples. This can be
documented in Creme's books, *The Reappearance of Christ,*
and *The Masters of Wisdom.*

How widespread is this New Age Movement?

According to Marilyn Ferguson and other New Age
sources, they are in every city and institution in the world.

Their people are in the United Nations, prominent scientific, legal and medical circles and even at the congressional and cabinet levels of the United States government.

Christians should remember that the motive behind the New Age Movement is Lucifer's desire to be worshipped as God.

Maitreya, if he is indeed the antichrist, will be worshipped. As Satan possesses Maitreya, he in turn will receive that worship he has sought since he was expelled from heaven.

CHAPTER 2

Awakening
to the New Age Movement

Although I had a strong biblical background as a child, I must confess that, like many of my peers, I paid scant attention to end-time prophecies in my adult years. This changed for me when I began to notice a profusion of materials in bookstores, both religious and secular, containing similar unique vocabularies and an apparent political platform.

Many of the books also contained postcards enabling one to obtain additional information, an old political organizer's trick to help compile a mailing list of sympathizers. I thought the proposals — even those appearing on Christian bookstore shelves — appeared suspiciously similar to what is described in Revelation 13:16-17:

> "And he causeth all, both small and great, rich and poor, free and bond, to receive a mark in their right hand, or in their foreheads:
>
> "And that no man might buy or sell, save he had the mark, or the name of the beast, or the number of his name."

These books, even the Christian ones, were calling for a New World Order with an accompanying global food redistribution program — aided of course, by modern technology, i.e., computers. This startled me, for even during my "wilderness years" I had retained an opinion that for a system such as that described in Revelation to come into being, it would necessarily require computer implementation.

I also understood, even as a child, that Christians were to resist this system with every ounce of their being. Therefore, I was particularly startled when I found one such book, by a Baptist writer, that told Christians they must champion this New World Order even if it meant imprisonment!

Many of these books either openly advocated Eastern religions or told Christians we had much in common with their essentials.

The vocabularies included such New Age "buzz" words as holistic, Spaceship Earth, Global Village, celebration/celebrative, transformation, crowded planet, paradigm, right brain/left brain/whole brain, matrix, linear thinking, dualistic, mechanistic, global thread, new vision, initiation, interdependent, new age, etc.

Since childhood I had been familiar with Paul's Thessalonian prophecies regarding end-time events:

> "Now we beseech you, brethren, by the coming of our Lord Jesus Christ, and by our gathering together unto him,

> "That ye be not soon shaken in mind, or be troubled, neither by spirit, nor by word, nor by letter as from us, that the day of Christ is at hand.

> "Let no man deceive you by any means: for *that day shall not come*, except there come a falling away [apostasy] first, and that man of sin be revealed, the son of perdition" (II Thessalonians 2:1-3, KJV).

Reviewing these New Age materials, I faced a growing and troubling certainty that what I was witnessing was indeed apostasy in the fullest sense of the word. My belief was strengthened by the fact that I found these neo-gnostic beliefs even in Fundamentalist publications, not to mention their widespread infestation of mainline Protestant and Roman Catholic publications.

What is apostasy? The scriptures are clear:

> "Who is a liar but he that denieth that Jesus is the Christ? He is antichrist that denieth the Father and the Son" (I John 2:22, KJV).

"And every spirit that confesseth not that Jesus Christ is come in the flesh is not of God: and this is that spirit of antichrist, whereof ye have heard that it should come; and even now already is it in the world" (I John 4:3, KJV).

Many of these same books — particularly the mainline Protestant ones — stated that we could worship God and call him by names such as Buddha, Tao, Shiva and a variety of other pagan monikers.

Of course, this is a clear violation of Isaiah 42:8:

"I am the Lord: that *is* my name: and my glory will I not give to another, neither my praise to graven images."

Further, we are scripturally admonished that they who worship idols worship demons, a warning evidently conveniently forgotten by far too many "modern" theologians:

"What say I then? that the idol is any thing, or that which is offered in sacrifice to idols is any thing?

"But I *say*, that the things which the Gentiles sacrifice, they sacrifice to devils, and not to God: and I would not that ye should have fellowship with devils.

"Ye cannot drink the cup of the Lord, and the cup of devils: ye cannot be partakers of the Lord's table, and of the table of devils" (I Corinthians 10:19-21, KJV).

But now I faced a situation where respected theologians were telling us we could partake of both tables. Was it a case of "evolved theology"? Or was it a case of apostasy? I strongly suspected it was the latter.

A theologian I am not, but the Lord did see fit to bless me with a fair amount of common sense and a legal education. From both standpoints — common sense and logic — this appeared to be apostasy in the clearest sense of the word.

Another thing I noticed was that the New Age books containing this exotic new theology had a vocabulary very similar to the books calling for the New World Order. I suspected a connection.

The pieces of the puzzle were still falling together when I chanced upon *The Aquarian Conspiracy* by Marilyn Ferguson. This book contains the same unique vocabulary as that of the others.

The author herself has great insight into this Movement and her book carries the message that radical change is upon all of us. She said:

> "A leaderless but powerful network is working to bring about radical change in the United States. Its members have broken with certain key elements of Western thought, and they may even have broken continuity with history."[1]

So they had broken with certain elements of Western thought! I wondered which ones. A hint appeared in the next paragraph:

> ". . . But whose perspective sounds so *mystical* that they hesitate to discuss it."

I turned to the section on "Spiritual Adventure." There I learned what they have broken with is exactly what I suspected based upon my collection of curios acquired from religious bookstores: orthodox religion! Mystical experiences and "experiential religion" were the new order of the day.

She noted that there has been alarm expressed in religious circles over the new spiritual mentality:

> "Not unexpectedly, some religious groups see the emergent spiritual tradition as a fearful threat to the Judeo-Christian tradition. The fundamental Berkeley Christian Coalition, sponsor of the Spiritual Counterfeits Project, devoted its August 1978 journal to this threat."[2]

I was relieved to see that somebody had shown some alarm. If the churches were not alarmed, they should be! How big is this Movement? Again, clues are given:

[1] *The Aquarian Conspiracy*, Marilyn Ferguson, p. 23.
[2] *Ibid.*, p. 369.

"They have coalesced into small groups in every town and institution. They have formed what one called 'national non-organizations.' Some conspirators are keenly aware of the national, even international, scope of the movement and are active in linking others."[3]

And, the Movement has widespread, powerful influence! She says so!

"There are legions of conspirators. They are in corporations, universities and hospitals, on the faculties of public schools, in factories and doctors' offices, in state and federal agencies, on city councils and the White House staff, in state legislatures, in volunteer organizations, in virtually all arenas of policy-making in the country.

"Whatever their station or sophistication, the conspirators are linked. . . ."[4]

"In bureaucracies, in every corner of government, human beings conspire for change. *An Aquarian Conspirator at the cabinet level of the United States government helped foster departmental* change by setting up staff workshops in human development, saying, 'If you want to change bureaucracies, you have to first change bureaucrats.' "[5]

The book liberally boasted of widespread infiltration at every level of society. I was not so sure it was the "benign conspiracy" she represented it to be.

Another important clue to the nature of this conspiracy was found in the chapter on "Spiritual Adventure." There she quoted from *The Aquarian Gospel of Jesus the Christ.* I decided to locate that source document for myself and the next day purchased a copy from a local religious bookstore.

Reading *The Aquarian Gospel,* I was in for new shocks. I read on page 16:

[3]*Ibid.*, p. 24.
[4]*Ibid.*, p. 24.
[5]*Ibid.*, p. 235.

"In the infinite One manifest we note the attributes of Force, Intelligence and Love, and a person may be in full accord with one of these attributes and not with the others. *One may enter fully into the spirit of the God of Force. . . ."*

A strange bell was rung for me by this particular passage. I opened my King James Bible and read Daniel 11:38:

"But in his estate shall he honour the *God of forces:* and a god whom his fathers knew not shall he honour with gold, and silver, and with precious stones, and pleasant things."

On page 14 in the introduction of *The Aquarian Gospel* I read:

"Jesus was not always Christ. Jesus won his Christship by a strenuous life, and in . . . chapter 55, we have a record of the events of his christing, or receiving the degree Christ. . . .

"We recognize the facts that Jesus was man and that Christ was God. . . ."

Again I looked at my Bible:

"Who is a liar but he that denieth that Jesus is the Christ? He is antichrist, that denieth the Father and the Son" (I John 2:22, KJV).

"And every spirit that confesseth not that Jesus Christ is come in the flesh is not of God: and this is that SPIRIT of antichrist, whereof ye have heard that it should come; and even now already is it in the world" (I John 4:3, KJV).

I could hardly believe my eyes. I had discovered two major tests of the antichrist in *The Aquarian Gospel* introduction alone. I read on through chapter 14 where I discovered an alleged colloquy between John the Baptist and his pagan "master." John asked why any new sacred books would be needed.

He was told, in part:

> "And so the Holy Ones have judged; when men have
> needed added light, a master soul has come to earth to give
> that light. Before the Vedic days the world had many
> sacred books to light the way; and when man needed
> greater light, the Vedas, the Avesta and the books of Tao
> Great appeared to show the way to greater heights. And in
> the proper place the Hebrew Bible, with its Law, its Proph-
> ets and its Psalms, appeared for man's enlightenment. But
> years have passed and men have need of greater light. And
> now the Day Star from on high begins to shine; and Jesus is
> the flesh-made messenger to show that light to
> men. . . . But in the ages yet to come, man will attain to
> greater heights, and lights still more intense will come.
> AND THEN, AT LAST, A MIGHTY MASTER SOUL
> WILL COME TO EARTH TO LIGHT THE WAY UP TO
> THE THRONE OF PERFECT MAN."[6]

Now I knew for sure that I was encountering a direct
satanic prophecy of his own chosen messenger to men — the
antichrist! I was sure that I needed to learn more of this so-
called "Age of Aquarius" or "Aquarian Conspiracy" and I
needed to do so quickly.

Lack of the proper reference label stymied my efforts for a
short while. Then I received a major break. At a political
party for a local candidate, I heard a woman I had known for
14 years address the crowd. She told us that she had been a
student of the "mind sciences" for the past 20 years.

Marilyn Ferguson had said that the "conspirators" com-
municated by code words and signals; and from the little
reading I had done, I was certain that "mind science" was one
of the words.

Approaching the woman cautiously but amiably, I mentioned that I had had an interest in the "mind sciences" since
reading *Psychocybernetics* years before. When I suggested
that we discuss the subject over dinner, she agreed.

We adjourned to a nearby delicatessen. There she told me

[6]*Ibid.,* p. 48, emphasis added.

that the mind sciences are part of the "New Age Movement," also known as the "Age of Aquarius," "Aquarian Conspiracy," "Human Potential Movement," "Holistic Movement," "Humanistic Psychology" and by several other but lesser important names as well.

She said they believe that the mind operates on principles just as the body does, and that it is necessary to know the principles if one wants the mind to work efficiently.

She gave several of these "principles," but only one truly caught my attention. That was the one she cited as the most important: karma. Admitting that it has something to do with Eastern religions, she insisted that it is much larger than the Eastern religions!

I told her I had read *The Aquarian Conspiracy*. Growing cautious, she said that book was not an accurate representation of the New Age Movement. Unwilling to reveal my suspicions of the Movement as yet, I told her I had enjoyed the book and innocently asked what was wrong with it. Much to my dismay, she told me that the New Age Movement was far larger than that book portrayed it as being. That worried me, for Ms. Ferguson had described the Movement as being so large that it had kept me awake worrying several nights.

I had heard enough! It was time to share my true feelings with her. I explained that my research combined with Bible studies had convinced me that this was the Movement of the antichrist. To my surprise she agreed. I showed her Daniel 11:38 relating to the God of Forces and the parallel passage in *The Aquarian Gospel*.

Complimenting me on my perceptiveness, she told me that I should also remember that in the New Age Movement as well as at Unity, which is a part of the Movement, they believe Jesus and the Christ are two distinct entities. I answered by showing her I John 2:22, which declares that particular teaching to be a mark of the spirit of antichrist.

Quickly perceiving that: (a) I did not wish to join the Movement; and (b) she had already told me far too much, she said it was difficult to converse with me because she had received "a vision of light" — a phenomenon many New Agers seem to have in common. She suggested I pray for wisdom to help me see the "hidden meaning" of those Bible passages.

Sharing with her a rule of construction for lawyers that I felt to be just as applicable to Bible research, I told her that the plainest meaning fitting the facts should be the one to govern.

She suggested that I familiarize myself with the history of how the Bible was written as well as how contradictory it was. I replied that I found nothing contradictory or illogical about it, and asked her if she had read the Bible all the way through. She said she had not because it might tend to confuse her. I suggested it would be logical to know its contents before offering criticism of it.

Our food arrived and we concentrated on eating for a few minutes.

Then to my surprise I heard her say: "It's just not right — not right. That book should *not* be allowed! It's too misleading!"

Unable to believe my ears, I asked what book she was referring to and she exclaimed: "The Bible!"

I asked her why she would say something like that and she replied: "The antichrist is *not* the negative thing the Bible's made him out to be!"

That statement literally changed the course of my life, causing me to lay aside my law practice and concentrate on researching and exposing the New Age Movement. If indeed there is a movement afoot that is larger than Eastern religions and larger than the gargantuan enterprise described in *The Aquarian Conspiracy*, then we need to expose it for what it is!

The Christian world — myself included — has been blissfully asleep for far too long. It is time that somebody sounds the alarm — awaking sleeping Christians to this Movement and warning innocent participants to come out of it.

The book of Daniel predicts that there will be those in the last days who will give such warnings:

> "And such as do wickedly against the covenant shall he corrupt by flatteries: but the people that do know their God shall be strong, and do exploits.

> "And they that understand among the people shall instruct many . . ." (Daniel 11:32-33, KJV).

This book is my attempt to assist in delivering this warning — "to come out of her" before it is too late for us and our children.

CHAPTER 3

The Age of Aquarius?
Or the Age of the Antichrist?

"Now we beseech you, brethren, by the coming of our Lord Jesus Christ, and by our gathering together unto him.

"That ye be not soon shaken in mind, or be troubled, neither by spirit, nor by word, nor by letter as from us, as that the day of Christ is at hand.

"Let no man deceive you by any means: for *that day shall not come*, except there come a falling away first, and that man of sin be revealed, the son of perdition" (II Thessalonians 2:2-3, KJV).

For nearly two thousand years, Christians have cherished the idea of the imminent return of the Lord Jesus Christ. In each new generation, believers have nourished the hope within their hearts that perhaps *they* would be alive when Christ returns.

The generation of the Apostle Paul's time was no exception. Therefore, Paul found it necessary in his Second Epistle to the Thessalonians to clarify end-time events for this congregation. He did this so that they would be encouraged to continue to work diligently and wait patiently for the return of Jesus.

Nineteenth-century America was also no exception. The early Adventist movement founded by William Miller experienced the "great disappointments" of 1843 and 1844. That movement was based upon the premise that the "Great Falling Away" or apostasy of Thessalonians had already occurred between the era of Constantine and the Reformation during a 1,260-year period. This "apostasy" would reveal the "Man of Perdition," whom they believed to be the Catholic pope. Therefore, the Millerites and similar religious movements, which have influenced the Church of God and the Seventh Day Adventist Church of today, lived in confidence that the imminent return of the Lord was near.

Many other Protestant movements similarly believed these prophecies met fulfillment in the Pope of Rome. Yet it seemed clear that the Old Testament prophecies regarding restoration of Israel to the Holy Land remained unfulfilled.

Interpreting this prophecy to mean a "spiritual Israel" rather than political Israel, the Adventists felt that all prophecies were fulfilled except for the "Great Commission" — the command to preach the gospel to all nations. They set themselves to the task of preaching this Adventist gospel of salvation to all, in hopes that this would bring about the imminent return of the Lord — a not unworthy objective!

With the physical and political restoration of Israel to the Holy Land in 1948 and her subsequent land gains in 1967 and 1973, the Adventist excitement quickly spread to other Protestant churches as well as among Roman Catholic prophecy enthusiasts.

Eschatology differences, as well as other doctrinal differences, however, continued to divide Christian denominations, resulting in name-calling on every side. Evangelical Christians of the non-dispensational persuasion fought Evangelicals who were dispensationally oriented. Mainline Protestants looked down on Evangelicals. Baptists took every opportunity to snipe at Charismatics, some of whom, in turn, questioned the salvation of all who failed to obtain the spiritual gift of speaking in tongues. The Roman Catholics took nearly every available opportunity to proclaim eternal hell fire for Protestants, while those Protestants, in their turn, proclaimed there would be even greater heat for Catholics.

What nearly every "Christian" name-caller overlooked were the plain and simple biblical specifications of the spirit of antichrist and the fact that a Movement meeting these specifications was growing under their noses and even influencing their churches.

The Apostle John told us:

"Beloved, do not believe every spirit, but test the spirits to see whether they are from God; because many false prophets have gone out into the world.

"By this you know the Spirit of God: every spirit that confesses that Jesus Christ has come in the flesh is from God;

"And every spirit that does not confess Jesus is not from God and this is the spirit of the antichrist, of which you have heard that it is coming, and now it is already in the world" (I John 4:1-3, NASB).

From this we know that we may expect the actual anti-christ to deny that Jesus Christ came in the flesh. We would expect him to say, for example, that Jesus was an ordinary man who merely had the "Christ Consciousness" come upon him. This was clarified by John in a later epistle:

"For many deceivers have gone out into the world, those who do not acknowledge Jesus Christ as coming in the flesh. This is the deceiver and the antichrist" (II John 7, NASB).

Furthermore, the antichrist would actually deny that Jesus was the Christ:

"Who is a liar but he that denieth that Jesus is the Christ? He is antichrist, that denieth the Father and the Son" (I John 2:22, KJV).

Clearly, if we are to be in a position to recognize the true "spirit of antichrist" and antichrist when he actually appears, we must be careful to adhere strictly to scriptural specifications, or face the awesome penalties that the same John outlined in the book of Revelation:

"For I testify unto every man that heareth the words of the prophecy of this book, If any man shall add unto these things, God shall add *unto him the plagues* that are written in this book:

"And if any man shall take away from the words of the book of this prophecy, God shall take away his part out of the book of life, and out of the holy city, and from the things which are written in this book" (Revelation 22:18-19, KJV).

In this Twentieth Century evidences of this "spirit of antichrist" are everywhere, probably even more than when the Apostle John wrote his letters. Not only is that "spirit" diligently at work among us today, it is quite likely that so is the antichrist himself.

It is the contention of this writer that for the first time since John penned his words, there is a viable movement — the New Age Movement — that truly meets the scriptural requirements for the antichrist and the political movement that will bring him on the world scene.

It is further the position of the writer that this most likely is the great apostasy or "falling away" spoken of by the Apostle Paul and that the antichrist's appearance could be a very real event in our immediate future.

It is further contended, contrary to past Christian thought, that this Movement has infiltrated all of Christianity, as well as Judaism, sneaking in the side door of our institutions. It has taken the form of Easternization of our churches, successfully permeating even Evangelical denominations. It is blatant among Roman Catholics and mainline Protestant denominations — particularly Episcopalians and United Methodists.

While Christians have been successfully diverted by the enemy into mutual accusations of each other being the "antichrist" or "satanic," the Old Deceiver himself has moved in the guise of promoting "true ecumenism." He encourages the fostering of Eastern religious values in first our cultural setting, then our seminaries, by subverting 2,000-year-long Judeo/Christian doctrinal traditions taught there to an acceptance of "pluralism" and attacks on God's Word and its translations.

Christian seminary students are now widely and commonly told that to truly worship God, we must "do theology" instead of "parroting old theology written for another age, another continent, and another culture." They are told that such "doing of theology" could well include finding Christ in the Bhagavad Gita, the Koran, the Vedas, the Upanishads and a variety of other Eastern, Hindu-based scriptures. They are told they may do honor to our Lord by calling him "Buddha," "Shiva," "Tao," "The Great Spirit" and by other pagan monikers.

This Movement has further infiltrated our society as well as our churches by using vehicles such as Holistic Health Centers, Montessori schools, Waldorf education, Transcendental Meditation (TM), mind-control courses, hunger projects, Whole Earth catalogs, many health food stores and vegetarian restaurants, disarmament campaigns, and nearly every other social cause, including animal liberation!

Make no mistake about it! The New Age Movement *is* a religion complete with its own Bibles, prayers and mantras, Vatican City/Jerusalem equivalents, priests and gurus, born-again experiences (they call it "rebirthing"), spiritual laws and commandments, psychics and "prophets" and nearly every other indicia of a religion.

Their version of the Ten Commandments is fascinating to say the least. They claim there is no such thing as murder or adultery. If one is murdered it is either happening because he wanted it to happen or because his bad "karma" was being worked out for him.

While their theology is obfuscated in deliberate gobbledy-gook, it is not complicated. A Christian may read the main tenets in the third chapter of the book of Genesis. Basically they involve (1) an attack on the authority of God's Word; (2) a denial that one will die (reincarnation); (3) a claim that man can be as a god himself; and (4) a deification of Lucifer and other demonic entities (the Masters of Wisdom theory).

The universal proclamation of the Movement is that man is God and "Man created God in his own image." The Movement worships pagan deities from Pan to Buddha and Shiva. They even worship Lucifer himself.

The political goals of the Movement include a mandatory New World Religion, establishment of a "universal credit card" system, establishment of a World Food Authority, World Health Authority, World Water Authority, etc.; establishment of a universal tax and a universal draft which is truly universal — everybody is eligible, worldwide!

The Movement is not new. Neither is it a passing fad. Sadly, most of its participants are innocently involved. Many are under the influence of sophisticated forms of mind control.

The *Mein Kampfs* of the Movement are numerous and becoming daily less subtle about its intentions. Disciples of the Movement speak proudly of having received a "vision of light." Many openly speak of their planned welcome for the antichrist or "New Age Christ."

As was indicated earlier the Movement was even bold enough to run full-page newspaper ads proclaiming "THE CHRIST IS NOW HERE." They openly deny that Jesus is the Christ and instead proclaim the deity of a "Maitreya the Christ" and that Jesus is *his* disciple! They openly worship a "God of Force" and "forces." Characterized by common mystical experiences, many of their number possess a plethora of psychic powers enabling them to indeed show "great signs and wonders" ranging from astral travel to psychic predictions.

Many among their number encourage the internal undermining of nations and they proudly proclaim the "subversiveness" of their Movement as if such a designation were a badge of honor. While they call for the division of large federated nation states such as Canada and the United States, at the same time they call for institution of a Planetary Guidance System or other form of world government. While they promote simple life-styles, at the same time they call for the interconnection of the entire world by incredibly sophisticated computers with snooping capacities that are Orwellian in scope.

It is a Movement that meets the test of prophecy as well as the tests of Hitler's National Socialism (Nazism). It is a Movement that has seen the deception of many — including many of its own who participate for the finest of motives.

Clearly, if we have such a movement that meets the biblical specifications of the antichrist, existing simultaneously in history with the fulfillment of other end-time prophecies such as those regarding the restoration of Israel, then Christians and indeed not just Christians, but all who seek the truth and have concerns for our future, should take a very careful look at that Movement.

The succeeding chapters will give you considerable information about this Movement necessary to assist you and your friends and family from being unwittingly sucked into Satan's master plan. Because of the limited size of this first edition, everything relevant about the Movement will not be included.

For example, I have had many requests to compile a listing of organizations. There is no need for me to do so because the New Agers have done an excellent job of this themselves. A limited bibliography is included that lists some of the recommended reference works for this purpose.

Above all, I commend to you the words of Jesus Christ in Luke 21:29-36:

> "Behold the fig tree, and all the trees;
>
> "When they now shoot forth, ye see and know of your own selves that summer is now nigh at hand.
>
> "So likewise ye, when ye see these things come to pass, know ye that the kingdom of God is nigh at hand.
>
> "Verily I say unto you, This generation shall not pass away, till all be fulfilled.

"Heaven and earth shall pass away: but my words shall not pass away.

"And take heed to yourselves, lest at any time your hearts be overcharged with surfeiting, and drunkenness, and cares of this life, and so that day come upon you unawares.

"For as a snare shall it come on all them that dwell on the face of the whole earth.

"Watch ye therefore, and pray always, that ye may be accounted worthy to escape all these things that shall come to pass, and to stand before the Son of man."

CHAPTER 4

The Movement: A Short History

A vast organizational network today, the New Age Movement received its modern start in 1875 with the founding of the Theosophical Society by Helena Petrovna Blavatsky. A basic teaching of this organization was that all world religions had "common truths" that transcended potential differences.

Strongly propounding the theory of evolution, they also believed in the existence of "masters" who were either spirit beings or fortunate men more highly "evolved" than the common herd. This was a doctrine which was to have a substantial impact on the development of Hitler's Nazism several decades later.

Madame Blavatsky worked in "telepathic communication," serving as a "fulcrum" for the masters starting in 1867 and continuing until her death in 1891. Achieving "illumination" or enlightenment was one of the Theosophists' goals. And that meant more than mere light bulbs to at least one of their more famous initiates — Thomas Alva Edison, who joined the organization and signed its pledge of secrecy in 1878!

Through the Theosophical Society, the budding Movement demonstrated hostility to Christianity from its beginning. In 1875 Helena Blavatsky wrote in her scrapbook:

> "The Christians and scientists must be made to respect their Indian betters. The Wisdom of India, her philosophy and achievement *must* be made known in Europe and America and the English be made to respect the natives of India and Tibet more than they do."[1]

From Buddhist High Priest Mohottiwatte Gunanana to Prince Emil of Wittgenstein, from General Abner Double-

---

[1] *Golden Book of the Theosophical Society* (1925), pp. 28, 29.

day (founder of baseball) to Swami Saraswati, the famous of East and West *did* meet in a concerted effort to eliminate orthodox Christianity. In fact, many theosophists intended to eliminate all Christianity — orthodox and otherwise. When two theosophists attempted to institute a branch of Theosophy — known as Esoteric Christianity — that would be a revival of gnostic Christian teachings along the line of the Kabala — a form of Christianity that is Christian in name only — they quickly found opposition from the remainder of the Society. An attempt was made to resolve the dispute by chartering a special branch to be known as the Hermetic Lodge.

However, Theosophical hatred of Christianity was so strong that even such a watered-down, hereticized version could not survive within the organization. A Theosophical Society brochure made clear the anti-Christian aims of that movement:

> ". . . To oppose the materialism of science and every form of dogmatic theology, especially the Christian, which the Chiefs of the Society regard as particularly pernicious; to make known among Western nations the long-suppressed facts about Oriental religious philosophies, their ethics, chronology, esoterism (sic), symbolism; to counteract, as far as possible, the efforts of missionaries to delude the so-called 'Heathen' and 'Pagans' as to the real origin and dogmas of Christianity and the practical effects of the latter upon public and private character in so-called Christian countries."

As a matter of fact, it saw "unity" between all religions, except those monotheistic religions worshipping the Lord of Hosts:

> "Esoteric Philosophy reconciles all nations, strips every one of its outward human garments, and shows the root of each to be identical with that of every other great religion. It proves the necessity of a Divine Absolute Principle in Nature. It denies Deity no more than it does the sun. Esoteric Philosophy has never rejected God in Nature, nor Deity as the absolute and abstract *Ens*. IT ONLY REFUSES

TO ACCEPT ANY OF THE GODS OF THE SO-CALLED
MONOTHEISTIC RELIGIONS, GODS CREATED BY
MAN IN HIS OWN IMAGE AND LIKENESS, A
BLASPHEMOUS AND SORRY CARICATURE OF THE
EVER UNKNOWABLE."[2]

This is an attitude that continues to prevail throughout
the New Age Movement. Everything is good except orthodox, monotheistic religions: Judaism, Christianity and
Islam.

Proudly drawing their inspiration from "spirits" or
"elementals," the leaders of the Theosophical Society believed they were under the direct supervision of "adepts"
and "initiates" belonging to a branch of "The Great White
Brotherhood." Following written orders from these spirit
beings, the New York-based leadership moved to India in
1875.

Another order from these demonic messengers told them
to keep the society and teachings secret — at least for the time
being. This was a dictum that was to prevail for 100 years —
until 1975 — the year initiates were at last permitted to make
the initiatory teachings public.

After the secrecy order came down, the Society began to
communicate by secret signs and words of recognition. This
practice continues today within the modern New Age Movement. It is specifically designed to keep information from
hostile investigators.

Freely acknowledging their demonic origins, the organization called one of its publications *Lucifer* for many years.

For all their zeal in stamping out Christianity for the sake
of religious "freedom," the early Movement had no such
qualms about stamping their own brand of religious in-
terference upon the unsuspecting Indian population:

> "For, both H.P.B. [Blavatsky] and Colonel Olcott saw
> that Theosophy could become a power to reorganize
> India's life on national lines once again, if only Indians ac-
> cepted, as a practical code of life, Theosophy in its en-

[2]*Ibid.*, pp. 63, 64.

tirety. . . ."[3]

Psychic phenomena and seemingly miraculous signs also characterized the early days of the Society. These included precipitating of letters, materializations of objects, and production of strange sounds. Those allegedly producing the phenomena, which opponents of the Society decried as fraud, were said to be in Tibet, whereas the phenomena itself appeared in India and Europe.

An important addition was made to the Society when Helena Petrovna Blavatsky met an English clergyman named C.W. Leadbetter. To his surprise, he received two letters signed "Master KH (Koot Hoomi) instructing him to leave immediately for India to assist the Theosophists there. These letters arrived the same day that Madame Blavatsky was leaving England for a return trip to India. Disregarding biblical warnings about those in the last days departing from the truth to follow the doctrines of seducing spirits and devils, the clergyman quickly renounced the faith of his fathers to go serve the "masters."

During these activities, Madame Blavatsky composed *Isis Unveiled* and *The Secret Doctrine* under the direction of "the masters." Although the books possess a scholarly appearance, they are in fact entirely the product of automatic (demon-manipulated) writing.

After Helena Blavatsky's death, the organization continued to prosper under the direction of Annie Besant. That is, until they made an abortive attempt to bring forth the antichrist. Their candidate they meticulously prepared for the job backed out on them. In 1929 Krishnamurti dissolved the accompanying Order of the Star consisting of his worldwide supporters. Perhaps some of the credit for the refusal might be attributed to his father, who fought Annie Besant and the Theosophical Society tooth-and-nail in an unsuccessful legal attempt to recover the children he had lost by Theosophical trickery.

The blow to the Theosophists was enormous, for no ex-

[3]*Ibid.*, p. 42.

pense had been spared in grooming Krishnamurti for the job. Sorbonne educated and genteel in appearance, he was an individual with the necessary presence to make the desired worldwide impact.

The disgruntled masters decided to pass the torch to another less rash than Annie Besant. It went to a former Christian teacher and former wife of an Episcopal rector named Alice Ann Bailey. Born to position and beauty in England, she spent part of her childhood in Montreal, where her father was employed as an engineer. Both parents died while Alice and her sister were still children.

Raised by other relatives, their treatment was not unkind and they were well provided for during their minority.

Alice evidently felt inferior to her sister, a beautiful and brilliant physician. If her autobiography is to be believed, she already had contact with a "master" while still in her teens — an experience she did not understand until much later. For a period of her life she aspired to Christian service and spent time in India for this purpose.

She married outside her own social class; however, the class difference had been provided for in the usual mode of raising a prospective husband's status: he went to America to study for the Episcopal rectorhood and Alice joined him there. Since Episcopalians and Anglicans were considered equal in the eyes of British social and religious society, this technically made the marriage consistent with her own class.

It was not a happy marriage for Alice. Her husband had only one major vice — wife beating. After several children and several severe beatings, which Alice tried to hide to protect his ministry, the estrangement finally was permanent.

During their separation, she resided in California and supported her growing family by working in a fish cannery. Hearing of two women in town who were English and of her same social class, Alice attempted to make their acquaintance. They were Theosophists and encouraged Alice to join their ranks. Hungry for companionship, she attended their meetings. The exotic teachings must have added interest to her monotonous life as a fish canner. After a monthly stipend began coming from her husband, Walter, she was financially free to quit the cannery and devote her time to her children and esoteric philosophy.

The "masters" had found another chosen vehicle to preserve their teachings and do their work. Recruiting as usual from the confused, the lonely, and those in despair, they found a woman, with all three symptoms, mentally ready to do their bidding. As a result, her sister, a successful physician and devout Christian, broke all contact with Alice and never spoke to her for the remainder of her life.

Since the "masters" had convinced Alice of the possibility of reincarnation, she took the break with her sister in stride, thinking she would re-establish contact in her next life.

Later in life Alice married Foster Bailey. The Baileys did more than anyone, except perhaps Helena Petrovna Blavatsky, to build the foundations for the "New Age." Alice wrote nearly two dozen books laying out the specific instructions for disciples of the "masters" in the latter part of the 20th century — our present time. Like Helena Petrovna Blavatsky, from that point forward in her life, Alice showed tenacious hatred for orthodox Christianity and fierce loyalty to the cause of occultism and Eastern mysticism.

Although she continued to label herself a Christian, an examination of her writings shows that she attached an entirely different meaning to the word than do orthodox believers. She taught the divinity of man and reincarnation as well as an attack on God's Word — the standard lies of the serpent of Garden of Eden days!

Her work was immense. She organized the Arcane School, the New Group of World Servers, Triangles, World Goodwill, and assisted with a host of other foundational activities to help build the "New Age."

Lucifer Publishing Company was established in 1922 to help disseminate her works. The name was changed the next year to Lucis Publishing Company for reasons unknown. (Maybe he wanted to use his nickname!)

Her work was much more low-profile and cautious than that of the flamboyant Annie Besant, who had helped precipitate the Krishnamurti embarrassment for the "masters." She concentrated on giving disciples directions for networking and infiltration. Time frames were established by the "masters." Work was to remain low-profile until 1975 — when the hitherto secret teachings about the "New Age Christ" and "Hierarchy" could be publicly disseminated by all available media.

These teachings omitted little or nothing. They ranged from the attitude of the Hierarchy toward Jews (negative) through dietary advice. Step by step they plotted the coming "New Age," with instructions for the institution of the necessary New World Order through the use of identifying rainbows. Plans for religious war, forced redistribution of the world's resources, Luciferic initiations, mass planetary initiations, theology for the New World Religion, disarmament campaign, and elimination or sealing away of obstinate religious orthodoxies — all were covered extensively in the Alice Bailey writings. Even the "sacredness" of the number of the beast — 666 — was covered in at least two places.

She discounted the possibility that the Movement might be embarrassed by these books falling into the wrong hands. Alice was confident that they would be incomprehensible to anyone but an initiate.

Had she been more familiar with the scriptures, she would have realized the folly of this position:

> "Many shall be purified, and made white, and tried; but the wicked shall do wickedly: and none of the wicked shall understand; but the wise shall understand" (Daniel 12:10, KJV).

Comparing the Bailey teachings with the state of the Movement and its constituent organizations, it is clear that her instructions have been followed meticulously. Her disciples are now on the last stages of the New Age scheme to take the world for Lucifer.

The year 1962 was another landmark year, for that was when the Scottish community of Findhorn — the Vatican City of the New Age Movement — was founded. The life-work of Peter and Eileen Caddy and their friend Dorothy McLean, the role of Findhorn was to help anchor "The Plan" on earth. Again, their work was performed by following meticulously the Bailey writings and "guidance" Eileen was receiving from spirit beings and what she calls the voice of "God."

Findhorn received an important new member in 1970 — David Spangler. Although many young people showed up daily at Findhorn, none received quite the royal welcome as did Spangler. Eileen Caddy had received "guidance" that David had the "Christ energies."

Therefore, upon his arrival at Findhorn with his "spiritual advisor," ex-Mormon Myrtle Glines, he was immediately inaugurated as the co-director of the Findhorn Foundation, where he was to remain for the next three years.

Spangler went into frequent transmission from demonic beings, including Maitreya, Rakoczi, and many others. Esoteric lore, from Tibetan Buddhism through UFOlogy, was actively pursued by the Findhorn initiates and would-be initiates. Clergy ranging from Episcopal priests through Methodist ministers and others came to Findhorn to lend their input and approval. Spangler made clear to those Findhorn residents and visitors — and a few years later to the entire listening world — that the true light of Findhorn was the light of Lucifer.

At the same time Findhorn was blossoming, esoteric groups around the world commenced their networking operations. Serving as a focal point for The Plan, Findhorn itself attracted visitors and residents from a worldwide base. Its residents meticulously studied and mastered the works of Alice A. Bailey, Helena Petrovna Blavatsky, Agni Yoga and a host of other esoteric "saints" and societies.

David Spangler wrote a book which purported to be a transmission from unearthly sources — or "his higher self."

Revelation: The Birth of a New Age quickly became mandatory reading for Findhorn residents along with the Blavatsky/Bailey works. Networking efforts ranged from Amnesty International, New Age brain trusts of Lucis Trust and the Stanford Research Institute (SRI) of Palo Alto, California. SRI itself proclaimed the inviolability of "spiritual forces" on its public lobby walls.

Linkages were formed with the International Cooperation Council. This 200-plus organizational network of networks is dedicated to the speedy implementation of "The Plan" — a plan which includes the bringing in of a New Age "Christ."

In 1973 David Spangler and other Findhornites left for the USA to form the Lorian Association. This was another Planetary Network designed to publicize the "spiritual" goals of the coming "New Age." Lorian Association is presently headquartered in Madison, Wisconsin. Spangler also calls Findhorn his home.

Similar to many dedicated New Agers, Spangler hails from a family which includes devout Christians. Jesus foresaw this division of earthly families:

> "Think not that I am come to send peace on earth: I came not to bring peace, but a sword.

> "For I am come to set a man at variance against his father, and the daughter against her mother, and the daughter in law against her mother in law.

> "And a man's foes shall be they of his own household.

> "He that loveth father or mother more than me is not worthy of me: and he that loveth son or daughter more than me is not worthy of me.

> "And he that taketh not his cross, and followeth after me, is not worthy of me" (Matthew 10:34-38, KJV).

The year 1975 was a banner year for the New Age Movement. That was when its disciples had permission from the deceased Alice Bailey to "come out of the closet" and spread the New Age message to the world. With *joie de vivre* they *did* go public. Spangler, Mark Satin, and a host of other New Age personages and organizations launched their public work.

It is interesting to note that Marilyn Ferguson also began publishing her *Brain Mind Bulletin* in 1975.

From 1975 through and including the present time the propaganda networking has coincided with other planning and organizational efforts.

One important para-military organization with ties to the New Age Movement has come into being — the Guardian Angels.

More ominous still are developments that have taken place under the auspices of the United States Military — the First Earth Battalion headed by recently retired Lt. Col. James Channon — who proudly proclaimed he was leading his "monk-warriors with the Force."

Most important New Age organizations have coalesced behind Planetary Initiative for the World We Choose. Planetary Initiative itself has organized "The World Council of Wise Persons." If their plans go according to schedule, Planetary Initiative will hold its World Congress in Toronto, Canada, on June 21, 1983, with a simultaneous meeting of the World Council of Wise Persons taking place in New York City at the United Nations headquarters.

However, we Christians must realize that God's timetable takes precedence over the New Agers' timetable. Clearly the times are in God's hands. Nothing can happen, the whole New Age Movement notwithstanding, unless he is ready. However, if God is ready, are we ready? It is time for a real soul-searching by all God's people.

CHAPTER 5

The Movement: An Overview

According to New Age sources, the New Age Movement is a worldwide network. It consists of tens of thousands of cooperating organizations. Their primary goal or the secret behind their "unity-in-diversity" is the formation of a "New World Order." The Movement usually operates on the basis of a well-formulated body of underlying esoteric or occult teachings.

Heavily drawing upon all forms of mysticism — Eastern and Western — the Movement could appear to the uninitiated as a loose coalition. However, there is extensive political collusion and agreement among its leadership.

Carefully structured along the lines set forth in the Alice Bailey writings, it includes organizations teaching mind control, holistic health, esoteric philosophy; scientific workers, political workers; and organizations dedicated to peace and world goodwill. It also includes many consumer, environmental and nutritional organizations as well as religious cults of every shade and description.

It has successfully infiltrated nearly every segment of our personal, religious, and professional lives.

The glue binding most New Age devotees is one of common mystical experiences. "Experiential religion" is considered vital within the Movement. A substantial proportion of those within the Movement strongly believe in psychic phenomena and say they do so because of "direct experiences."

Those among their number who have not participated in the communal tripping of the "Light Fantastic" are encouraged to try meditation, LSD, or any one of the scores of "psychotechnologies" promised to induce "transformation" — a euphemism for progressively deeper levels of demonic influence.

The New Age Movement, called by Marilyn Ferguson *The Aquarian Conspiracy*, and deriving its name from the so-called Age of Aquarius, encompasses a number of groups and submovements, such as: the Holistic Movement, Humanistic Psychology, Transpersonal Psychology, Humanistic Movement, New Thought, Third Wave, Third Force, The New Spirituality, the Human Potential Movement, Secular Humanism, and Humanism.

Contrary to the assertions of New Agers that their conspiracy lacks dogma, there *is* a discernible body of teachings dominant within the Movement. While many paths may be employed to reach the trance-like state they encourage, once that state is reached, the paths are nearly identical from that point forward. As Alice Bailey said, "[T]he emphasis in all esoteric schools is necessarily, and rightly, laid upon meditation."[1]

Besides the writings of Helena Petrovna Blavatsky and Alice A. Bailey, the bulk of New Age doctrine is derived from the works of George Gurdjieff, Pierre Teilhard de Chardin, P.D. Ouspensky, H.G. Wells, Nicholas Roerich (the Agni Yoga teachings), and David Spangler. The esoteric thrusts of the Movement as well as the aims of its groups are largely derived from the Alice Bailey books. Its overall direction and tactical strategy may be found in *The Open Conspiracy: Blueprints for a World Revolution* by H.G. Wells. The "New Revelation" of the Movement has come forth in the prolific prose and poetry of Spangler.

Marilyn Ferguson's *The Aquarian Conspiracy*, an important New Age manifesto, attempts to announce and popularize what the New Agers chose to publicly display in their Movement. Heavily extolling the joys of "altered states of consciousness," her book contains more euphemisms than facts when it comes to describing the promised land of the New Age.

Millions of human beings are actively involved with the

---

[1]From *The Externalisation of the Hierarchy* by Alice A. Bailey, Lucis Publishing Company, New York City (originally incorporated as the Lucifer Publishing Company), quoting from page 17.

New Age Movement in all its phases and levels of activity. The hierarchy of the Movement has successfully managed to draw from a full spectrum of society to implement eventual aims that can only benefit a small percentage — if anyone at all. Millions have been deceived into supporting projects designed to eventually strip even themselves of their civil liberties, much of their property, their preferred religion, and perhaps even their lives.

While euphemistically professing peace and love, the Movement has blinded even many of its sincere adherents from seeing its plain declarations for what they actually are. In trance-like rapture they openly cheer while "Aryanism," "the out-worn Jewish dispensation," "mass planetary initiation," "cleansing action" are sold to them as desirable positions and programs. While these same individuals would rightfully picket to prevent a Nazi demonstration, they fail to see that point-for-point the program of the New Age Movement has complete identity with the programs of Hitler.

Supporters of anti-hunger programs are urged to back measures for abortion, artificial insemination, forced limitation of family size, genetic control, and even death control.

Disarmament is a major component of the New Age Movement. Most of the rank and file supporters of this measure are sincere. However, I am sure most of them would lose their enthusiasm if they became aware of the scheme in its entirety. For the very same books that lay out the freeze campaign as a necessary step towards implementing a planetary government and a New World Order also state that the bombs will be used to keep religious groups in line once out of the hands of individual nation states.[2]

While professing to decry the abuses of Hitler, at least one

[2]See *The Externalisation of the Hierarchy* by Alice A. Bailey. You will find the freeze campaign outlined as step no. 9 towards implementing the "New World Order." This is found on page 190-191. Turn to page 548 and you will see an extollation of the atomic bomb as something developed by the occult "Hierarchy" and the plans for use or threatened use on obstinate religious groups who will not relinquish their right to speak out on political/social issues.

important leader of the Movement has not-so-subtly informed New Age disciples that Hitler was one of their own and a disciple at that.[3]

While professing to support equality, the Movement's seminal writings openly call for the triumph of Aryanism and the domination of Caucasians over other "root races." The New Age is, according to the "Tibetan Master," an age of Occidental racial triumph.[4] We are all to be considered equal in the New Age to be sure — *but at varying stages of evolutionary development!*[5]

While professing support for religious liberty in their public releases, the Alice Bailey books which are meticulously followed within the Movement call for complete abridgement of this freedom. They openly and boldly set forth plans for a new mandatory world religion — a religion completely breaking with the concept of Jesus as the Christ and God as the Father. Jews and Christians — Roman Catholic and Protestant alike — as well as uncooperative Moslems are openly

[3]See *Running God's Plan* by Foster Bailey, pp. 14-15. This book is published by Lucis Trust. Foster Bailey was an attorney, a former officer of the American Theosophical Society under the international direction of Annie Besant, and most importantly, the husband of Alice A. Bailey. The Baileys broke with the Theosophical Society after Alice became the subject of transmissions by the "masters." They formed Lucis Trust, which is the single most important organization within the Movement, as the custodian of the Alice Bailey writings. While Bailey does not mention Hitler directly in this particular passage, nevertheless, one hardly needs a Ph.D. in history to sort out his statements that a previous attempt had been made to unify Europe "by uniting the peoples living in the Rhine River valley using that river as a binding factor. It was an attempt by a disciple but did not work. Now another attempt is in full swing. . . ." This particular paragraph was penned by Foster Bailey in 1972. Foster Bailey died in 1977 and the work at Lucis Trust has continued under the direction of Mary Bailey, Foster Bailey's widow. After the death of Alice Bailey in 1949, Foster Bailey eventually married Mary Bailey, another staunch female esotericist.

[4]See *Initiation, Human and Solar* by Alice Bailey (transmitted "telepathically" by the "Tibetan Master"), page 182. According to this, the "New Age" is to be an age when "[A]bove all . . . which brings opportunity to the occidental races, and through the medium of this life force of executive organization, of government by rule and order, by rhythm and by ritual, will come the time wherein the occidental races — with their active, concrete mind, and their vast business capacity — can take initiation."

[5]See *The Externalisation of the Hierarchy*, page 190 (paragraph no. 4) which states that "The new world order will be founded on the recognition that all men are equal in origin and goal *but that all are at differing stages of evolutionary development.*"

slated for persecution and even a "cleansing action" should they fail to cooperate.[6]

In fact, Jews are no better off with the New Agers than they were under their predecessors the Nazis. The New Agers also maintain the traditional occult doctrine of a blood taint resting on those of Jewish extraction.[7]

New Age esoteric leaders such as Benjamin Creme have openly attempted to deify Lucifer.[8] At the same time they have subtly demoted Jesus — phasing him out by reducing him to the rank of a relatively low-level "Master of Wisdom."

Considering that it meets every test of Bible prophecy regarding the coming antichrist as well as every test of Nazism, it is incredible that the Movement has been able to achieve such power and influence. An imminent coup by a New Age cabal is not outside the range of probability.

Organizations as diverse as Amnesty International, Greenpeace, the Sierra Club, Children of God, and Zero Population Growth openly and proudly bill themselves as "New Age." So do another approximately 10,000 organizations within just the United States and Canada — not including the branches of these organizations — many of

[6]See *The Rays and the Initiations* by Alice A. Bailey, Lucis Publishing Company, New York, pp. 754-755. This defines the surfacely innocuous line of the "Great Invocation" calling for "sealing the door where evil dwells." This includes doing away with the religious citadels of Judaism, Christianity, and Islam.

[7]See, for example, *The Rays and the Initiations* by Alice A. Bailey, pages 705-706, which states that the New "Christ" will not be Jewish as the Jews have forfeited that privilege and must "pass through fires of purification." These particular passages were written in 1949 when the entire world knew exactly what had happened to Europe's Jewish population.

[8]See *The Externalisation of the Hierarchy*, page 107, which states that Lucifer is the ruler of humanity. In a November 9, 1982, radio interview over WLAC, Nashville, Benjamin Creme told the entire Bible belt that Lucifer came to planet earth from planet Venus 18½ million years ago and made the supreme sacrifice for us. David Spangler in his *Reflections on the Christ* devotes an entire chapter to "Lucifer, Christ and God." He states on page 44-45 that the required initiation to enter the New Age is Luciferic. *Reflections* is published by the Findhorn Foundation. Findhorn may accurately be described as the "Vatican City" of the New Age Movement.

which are located in every major city.[9]

These organizations have achieved "synergy," thereby maximizing their strength to enormous proportions through a process of networking. This structure is difficult to depict on an ordinary organizational chart. Sociologically described as "Segmented Polycentric Integrated Networks" (SPIN), Marilyn Ferguson says that the "organization chart of a SPIN would look like 'a badly knotted fishnet with a multitude of nodes of varying sizes, each linked to all the others, directly or indirectly.' "[10]

And there is no single leader or organization indispensable to the functioning of this New Age "network of networks."

> "Each segment of a SPIN is self-sufficient. You can't destroy the network by destroying a single leader or some vital organ. The center — the heart — of the network is everywhere. A bureaucracy is as weak as its weakest link. In a network, many persons can take over the function of others. This characteristic is also like the brain's plasticity, with an overlap of functions so that new regions can take over for damaged cells.

> "Just as a bureaucracy is less than the sum of its parts, a network is many times greater than the sum of its parts. This is a source of power never before tapped in history: multiple self-sufficient social movements linked for a whole array of goals whose accomplishment would transform every aspect of contemporary life."[11]

Jim Jones was an excellent case in point. Prior to the

[9]According to the *Spiritual Community Guide #4*, 1979, one could order the NAM (New Age Media) *International New Consciousness Directory*. According to the advertising blurb, "The first edition of this year's directory features the names and full addresses (only) of approximately 10,000 New Age organizations with their branches throughout the United States and Canada, and some overseas." Orders and inquiries for this directory were to be directed to NAM Directory, Box 1080-G, San Rafael, California 94902. That particular edition was sold for $25.00.

[10]Quoting from *The Aquarian Conspiracy*, page 216. Marilyn Ferguson was in her turn quoting anthropologists Luther Gerlach and Virginia Hine.

[11]*Ibid.*, pp. 216-217.

Guyana suicide/murder fiasco, the New Agers were most proud to claim him as their own. In fact, they gave his organization the label of a New Age "spiritual" center.[12]

Spiritual Community Guide (Handbook for the New Age) listed People's Temple as a "center" in their 1972 and possibly later editions. According to them, Jones' role was to "teach Christian socialism in preparation for the New Age."[13]

Of course, once Jones lost his sanity and his favorable public image, the rest of the New Agers never mentioned him again, except to point to him as an example of the dangers of religious fundamentalism. *New Age Magazine* as well as several other New Age publications, quickly and with real *chutzpah*, moved to turn a potential public relations disaster into a propaganda victory.

The New Age Movement *is* different. Because of those differences we tend not to recognize it for the true danger it actually poses. As Marilyn Ferguson euphemistically said in quoting anthropologist Virginia Hine:

> " 'Because SPINs are so qualitatively different in organization and impact from bureaucracies,' Hine said, 'most people don't see them — *or think they are conspiracies*. Often networks take similar action without conferring with each other simply because they share so many assumptions. It might also be said that the shared assumptions *are* the collusion.' "[14]

Networking is not a passing fad; it is the key to success

[12]The role of the centers is to anchor "The Plan" on earth. As David Spangler once said, "The value of the New Age centers is that they are developing around people and places relatively uncontaminated by the taught forces, energies, and patterns of the past. Not being a part of the old web of power lines and influence, these new centers are not faced with having to overcome the inertia and ambiguous energies from past patterns. Thus a new world is being born and shall be born. . . ." (Quoting from *The Magic of Findhorn* by Paul Hawken, Bantam Edition, 1976, New York, p. 327.)

[13]From page 25 of *Spiritual Community Guide*, copyright © 1972 by "The Spiritual Community," Box 1080, San Rafael, California 94902.

[14]*The Aquarian Conspiracy*, p. 217.

for the Aquarian Conspiracy or the New Age Movement:

> "The Aquarian Conspiracy is, in effect, a SPIN of SPINs, a network of many networks aimed at social transformation. The Aquarian Conspiracy is indeed loose, segmented, evolutionary, redundant. Its center is everywhere. Although many social movements and mutual-help groups are represented in its alliances, its life does not hinge on any of them."[15]

While Marilyn Ferguson and others have protested that the Movement is both leaderless and unstructured, their statements are belied by the abundance of network council organizational charts, matrixes, statements of purpose, and directories — all showing both leadership and structure to an advanced degree.

"Network" as well as "synergy" are magic words for New Agers. By networking they have achieved a synergetic effect that makes them nearly unstoppable. By networking they have indeed achieved a lack of dependency on any one group or leader.

As they continued undaunted by the Jim Jones affair, they probably can and will go on unaffected by anyone else committing a similar *faux pas* in the eyes of the public. Perhaps they will again even exploit such a similar disaster by publishing books and articles proclaiming that unfortunate experience to be a danger of "religious fundamentalism."

Frustratingly, most of the participants in these New Age networks are quite innocently involved. Either they do not know the true aims and intents of its leadership or, more often, they are operating under the influence of extremely sophisticated forms of mind control.[16]

Classes such as TM, Silva Mind Control, EST, Life-

---

[15]*Ibid.*, p. 217.

[16]Typically, in many New Age sessions, particularly within the New Age cults, participants are taken under progressively deeper levels of hypnosis and not brought back out! One such session witnessed by me personally in Oklahoma City saw the "guru" take his audience under several levels of hypnosis by putting them in a "relaxation" state. Techniques of clairvoyance were taught while they were under as well as religious/political propaganda. They were never brought back up!

springs, Arica and dozens of other such "psychotechnologies" help the trainers induce the desired trance-like state in the would-be initiate.

However, many abandon the New Age Movement when tactfully presented with its true facts.

Truly the conspiring spirit behind the New Age Movement, as well as many of its theoreticians, leaders, and occult predecessors, has successfully exploited the principle of "divide and conquer." They have succeeded in persuading Christian to fight against Christian. While the Christians were preoccupied with each other, their churches were nearly all infiltrated with the New Age philosophies and social-political programs. Judaism was also infiltrated.

The New Age teachings are the same old lies that have been about since the snake beguiled Eve in the Garden of Eden: "Thou shalt not surely die . . . and thou shalt be as gods." Combine that line together with an attack on God's Word and understand the reason why Lucifer was originally expelled from Paradise and you will perfectly understand the philosophies and goals of the New Age Movement.

The political goal of the Movement is global control. Although this goal has never before been achieved, they think the times are ripe and they may well be right.

> "Global communications have encircled our world beyond any possibility of retreat. Now the whole planet is alive with instantaneous links, networks of people poised for communication and cooperation."[17]

And as Marilyn Ferguson further noted, the base has been carefully constructed for many years:

> "Cultural transformation announces itself in sputtering fits and starts, sparked here and there by minor incidents, warmed by new ideas that many smoulder for decades. In many different places, at different times, the kindling is laid for the real conflagration — the one that will consume the old landmarks and alter the landscape

---

[17]*Ibid.*, p. 35.

forever."[18]

While the writings are probably deliberately scattered, nevertheless, there is a discernible political program emanating from the New Agers. They propose to establish gigantic global agencies such as a World Food Authority, World Water Authority, and an authority to administer a universal draft and a universal tax.[19] They have pointed to such legislative proposals as the Peace Academy as proof of their success in advancing towards the New World Order. They intend to give us a "Universal Credit Card" not to mention a "New World Religion."[20]

The structures New Agers propose are both Orwellian and apocalyptic in their scope, organization, and possibilities. Proposing the dissolution and/or destruction of individual nation states in the interests of peace and conservation, New Age spokesmen openly discuss their replacement with a bioregional parliament and a "Planetary Guidance System."[21]

As already mentioned, its big push is through a vehicle known as Planetary Initiative for the World We Choose. Planetary Initiative's "World Council of Wise Persons" membership reads like a New Age *Who's Who.*[22]

[18]*Ibid.*, p. 37.

[19]David Spangler spoke in Southfield, Michigan, on February 1, 1982. At that time he told those present that the New World Order would consist of very large global agencies. We would have to manage on a large scale. He said that both the United Nations and the multi-national corporations have been training grounds for the coming globalization.

[20]See, for example, Buckminster Fuller's *The Critical Path*, St. Martin's Press, copyright © 1981. Computer use and its maliciously planned destructive impact on religion are discussed on pp. xxvii, xxviii, 215, 217, 218.

[21]See for example Mark Satin's *New Age Politics*, chapter 17 "Planetization: Celebration of Unity." Satin quotes Club of Rome sources, Richard Falk of the Institute for World Order, Donald Keys of Planetary Citizens (also Planetary Initiative for the World We Choose), Barbara Ward and Gerald & Patricia Mische as being in support of such a structure. All are prominent within the New Age Movement.

[22]Incredible, but true! Norman Cousins is heading the invitor committee, according to Issue #2 of their newspaper, *The Initiator*. Buckminster Fuller and Dr. Carlos Romulo of the Philippines had accepted as of late winter-early spring, 1982. They plan to hold a simultaneous meeting of the World Council of Wise Persons in tandem with the "culminating global congress" of Planetary Initiative in Toronto. Of course this will take place at the time of "Summer Solstice," 1983.

While it is all too common for New Agers to ridicule orthodox Christians and particularly fundamentalists as being "fanatical and unsophisticated," their own beliefs surpass the "bizarre." They calmly discuss not only Luciferic initiations, but "raising the fires of Kundalini," chakras, and "Maitreya the Christ."

They rationalize the concepts of initiation and secret ritual by claiming a need for the "geniuses" among us to have their own private language and code. The Movement has managed to win many of the very cream of our intellectual crop by flatteries. The flattery is the same as that employed by the serpent to Eve — "Thou shalt be as gods." As the book of Daniel says:

> "And such as do wickedly against the covenant shall he corrupt by flatteries: but the people that do know their God shall be strong, and do exploits" (Daniel 11:32, KJV).

In fact, the New Agers claim they are a "new species." They have "evolved" into *homo noeticus*. They "evolved" by employing mind-expansion techniques such as meditation and the "other disciplines."[23]

Such talk is chillingly reminiscent of Hitler's "master race" theories. And it should be for it is identical. Both theories — Nazi and New Age — are based on a fable of "Aryanism," a belief that out of the mists of Atlantis emerged Aryan man. Other "sub-races" also survived the Atlantis cataclysms; however, the Aryans were the most highly "evolved."

In agreement with Hitler's Nazi doctrines, New Agers also believe that superior mutation of Aryan man can only come through "consciousness expansion." One could smile at such nonsense were it not for the all-too-poignant memories of the masses who worshipped and blindly followed Hitler.

One is also forced to pause when he sees the extensive organizational efforts of determined New Agers. Planetary Initiative and its World Council of Wise Persons are synergis-

---

[23]This surprising statement is taken from John White's introduction to the 1979 *International Cooperation Council Directory*. Presently known as the Unity-in-Diversity Council and under the direction of Leland Steward, it is actively and openly on the "Maitreyan path."

tically enhanced by the parallel operation of networking organizations such as New World Alliance, Club of Rome, World Goodwill, Lucis Trust, and thousands of others.

New Age communication employs a specialized vocabulary extensive enough to require a separate New Age Dictionary which helps worldwide New Agers speak each other's language.[24]

The Movement teaches the Law of Rebirth or reincarnation. This is basically a teaching that man does not really die, but that he instead is endlessly reborn into new life cycles until such time as he perfects himself sufficiently to qualify for endless rest *(Nirvana)*. Of course, this just happens to match one of the lies of the serpent in the Garden of Eden in telling Eve "you shall not surely die."

The Movement teaches that the Trinity is inferior to an entity known as "The Solar Logos." In fact, the Alice Bailey writings contain in at least two places elaborate organization charts of the "gods" and "masters." The "Solar Logos" is just a notch above the Trinity — a false trinity that does not match our Holy Trinity in that instead of being a personal godhead there is a "Solar Trinity or Logoi" consisting of:

I	The Father	Will
II	The Son	Love-wisdom
III	Holy Spirit	Active Intelligence

After the Solar Trinity come the "Seven Rays" and below that, but deriving "authority" directly from "The Solar Logos" is "S. Sanat Kumara (a scrambling of Satan)." According to Benjamin Creme, David Spangler, the Alice Bailey writings, and the Helena Petrovna Blavatsky writings, this so-called Sanat Kumara is our "God," the "Ancient of Days" and the "One Initiator." Probably, more truthfully,

---

[24]Yes Virginia, there really is a *New Age Dictionary! The New Age Dictionary* was compiled by Alex Jack, the Associate Editor of *East West Journal,* another prominent New Age magazine. It is published by Kanthaka Press of Brookline Village, Massachusetts, and was copyrighted © in 1976 ("The Year of the Dragon"). It contains thousands of entries in its 224 pages. Needless to say, it is an invaluable reference for those wishing to research the New Age Movement.

the "Venus" link of occultism gives us a better clue as to who Sanat Kumara really is. For "Sanat Kumara" is allegedly "the eternal youth from the Planet Venus." Lucifer is also known in occultdom as "Venus." Therefore, Sanat Kumara is merely another name for Satan or Lucifer.

The same chart also contains several lower levels of assorted "Kumaras," "departmental heads," "Manus," "Bodhisattvas," and "Mahachohans," and beneath them, in their turn, many "masters."

Guess who is at the bottom of this chart? None other than "The Master Jesus!" They have demoted our Lord and Savior to the lowest possible spot on their "Hierarchy of Masters!" Furthermore, adding insult to injury, he is shown as reporting to an entity known as the "Venetian Master."

This is clearly the preaching or teaching of "another Jesus" as warned against in II Corinthians 11:3-4, which states:

> "But I fear, lest by any means, as the serpent beguiled Eve through his subtilty, so your minds should be corrupted from the simplicity that is in Christ.

> "For if he that cometh preacheth another Jesus, whom we have not preached, or if ye receive another spirit, which ye have not received, or another gospel, which ye have not accepted . . ." (KJV).

The same organizational chart has separate listings for Jesus and the Christ — a distinct mark of the spirit of antichrist:

> "Who is a liar but he that denieth that Jesus is the Christ? He is antichrist, that denieth the Father and the Son" (I John 2:22, KJV).

Another key component to the Movement is a boundless belief in evolution. In fact, it is central to their theology. The Movement teaches that we have all evolved, but some of us have evolved more highly than others — just as some of us "manifest our divinity" more than others.

It is interesting to note that several of the signers of the

1973 *Humanist Manifesto* are also actively involved in Planetary Initiative for the World We Choose — the big, in-vogue political vehicle for the would-be forces of "Maitreya the Christ."

These esoteric teachings, founded on a base of Eastern mysticism, include a belief in the "Law of Avatars." This teaching states that at the start of every New Age the "Solar Logos" sends "The Christ" or a lesser avatar to overshadow a human being, and working through that person, imparts necessary teachings to the world to help its citizens move forward into the New Age.

When Benjamin Creme, spokesman for the so-called Maitreya the Christ spoke in Detroit on November 4, 1981, he was asked if he had ever met the Christ.

His answer was revealing. He said, "No, I've never met the Christ, but I've met the human body he is inhabiting several times — but never as the Christ."

This reveals the real nature of the antichrist and the power behind the New Age Movement in general. It constitutes nothing less than old-fashioned demonic possession. The person who will eventually be the antichrist and consequently the chief spokesman for Satan will be an adult who freely and voluntarily decided to assume the spirit of Satan.

The Movement teaches that man is saved by initiation and works rather than through the grace of God and faith in the sacrifice of Jesus Christ. Initiation is considered by them to be the heart and core of the planned New World Religion.

This initiation has been clearly defined as "Luciferic" in the Helena Petrovna Blavatsky, Alice Ann Bailey, and David Spangler writings. Sadly, the New Age Movement has infiltrated even many of our Christian denominations with this pagan concept.

Another key teaching of this Movement is that all things are "interconnected" or "interdependent." This is known in the New Age Movement as the Doctrine of Wholeness. This is also called the Doctrine of At-One-Ment, which is a probable perversion of the Christian doctrine of atonement. Its relationship to the Holistic Movement is clear.

The New Age Movement's deep and abiding hatred for Jews, Catholics, Protestant fundamentalists, and orthodox Moslems in particular, and all Christians in general has been reaffirmed in the numerous David Spangler writings and tapes as well as those of other current New Age leaders.

Further, the Movement's theology contains a strong belief in an "inner government" of our planet by a hierarchy of spirits or alleged "masters of wisdom."

One has only to read *The Spear of Destiny* by Trevor Ravenscroft, *The Occult and the Third Reich* by Jean-Michel Angebert, *Hitler, the Occult Messiah* by Gerald Suster, and *Gods and Beasts, the Nazis and the Occult* by Dusty Sklar to quickly come to the horrible realization that the basic doctrines of the New Age Movement were also the teachings that formed the ethos of Nazism.

The danger to Jews, Christians, and even orthodox Moslems from this New Age Movement should not be underestimated. The Movement is working quickly and efficiently to execute its scheme to take control of the world for "Maitreya," not so-subtly, calling it "The Plan."

If "The Plan" proceeds on schedule, they may well be in the driver's seat by June 21, 1983, the date of their planned World Congress to be held in Toronto, Ontario, Canada.

Much of the leadership behind this Initiative has already taken public stands in favor of "Maitreya the Christ."

They have made flat statements in writing that they plan to outlaw the present religious practices and symbols of orthodox Jews and Christians.

They claim that master "messiahs" will appear to adherents of all the present major world religions to persuade them of the "truths" of the New World Religion and its "New Relevation." In fact, "continuity of revelation" is to be a key doctrinal note of the "New World Religion."

They have also stated that angels will appear with "Maitreya" at the time of his declaration and attempted implementation of the New World Religion.

Christians should not be deceived should such an occurrence take place, for the Bible clearly warns us that Satan is able to appear as an angel of light and has the power to make his lesser agents and ministers appear likewise in the same light.

The Movement has threatened violence and even extermination of Jews, Christians, and Moslems failing to cooperate with "Maitreya" and the New World Religion. The threat is contained in several places in the Alice Bailey writings and reiterated in the David Spangler writings, which state that those of us who refuse to accept the "Christ" will be sent to another dimension other than physical incarnation, out of physical embodiment, to another level of vibration where we will be happier!

The threat is also repeated in the Agni Yoga (Nicholas Roerich) teachings, another cornerstone work of the "New Age."

The Movement is profoundly antisemitic, all the way through to its esoteric core. Many lesser-level initiates in the Movement are unaware of the situation. The Movement's theoreticians, including Spangler, also speak freely of the need to maintain Aryan purity — which was Hitler's justification for exterminating the Jews.

Despite their current talk of need for "religious freedom" from the "persecutions" of the Moral Majority, the Movement advocates just the opposite. Its views are reiterated frequently by prominent New Age spokesmen such as Gregory Bateson, David Spangler, and Foster Bailey (Bateson and Bailey are now both deceased): that religious freedom and the separation between Church and State must end in the New Age.

Buckminster Fuller has also incorporated such teachings into his "design science" proposals for the "New Age."

The Movement has campaigned long and arduously for disarmament. This is considered a key step to the implementation of their hoped-for "New World Order."

"9. In the preparatory period for the new world order there will be a steady and regulated disarmament. It will not be optional. No nation will be permitted to produce and organise any equipment for destructive purposes or to infringe the security of any other nation. One of the first tasks of any future peace conference will be to regulate this matter and gradually see to the disarming of the nations."[25]

How sincere they are about a nuclear-free world, however, is unfortunately well-demonstrated within the pages of the very same Alice Bailey book:

"The atomic bomb (though used only twice destructively) ended the resistance of the powers of evil because its potency is predominantly etheric. Its uses are twofold at this time:

"a. As the forerunner of that release of energy which will change the mode of human living and inaugurate the new age wherein we shall not have civilisations and their emerging cultures but a world culture and an emerging civilisation, thus demonstrating the true synthesis which underlies humanity. *The atomic bomb emerged from a first ray Ashram* [will-to-good, Shamballa (force, violence) energies], *working in conjunction with a fifth ray group* [scientific workers]; from the long-range point of view, its intent was and is purely beneficent.

"b. As a means in the hands of the United Nations to enforce the outer forms of peace, and thus give time for teaching on peace and on the growth of goodwill to take effect. The atomic bomb does not belong to the three nations who perfected it and who own the secrets at present — the United States of America, Great Britain and Canada. *It belongs to the United Nations for use (or let us rather hope, simply for threatened use when aggressive action on the part of any nation rears its ugly head).* It does not essentially matter whether that aggression is the gesture of any particular nation or group of nations or whether it is generated by the

[25]*The Externalisation of the Hierarchy* by Alice A. Bailey, p. 191.

political groups of any powerful religious organisa-
tion, such as the Church of Rome, who are as yet
unable to leave politics alone and attend to the business for which all religions are responsible — leading
human beings closer to the God of Love."[26]

[26]*Ibid.*, p. 548.

CHAPTER 6

The New Age and Prophecy

It becomes very evident as one studies the basic literature of the New Age Movement that its leadership proposes to implement all the systems of the antichrist warned of in the Bible, particularly those presented in Revelation, chapter 13.

New Agers have publicly made their intent known to abolish cash money. They have said they propose to implement a "more rational means of exchange," such as a computerized barter system.

Books by Buckminster Fuller clearly spell out an intent to give every world resident a number and require the usage of this number in all financial transactions of any sort — including minor purchases — with a universal "credit card."

The Movement has also been promoting the establishment of gigantic global agencies for controlling the distribution of food and other vital resources. The motivation behind this proposal may be gleaned from the Fuller writings: in order to control the world, one must also control the world supply routes.

The New Agers have stated that we will soon enjoy a "New World Order" that will be a synthesis of the parliamentary/Commonwealth of Nations system of Great Britain, the socialism of Russia and the heterogenous mixtures of the United States.

Another goal of their "hierarchy" for this "New World Order" is that of a unified Europe. This sounds strangely like the beast that came out of the water in Revelation 13: it had feet like a bear (Russia?), spoke like a lion (Britain?), was like unto a leopard (United States?) and had ten horns and seven heads. As to the seven heads, the New World Order will supposedly be one in which the "mysteries" are restored. The seven past governments of which Rome was the sixth and Hitler the seventh were all pagan, mystery-religion governments.

In the Book of Revelation the government of the antichrist is to be headed by "the beast that was dead and came back to life." After extensive research, it is safe to say that the New Age Movement is identical in both belief systems and cosmology to the Nazism of Hitler — which I believe is the beast that was dead and came back to life. It is also interesting to note that Nazism was commonly referred to as "the beast" and according to Trevor Ravenscroft in *The Spear of Destiny*, Hitler knowingly tried to invoke the spirit of the "beast from the pit."

Similarly in this day and age many New Agers are deliberately trying to "invoke" a presence — the presence of "Maitreya the Christ" or an antichrist.

The October 1982 issue of the *Reader's Digest* carried a full-page, full-color copy of "The Great Invocation," the New Age prayer to "Maitreya the Christ" to invoke his presence on earth.

Benjamin Creme has stated, as do the Alice Bailey writings, that the "Great Invocation" will be the new world prayer after the advent of "Maitreya," whoever he is.

And similar to Nazism, the New Agers — or top level New Age esotericists, that is — do have a war planned for our future. The precise nature of this planned conflict may be gleaned from the Alice Bailey writings:

> "Years ago I said that the war which may follow this one would be waged in the field of the world religions. Such a war will not work out, however, in a similar period of external carnage and blood; it will be fought largely with mental weapons and in the world of thought; it will involve also the emotional realm, from the standpoint of idealistic fanaticism. This inherent fanaticism (found ever in reactionary groups) will fight against the appearance of the coming world religion and the spread of esotericism. For this struggle certain of the well-organised churches

through their conservative elements (their most powerful elements), are already girding themselves. . . . Fanaticism, entrenched theological positions, and materialistic selfishness are to be found actively organised in the churches in all continents and of all denominations. They can be expected to fight for their established ecclesiastical order, their material profit and their temporal rule, and already are making the needed preparation.

"The coming struggle will emerge within the churches themselves; it will also be precipitated by the enlightened elements who exist in fair numbers already, and are rapidly growing in strength through the impact of human necessity. The fight will then spread to thinking men and women everywhere who — in a protesting revolt — have denied orthodox churchianity and theology."[1]

The reason why Alice Bailey might have anticipated such trouble from the churches is found on page 544 of the same book. There she states the three planned activities of this "New Age Christ":

"1. *The reorganisation of the world religions* — if in any way possible — so that their out-of-date theologies, their narrow-minded emphasis and their ridiculous belief that they know what is in the Mind of God may be offset, in order that the churches may eventually be the recipients of spiritual inspiration.

"2. *The gradual dissolution — again if in any way possible — of the orthodox Jewish faith, with its obsolete teaching*, its separative emphasis, its hatred of the Gentiles and its failure to recognise the Christ. In saying this I do not fail to recognise those Jews throughout the world who acknowledge the evils and who are not orthodox in their thinking. . . .

"3. Preparation for a revelation which will inaugurate the new era and set the note for the new world religion."

Another reason why she might have logically expected or-

[1]*Externalisation of the Hierarchy* by Alice A. Bailey, pp. 453-454.

thodox religious opposition has to do with the economic system she proclaims will be set up by the so-called "Hierarchy":

"When the 'adjuster of finances' (as an advanced disciple from this Ashram is called in the Hierarchy) appears, he will find conditions greatly changed from those now prevalent, and this to the following extent:

"1. The principal of barter and exchange (to the benefit of all concerned) will control.

"2. Owing to the development of atomic energy on behalf of human welfare, national currencies will have been largely superseded, not only by a system of barter but by a universal monetary exchange — representative of bartered goods when they are relatively small and unimportant — and by a planned scale of related values. National material assets and the needed commodities will all be provided for under an entirely new system.

"3. Private enterprise will still exist, but will be regulated; the great public utilities, the major material resources and sources of planetary wealth — iron, steel, oil and wheat, for instance — will be owned in the first place by a governing, controlling international group; they will, however, be prepared for international consumption by national groups chosen by the people and under international direction."

If the foregoing sounds reminiscent to those who have had some exposure to biblical prophecy, it should. It is chillingly similar to Revelation 13:16-17:

"And he causeth all, both small and great, rich and poor, free and bond, to receive a mark in their right hand, or in their foreheads:

"And that no man might buy or sell, save he that had the mark, or the name of the beast, or the number of his name."

The New Agers even have a perspective on the war of Armageddon. However, their scenario differs from the biblical account. In reading the following passage, it should be kept in mind that "Black Lodge" or "Black Forces" means the religious orthodox forces whereas "White Lodge" or "White Forces" is used by the New Agers to refer to themselves. The term "Black Magician" as used in the following context also refers to religious orthodoxy:

> "You might well say here: We have also been taught that there exist those who work in the four ethers and who undoubtedly perform magical deeds, yet who do not possess this essential purity and loving-kindness to which reference has been made. This is undoubtedly true; they belong to a group of workers in matter whom we call Black Magicians; they are highly developed intellectually and can motivate mental substance or mind stuff in such a manner that it can achieve objectivity on the physical plane and bring about their deep intent. About this group there is much misunderstanding and profound ignorance. It is perhaps as well, for their destiny is tied up with the future race, the sixth, and their end and the cessation of their activities will come in that far distant aeon which is technically called the Sixth Round. The final break or division between the so-called black and white forces, for this particular world cycle, will take place during the period of the sixth root race in the present round. Towards the close of the sixth root race, before the emergence of the seventh, *we shall have the true Armageddon about which so much has been taught.* A small cycle, corresponding to this final battle and cleavage, will appear during the sixth subrace which is now in process of formation. *The world war, which has just taken place and our present cycle of separativeness and upheaval, do not constitute the true Armageddon.* The war which is told to us in the Mahabharata and the present war had the roots of their trouble and the seeds of the disasters which they brought about, one in the lower and one in the higher astral world."[2]

They have spoken correctly by stating this would be a war as no other. The Book of Revelation, however, claims that this final world battle will see Lucifer and his followers defeated by

[2]From *A Treatise on White Magic* by Alice A. Bailey, pages 543-544.

God himself.

"For they are the spirits of devils, working miracles, which go forth unto the kings of the earth and of the whole world, to gather them to the battle of that great day of God Almighty.

"And he gathered them together in a place called in the Hebrew tongue Armageddon.

"And I saw the beast [antichrist], and the kings of the earth, and their armies, gathered together to make war against him [Jesus Christ] that sat on the horse, and against his army" (Revelation 16:14, 16; 19:19, KJV).

Following is a chart which will give you a correlation between biblical prophecy and the New Age Movement. This chart relates to the end-time events and the facts regarding the New Age Movement which fit those prophecies.

PROPHECY	NEW AGE/CREME FULFILLMENT
"Here is wisdom. Let him that hath understanding count the number of the beast: for it is the number of a man; and his number is Six hundred three score and six (666)" (Revelation 13:18, KJV).	Alice Bailey on pages 79-80 of *The Rays and the Initiations* calls 666 a sacred number and shows how they use occult numerology to calculate it. In *A Treatise on Cosmic Fire* on page 306 she said that 666 "holds the mystery hid of one of the three heavenly men." *The Keys of Enoch*, another New Age "Bible," instructs the reader to use the numerical sequence 6-6-6 as frequently as possible. Use of the number is to attract "higher intelligence" from either another dimension or outer space to our planet.
"The earth also is defiled under the inhabitants thereof; because they have transgressed the laws, changed the ordinance, broken the everlasting covenant" (Isaiah 24:5, KJV).	The New Age Movement uses rainbows (the everlasting covenant pursuant to Genesis 9:15-17) to signal their building of the Rainbow Bridge (antahkarana) which is a bridge between the personality (man) and the soul (Lucifer).

"And he doeth great wonders, so that he maketh fire come down from heaven on the earth in the sight of men" (Revelation 13:13).

"And deceiveth them that dwell on the earth by the means of those miracles which he had power to do in the sight of the beast; saying to them that dwell on the earth, that they should make an image to the beast, which had the wound by a sword, and did live. And he had power to give life unto the image of the beast, that the image of the beast should both speak, and cause that as many as would not worship the image of the beast should be killed" (Revelation 13:14-15, KJV).

"And he causeth all, both small and great, rich and poor, free and bond, to receive a mark in their right hand, or in their foreheads: And that no man might buy or sell, save he that had the mark, or the name of the beast, or the number of his name" (Revelation 13:16-17, KJV).

The New Age Movement has devoted a great deal of research and attention to the use of holographic images (three dimensional images created by use of laser beams). According to David Spangler, in a meeting in Southfield, Michigan, on February 1, 1982, laser beam projectors have been installed for their use on top of the Cathedral of St. John the Divine (Episcopal) in NYC. Lighting experts say these may be used (1) to be beamed on a satellite and coming back through the ionosphere. The light rays will be bent in such a manner as to make it appear that actual flames are coming from the skies and to project a three-dimensional holographic image that could be viewed by up to one-third the earth's surface at any given time. Sound technology is available to make the image speak in the language of areas beamed to.

Benjamin Creme, David Spangler, Alice Bailey, Helena Petrovna Blavatsky, et al, have all said that "initiation" will be the heart and core of the "New World Religion." David Spangler has defined that initiation as a Luciferic initiation and for those who cannot accept the "New Christ" — they will be sent to another dimension other than physical incarnation, according to Spangler. Creme says that cash will be abolished and the world will go to a more rational means of exchange, such as a computerized barter economy. Creme has said that the "initiations" will be given on a mass planetary basis in a "revitalized Christian church" and in the Masonic lodges and other esoteric organizations. Creme said there would be the "sword of cleavage" for all who would not go willingly into the future with this so-called new "Christ."

"And I stood upon the sand of the sea, and saw a beast rise up out of the sea, having seven heads and ten horns, and upon his horns ten crowns, and upon his heads the name of blasphemy. And the beast which I saw was like unto a leopard, and his feet were as the feet of a bear, and his mouth as the mouth of a lion: and the dragon gave him his power, and his seat, and great authority" (Revelation 13:1-3).

Per Alice Bailey in *The Rays and the Initiation,* etc., the New World Order will be a synthesis between the USSR (feet like a bear), Great Britain with its commonwealth of nations (spot like a lion), and the United States with its heterogenous mixture of people (like unto a leopard?). It will also feature a unified Europe. In *The Aquarian Conspiracy,* by Marilyn Ferguson, she stated that Europe was eminently presuitable for launching the new "political-spiritual" entity. Foster Bailey, husband of Alice Bailey, wrote in his book *Running God's Plan* (copyright © 1972, Lucis Trust), that one of the goals of their so-called Hierarchy was to have a unified Europe and that a previous attempt had been made by a disciple, using the Rhine River as a unifying factor — but that attempt was unsuccessful. (The beast that was dead and came back to life — Nazism? — Hitler tried to unify Europe using the Rhine River as a unifying factor! Hitler was into exactly the same brand of occultism as the New Age Movement — Gnosticism and mysticism. The plans of Alice Bailey which are followed with precision by the New Age Movement, are *identical* to Nazism.)

"And there are seven kings: five are fallen, and one is, and the other is not yet come; and when he cometh, he must continue a short space. And the beast that was, and is not, even he is the eighth, and is of the seven, and goeth into perdition" (Revelation 17:10-11).

The five preceding kings were all Babylonian philosophy empires based on the Mystery Traditions, which is also what occultism and the New Age Movement are based upon. The sixth kingdom was obviously Pagan Rome. Many Bible scholars have interpreted the Vatican as being the seventh, but I must reject that interpretation (however, the Vatican has seen occult infiltration, as have probably all other denominations of Christianity) as the Vatican continued longer than the other six empires put together and the Bible said "a *short* space." Hitler continued for a short space, also tried to make the old mystery teachings the state religion, was hostile to orthodox Christianity and to Judaism. The New Age goals and teachings from promotion of Aryanism and a super-race to use of swastikas are identical to Nazism. Also to be remembered is the fact that the Vatican never taught reincarnation — this is a New Age or Mystery teaching. It is much more probable that the interpretation is that of an identical government or political system to that of the seven — all mystery teaching governments, including Hitler!

"For when they shall say, Peace and safety; then sudden destruction cometh upon them, as travail upon a woman with child; and they shall not escape" (I Thessalonians 5:3, KJV).

The New World Order, complete with the proposed Nuclear Freeze or disarmament campaign, is laid out on pages 190-191 of *The Externalisation of the Hierarchy* by Alice A. Bailey. On page 548 of the same book, she states that the nuclear bomb was a great advance for humanity, that their "hierarchy" helped develop it working through the fifth ray or scientific workers. She went on to say that when they put the bomb into the hands of the "United Nations," that it could be used or threaten to be used "whenever aggression rears its ugly head" and that it did not matter whether that "aggression" came from nation-states or from powerful religious groups such as "the Church of Rome who did not know how to leave politics alone and attend to the business for which religious groups were responsible." Creme is a disciple of Alice A. Bailey as is David Spangler and this is from the book Creme recommended in his bibliography to give more information on the new "Christ." Also there is extensive New Age literature on the use of atomic weapons.

"Let no man deceive you by any means: *for that day shall not come*, except there come a falling away first, and that man of sin be revealed, the son of perdition; Who opposeth and exalteth himself above all that is called God, or that is worshipped; so that he as God sitteth in the temple of God, shewing himself *that he is God*" (II Thessalonians 2:3-4, KJV).

The "Secret Doctrine" of the New Age Movement and of occultism includes a teaching that the Trinity (not to be confused with our Trinity, for they have totally perverted the persons and purpose of the triune Godhead) is inferior to something known as "The Solar Logos." In Alice Bailey's books, *The Initiations: Human and Solar* and *A Treatise on Cosmic Fire*, this organizational chart may be found and possibly in the Helena Petrovna Blavatsky books also.

"Who is a liar but he that denieth that Jesus is the Christ? He is antichrist, that denieth the Father and the Son" (I John 2:22, KJV).

Benjamin Creme, as well as the rest of the New Age Movement, with the exception of those who have not been initiated to this point, consistently deny that Jesus is the Christ and they insist that Maitreya is the Christ and Jesus is his disciple. This is a central point of the Secret Doctrine as well as a central teaching of Unity and other New Age churches — that the Christ consciousness resides in each of us individually (doctrine of God Immanent) and there can be a Christ other than Jesus — that Buddha was a Christ, Krishna was a Christ, etc.

"And every spirit that confesseth not that Jesus Christ is come in the flesh is not of God: and this is that spirit of antichrist, whereof ye have heard that it should come; and even now already is it in the world" (I John 4:3, KJV).

The New Age Movement people, including Benjamin Creme and David Spangler, as well as Unity and many theologians who have infiltrated other denominations say that Jesus Christ did not come in the flesh — that the Christ Consciousness descended upon him at the time of his baptism and stayed with him until the time of his crucifixion. More outrageously still, Creme said that Jesus did not earn the right to keep his resurrected body and that he is presently living in a 640-year-old Syrian body in the Himalayan mountains.

"And the rest of the men which were not killed by these plagues yet repented not of the works of their hands, that they should not worship devils, and idols of gold, and silver, and brass, and stone, and of wood: which neither can see, nor hear, nor walk: Neither repented they of their murders, nor of their sorceries, nor of their fornication nor of their thefts" (Revelation 9:20-21, KJV).

The New Age Movement is both pantheistic (worship of many gods) and animistic (worship of inanimate objects and of animal and plant life). They deify Lucifer and in fact David Spangler has said we *must* take a Luciferic initiation if we wish to enter the New Age alive. They have resurrected every pagan god that was ever worshipped and a variety of new ones, as well. As far as sorceries are concerned, they are the *modus operandi* of the New Age Movement, as much attention is given to psychic phenomena and "consciousness raising."

"And the king shall do according to his will; and he shall

Maitreya has claimed through transmissions from Benjamin

exalt himself, and magnify himself above every god, and shall speak marvellous things against the God of gods, and shall prosper till the indignation be accomplished: for that that is determined shall be done" (Daniel 11:36, KJV).

"But in his estate shall he honour the God of forces: and a god whom his fathers knew not shall he honour with gold, and silver, and with precious stones, and pleasant things" (Daniel 11:38, KJV).

"And he shall speak great words against the most High, and shall wear out the saints of the most High, and think to change times and laws: and they shall be given unto his hand until a time and times and the dividing of time" (Daniel 7:25, KJV).

Creme that Jesus is one of his disciples and that he is at the head of a hierarchy of "gods" or "masters."

The Aquarian Gospel of Jesus the Christ, allegedly transcribed from the "Akashic Records" by "Levi" (Leo Dowling) states on page 16 of the introduction by Eva Dowling that one may enter fully into the spirit of the "God of Force." The entire theme of occultism, Luciferianism, and cultism connected with the New Age Movement is learning how to manipulate the "Force." New Agers do not believe in a personal transcendent God to whom we are all accountable. They believe that God is a neutral force which can be manipulated either for good or evil.

According to Benjamin Creme, there will be the "sword of cleavage" for all who refuse to accept Maitreya the Christ. Alice Bailey said in her books that the next great war would be in the field of world religions. She stated that the three goals of the so-called new "Christ" included restructuring Christianity and abolishing orthodox Judaism.

The New Agers, including Bailey, Creme, and David Spangler, have laid out plans consistent with what they call "The Plan" which include abolishing traditional religious holidays and substituting New Age pagan festivals in their place. For example, they have said that Good Friday and Christmas will have to go.

CHAPTER 7

Structure and Front Organizations

The New Age Movement is characterized by a large corps of participants who truly believe they are working for the good of the world and the good of themselves.

While there are thousands of diverse organizations banded together to mutually promote the New Age through a system of networking, the real power in the Movement presently appears to be in the hands of those behind the Planetary Initiative for the World We Choose.

They went public in a big way on February 8, 1982, holding their reception/cocktail party in The Cathedral of St. John the Divine, Episcopal, New York City. Some of the most influential names in the world sponsored this party as well as endorsed the concept and organization of Planetary Initiative for the World We Choose.

The work of Planetary Initiative (PI) followed years of preparation by the Network of World Servers, set up by Alice A. Bailey in 1925. The role of the World Servers (also called "Servant of the World") was to act as the "vanguard for the reappearance of the Christ. . . ." The organization controlling PI, which coordinates the efforts of the networking groups, is called Planetary Citizens. One of the official purposes of Planetary Citizens is to aid the "world servers" everywhere.

As with most operations aspiring to world domination, one would expect a police/military arm somewhere in the picture. At least two have come to my personal attention to date: the Guardian Angels and the First Earth Battalion. Both groups enjoy the support — financial and otherwise — of the New Age Movement and both groups spread the New Age concepts as well as demonstrate a highly visible New Age presence.

The Guardian Angels have rapidly expanded to over 40 American cities and several Canadian cities and Curtis Sliwa has made public statements that he intends to go worldwide with 100,000 Guardian Angels.

The First Earth Battalion — sponsored by the United States military and enjoying good reviews from the War College in Pennsylvania — openly claims through its leader, Jim Channon, to be a battalion of New Age Samurai.

Even more startling is another parallel to Nazism — attempts to swell their ranks with prisoners, especially convicted felons. There are literally dozens of New Age prisoner recruiting efforts ranging from in-prison mind-control programs such as EST and Silva to encouragement of Transcendental Meditation (TM). Allegedly introduced to help curb recidivism, they are actually designed to give ex-convicts the mystical experiences that help enhance their desired solidarity with other rank-and-file New Agers.

Adopt-a-prisoner programs and prison ashram projects are also popular ways of reaching the prisoners. Sadly this is an area that Christians have all too often abdicated to those with less than honorable motives for the fate of the prisoners' eternal souls.

The Movement has enjoyed a well-organized and orchestrated propaganda drive since 1975. Various aspects of the drive have been conducted on a subtle level for many years; and the occult motives of the Movement have been kept largely hidden from public view during that time. Since 1975, however, the New Agers have been open about their aims for a "cleansing action" against the "negative elements" of religion and other opposition to the world-domination goals of the Movement.

This propaganda effort has utilized sophisticated, cleverly veiled rationales for the persecution of Christians and Jews in the near future. New Agers now widely believe that Christainity is bad because "it promotes cruelty to little animals," "it is bad for one's mental adjustment," "it is separative and anything separative is evil," etc.

Some of the other items to be covered in the propaganda drive to prepare the world for the so-called new "Christ" includes teachings on:

1. Evolution of consciousness.
2. The interrelatedness of the individual soul to all souls.
3. The "kingdom of God" as simply the appearance of soul-controlled men on earth in everyday life — "WE ARE ALL DIVINE."
4. The idea that there are some on earth who have reached relative perfection — "SOME OF US ARE, HOWEVER, MORE DIVINE THAN OTHERS."
5. The belief that there are individuals who have reached total perfection or "Christ Consciousness" — "ONE OF US IS PERFECT AND SHOULD BE KING!"
6. A recognition that there has always been a "plan" (The Plan) and that this plan has been present — but unrecognized — throughout history.
7. Mind control.
8. Holistic health.
9. Color therapy and music therapy.
10. Iridology.

This chapter is necessarily an encapsulated statement of some of the features of the New Age Movement that are important to Christians. This Movement has successfully infiltrated all of Christendom and is bold enough to sponsor full-page ads proclaiming "The Christ Is Now Here."

While New Agers know their Movement is worldwide and powerful, too many Christians are still sound asleep, thinking that nothing prophetic is happening, while their children and sometimes even themselves are lured by the deceptively smooth flatteries of this Movement.

We can still wake up. We do not have to be deceived by the flattering lies of this Movement that we shall not surely die and we shall be as gods ourselves. We can shake off our embarrassment at being called "fundamentalist." We can and must realize that there is nothing inherently wrong with fundamentalism. If anything, we are not fundamentalist enough in that we have hide-bound interpretations and eschatologies that too often conflict with the plain words of scripture.

We must realize that we have been the victims of a gigantic propaganda drive directed against all Jews and Christians in general and fundamentalists in particular. Not until we ourselves realize what is going on will we be able to assist our friends and children who have been unwittingly involved. A time of alertness and repentance is required for all God's children so that we might be counted "worthy to stand all these things" and prepare for our ultimate reward paid for with the precious blood of our Savior Jesus Christ.

In the process of investigating the New Age Movement, I must confess that I became fairly hardened to messages from their numerous false Christs. I had accumulated an abundance of material containing incredible heresies. Many bore purported signatures of "Jesus" with acknowledgements by purported distinguished authors including the "Holy Spirit."

Clearly the landscape of the "New Age" was dotted with false avatars and Christs of every shape and description. For the sake of thoroughly documenting my point that we were indeed in an age of many false Christs and messiahs, I made a habit of acquiring their materials.

Therefore, I was somewhat less than attentive when I found a book in a local New Age bookstore entitled *The Reappearance of the Christ*, by Benjamin Creme. I did purchase it however, and added it to my ever-growing New Age collection.

Later, while computer cataloging my collection, I was forced to skim its contents to make a brief description for entry purposes. Thereupon, I realized that this was not an average New Age book about the average false Christ. This book was clearly special. It appeared that this so-called Christ was saying he would do the very things the Bible alerted Christians to watch for in the coming antichrist.

An appendix entitled *How the Plan Is Working Out* was authored by Peter Liefhebber, a prominent European journalist, and co-authored by Creme himself. It boldly claimed as proof their plan is working the following facts: activities of the International Legal Commission (consultants to the United Nations); the North-South Commission, consisting of 18 international politicians under the chairmanship of former German Chancellor Willy Brandt; an American Presidential Commission report on global malnutrition; a UNICEF report; activity in support of the New International Economic Order, including a periodic supplement report by 16 major newspapers; statements by Brazilian archbishop Dom Helder Camera (a Pierre Teilhard de Chardin admirer); statements by Nobel Prize winner Professor J. Tinbergen (also affiliated with the Club of Rome); activities and enrollment in the Hunger Project; European Economic Commission activities; and activity by the World Council of Churches.

It also claimed as proof of Maitreya's presence the absence of California earthquakes, claiming Maitreya had caused the Mt. St. Helens volcanic explosion to reduce geological pressure! Although the earthquake part was hard to take, many of the other facts cited were not. These were tiny aspects of the overall line of logic appearing on even Christian bookshelves calling for marshalling and globalization of the world's resources. The very items I would have sworn were part of a plan Creme was openly bragging about were indeed part of a plan!

The same appendix ominously stated:

> "All these statements and developments are signs of a dawning awareness of the position in which our society finds itself; it is indeed a matter of 'share or die.' In this awareness, however, lies the implication that it is still possible to change course. That possibility will become a certainty as soon as man has pledged himself in support of Maitreya."

Throughout history there have been a number of false Christs. Their usual tactic is to come along and insist that they are either Jesus or some type of an Eastern avatar.

Another characteristic of these false Christs is that they are far from bashful. They appear, collect dollars and accolades from their faithful and allow their supporters to house and feed them in a manner fit for a king.

Here we had a somewhat different situation: an advance man for a false Christ who transmitted messages claiming Jesus was not the Christ. One such transmission from Maitreya through Creme dated November 10, 1977, declared:

> "Those who look for Me in terms of My beloved Disciple, the Master Jesus, will find his qualities in Me."

This should be of great interest to Bible scholars because of the biblical test of antichrist found in I John 2:22:

> "Who is a liar but he that denieth Jesus is the Christ? He is antichrist, that denieth the Father and the Son" (I John 2:22, KJV).

Skimming Creme's book further, I learned that *this* false Christ intended to inaugurate both a new world government and a new world religion. This religion would feature "mass planetary initiations." Initiation would, in fact, be the heart and core of the new world religion. They were going to change times and laws. Traditional Jewish and Christian holidays would be replaced with pagan festivals such as Wesak Festival and a Festival of the Christ — to be celebrated at full moons, of course.

Creme reiterated the standard New Age teaching that we are entering the Age of Aquarius. This New Age will be inaugurated by Maitreya and there will be a necessary "sword of cleavage" for all refusing to cooperate with Maitreya.

Clearly this book deserved more than a superficial reading. It apparently required serious study. I resolved to do just that and the book accompanied me day and night until it was inadvertently misplaced. Returning to the place of purchase for a replacement I was told the book was out of stock. However, I was still in luck because Benjamin Creme was coming to Unity and I could hear him for myself!

The cashier handed me a brochure proclaiming, "THE EMERGENCE OF THE WORLD TEACHER." I read the brochure in stunned silence. It was one thing to read a book by an apparently strange English writer with a Los Angeles publisher. Somehow, I expected that type of input from such exotic sources. It was something else, however, to hold in my hand a brochure announcing his presence in the near future within the confines of a local *and* prominent religious organization.[1] I felt this was a sign that things were much more advanced than even I had previously believed.

I located a copy of Creme's book in another store and also purchased some of the titles he set forth in his bibliography. Creme had noted that he was a follower of Alice Bailey's esoteric writings. One familiar with the Movement and the Bailey teachings cannot help but note the close patterning of developments within the New Age Movement along the lines set forth by Mrs. Bailey. She is literally followed like a recipe.

Was Maitreya coming to inaugurate a New Age of peace and light? Or was he coming to inaugurate a reign of terror? The answers are contained within the Alice Bailey writings.

Creme had recommended *The Externalisation of the Hierarchy* by Alice A. Bailey. I must confess it was an excellent source of information! I learned that the New Age Movement was at its esoteric core profoundly anti-Christian, antisemitic, and even anti-Moslem (orthodox Moslem, that is — not Sufism).

Bailey's books, allegedly transmitted to her through the "Tibetan Master DK," openly promoted the concept of Aryanism — a major doctrine of Hitler's Third Reich!

[1]Since I launched a public attack on the New Age Movement, the local minister of Unity (his church openly bills itself as a "New Age Center") publicly denied they had sponsored Creme. He claimed the sponsorship was by another but refused to say who that "other" had been. Creme, in the same three-way radio debate between myself, Creme, and Rev. Williamson, said he could not recall off-hand if Unity had sponsored him on that occasion, but other Unity ministers and churches had sponsored him and he completely endorsed all Unity stood for. Rev. Williamson refused to denounce Creme and even conceded that Maitreya might be the Christ — even though he admittedly was not Jesus!

The Movement was sounding amazingly like Nazism and Maitreya was sounding more and more like another Hitler. I invested in a few books on the occult background of the Third Reich and my suspicions were confirmed. The parallels were covered in a tabulation in another chapter of this book and the reader should study them carefully.

Although religious fundamentalism has been paralleled with Nazism, nothing could be further from the truth. Nazism was an elaborate synthesis of neo-paganism, gnosticism, consciousness-expansion techniques and the occult. The same things may be said of the New Age Movement.

As Dr. Lewis Sumberg once noted:

> "The ability of neo-Paganism to reaffirm itself militantly and contest with Christianity for men's minds and bodies tells us that the Nazi nightmare is the most recent but not the final act in a larger human tragedy that is still being played out. It would be foolish to see the phenomenon as a specifically 'German problem'; how unbelievably shallow the Christian faith and ethic are was amply demonstrated by the unparalleled recrudescence of neo-Paganism everywhere the swastika went.

> "The rise of occultism and the practice of the black arts by the myriad secret societies — particularly the kind represented by satanism — was noted everywhere in the Germany of the 1920s. That we are witnessing much the same phenomenon in the United States today in the ominous and prodigious growth of politico-religious elitist cults represented by satanism, by Manson-type 'families,' and by the epidemic of occult-inspired political assassinations, should cause civilized men the gravest concern. The authors are doubtless right in predicting that certain practitioners of the black arts will yet play a major role in determining the shape of a not-too-distant future."[2]

[2]From *The Occult and the Third Reich* by Jean-Michel Angebert (joint signature of two French scholars) with introduction by Lewis A.M. Sumberg, Chairman of the History Department of the University of Tennessee. This book is an excellent overview of the occultic roots of Nazism. The one quarrel I would

Near-horror gripped me as I read the sourcebook for this quote — *The Occult and the Third Reich*. If I possessed fewer scruples, I could have easily whited out every reference to Nazism, the Third Reich, and Germany and replaced it with The New Age Movement — a worldwide phenomenon — and re-released it as an up-to-date, authoritative text on the New Age Movement. There was absolutely no question about it. The cosmology and cosmogony of the New Age Movement and Nazism were identical. From the "Master Race" theory through evolution through swastikas, there was total identity between these two political movements. Tibetan Buddhism and Theosophy played an important role in each. Initiates, adepts and masters were an important part of each. The pieces of the puzzle were beginning to come together.

I reread the Book of Revelation, where I saw:

> "And the angel said unto me, Wherefore didst thou marvel? I will tell thee the mystery of the woman, and of the beast that carrieth her, which hath the seven heads and ten horns.

> "The beast that thou sawest was, and is not; and shall ascend out of the bottomless pit, and go into perdition: and they that dwell on the earth shall wonder, whose names were not written in the book of life from the foundation of the world, when they behold the beast that was, and is not, and yet is.

> "And here is the mind which hath wisdom. The seven heads are seven mountains, on which the woman sitteth.

> "And there are seven kings: five are fallen, and one is, and the other is not yet come; and when he cometh, he must continue a short space.

have with the writers is that they tend to adopt an assumption prevalent among occultists that there is a good and bad side to "The Force." I would argue that it was more a matter of the degree of initiation, particularly all the more so now that so many New Agers openly adulate Lucifer. The edition quoted from was copyrighted © 1974 by MacMillan Publishing Co., Inc. McGraw-Hill also has published a paperback edition of this important work.

"And the beast that was, and is not, even he is the eighth, and is of the seven, and goeth into perdition" (Revelation 17:7-11, KJV).

There were seven kings. The New Agers had said their Movement was as old as Atlantis and enjoyed a post-diluvian renaissance and worldwide diffusion at the time of the founding of Babylon! There were seven Babylonian or gnostic (mystery-teaching) empires. Five are fallen — the five gnostic empires preceding Rome. The one in existence at the time of John's vision was obviously pagan Rome. The Apostle John wrote the book during the Roman persecution of the Christians.

The one that was not yet come "and when he cometh, he must continue a short space" — could it possibly have been Hitler? Who was the beast that was dead and came back to life?

I discounted the possibility of it being somebody physically dying and coming back to life for the reason that reincarnation was never a traditional biblical or Judeo/Christian teaching. It seemed more proper to describe a doctrine of gnosticism and Eastern mysticism. I knew also that many fundamentalists had interpreted that beast or the woman riding the beast as the Vatican. I had to discount the Vatican entirely as actually being the beast, for it had continued longer than most of the other empires combined.

The Bible had distinctly said that king would continue only a "short space." Likewise, I had to discount communism as being the beast for the reason that its teachings were not analogous to those of the other six mystery-teaching empires. Neither could anyone say with accuracy that it had been "dead." Communism has enjoyed excellent health since its inception and prophetically is to meet its Waterloo at the time of a future invasion of Israel.

Nazism was another story. Nearly everyone has enjoyed the illusion that it was dead and buried. Morever, Hitler had actively tried to invoke the spirit of the beast from the pit.[3]

The Third Reich had practiced unmatched barbarity towards its Jewish population as well as towards others classified as "subhuman."

Yes, the pieces were fitting. That beast must be Nazism — worldwide Nazism without Switzerland to run to — and the antichrist, whoever he is, the next Führer.

Painstakingly I collected every available scrap of information on the mystical roots of Nazism and compared it all to the data in my possession on the New Age Movement. I sought the assistance of political science experts who concurred that what I was showing them was indeed Nazism revived — in its purest sense.

With this preparation behind me, I attended the Creme lecture. Approximately 750 to 800 people were present at that Detroit gathering. I had known many among them personally for a number of years. The crowd ranged from influentials to those on welfare. Detroit's New Age elite had turned out in force. Anti-hunger organizations flanked the lobby distributing their literature. The program director for the Southeastern Michigan Holistic Health Association was assisting with the preparations and the question and answer period.

The Planetary Initiative for the World We Choose organizers were present and showing their approval for the proceedings by leading the crowd in cheers and standing ovations. Some of the nice people I had met in a Hunger Project meeting were there — with starry-eyed expressions. Prominent lawyers and physicians were in attendance. The entire Course-in-Miracles class from Detroit Unity Temple was also there.

Heavily incensed with the same brand as that used in occult bookstores, the hall had a familiar odor. The audience was truly representative. Rich and poor, black and white, powerful and powerless — it was a readily accessible

---

[3]See *The Spear of Destiny* by Trevor Ravenscroft, copyright © 1973 by Trevor Ravenscroft.

power base for Maitreya and his spokesmen.

With a wave of the hand, Creme seemed to instantly mesmerize a vast majority of the crowd. As he spoke, the audience's collective trance deepened.

Calling upon the Lord to spare me from this man's evil influence, I remembered Daniel's prophecy that the final world dictator would have power that was not his own:

> "And in the latter time of their kingdom, when the transgressors are come to the full, a king of fierce countenance, and understanding dark sentences, shall stand up.

> "And his power shall be mighty, but not by his own power: and he shall destroy wonderfully, and shall prosper, and practise, and shall destroy the mighty and the holy people.

> "And through his policy also he shall cause craft to prosper in his hand; and he shall magnify himself in his heart, and by peace shall destroy many: he shall also stand up against the Prince of princes; but he shall be broken without hand" (Daniel 8:23-25, KJV).

Clearly Creme had a power that was not his own — an evil, hypnotic presence.

I remembered eye-witness accounts of Hitler's hypnotic powers with awe. According to Ravenscroft, Hitler had deliberately invoked the spirit of Lucifer.

In a recent radio interview, Benjamin Creme stated to a listening audience of 28 states and 11 foreign countries that Lucifer came from the planet Venus, 18½ million years ago. He went on to say that Lucifer had made the supreme sacrifice for our planet and was both the prodigal son and the sacrificial lamb.

According to Creme, Lucifer is in charge of our planetary evolution. Interestingly enough, this was the same thing that he said about someone he called "Sanat Kumara." At the time of his Los Angeles lecture, he had said Sanat Kumara was our god. Maitreya was to lead the initiates before the feet of Sanat

Kumara.

Since there is obvious identity between Sanat Kumara and Lucifer, it appears that Maitreya and his spokesmen are involved with the same source of power as was Hitler — Lucifer. Clearly then, like Hitler before them, Creme, and Maitreya were enjoying power that was not their own.

Prior to the meeting and during the intermission, those in attendance were handed a brochure regarding the New Group of World Servers. An apparent 6-6-6 symbol enclosed in a triangle and a circle graced the leaflet. It stated that the New Group of World Servers was to be the vanguard for the reappearance of the Christ. It further said that while some organizations and religious experiments were good, others were undesirable and would have no part in the New Age. The ones that were not desirable were those that "spread the virus of hatred and separation."

This is exactly what Alice Bailey ascribed as fault to orthodox Jews, Christians, and Moslems. The brochure was openly based on the Alice Bailey teachings as is the entire concept of "World Servers." Alice Bailey organized the New Group of World Servers under the direction of her "Tibetan Master." The brochure also contained a recommended reading list for "more information." Marilyn Ferguson's *The Aquarian Conspiracy* was at the top of it.

The verbal content of Creme's speech could only be classified as bizarre. However, the apparently bewitched audience failed to see it that way. According to Creme, the world could expect Maitreya the Christ within a few short months. The Christ and Jesus would stand side by side, thus ending the controversy as to whether Jesus was the Christ once and for all. Further, Jesus had never left the earth. Having been reincarnated, he was living in a 640-year-old body in the Himalayas — a Syrian body at that. While Jesus had had a resurrected body after the crucifixion, he had to forfeit that body because "he had not earned the right to keep it" for the reason that "Jesus was only a fourth level initiate, whereas Gautama Buddha was a sixth level initiate. However, Lord Maitreya himself was a seventh level initiate and the only one eligible for such a high level of initiation."

Listening to Creme in horrified fascination, I was reminded of the prophecies of Daniel 11:36 and II Thessalonians 2:4:

> "And the king shall do according to his will; and he shall exalt himself, and magnify himself above every god, and shall speak marvellous things against the God of gods, and shall prosper till the indignation be accomplished: for that that is determined shall be done" (Daniel 11:36, KJV).

> "Who opposeth and exalteth himself above all that is called God, or that is worshipped; so that he as God sitteth in the temple of God, shewing himself that he is God" (II Thessalonians 2:4, KJV).

I also gained a fresh appreciation for the stern warnings not to add or subtract from the Book of Revelation. It was becoming increasingly apparent to me that the prophecies were being fulfilled in a very literal manner.

I also gained a fresh respect for the inspired words of the Apostle Peter who said:

> "We have also a more sure word of prophecy; whereunto ye do well that ye take heed, as unto a light that shineth in a dark place, until the day dawn, and the day star arise in your hearts:

> "Knowing this first, that no prophecy of the scripture is of any private interpretation.

> "For the prophecy came not in old time by the will of man: but holy men of God spake as they were moved by the Holy Ghost" (II Peter 1:19-21, KJV).

Many times during that evening I was scarcely able to contain my anger. People were present who were extremely active in the fight against the Moral Majority. One of the staunchest campaigners in this effort jumped to his feet and led the crowd in a standing ovation for Creme's remarks that all false Christs and false teachers about the Christ would "disappear" when Maitreya made his declaration.

Creme received another round of applause when he stated "democracy will disappear." It was easy to understand why Creme had expressed such hostility to the Bible and particularly the fundamentalist interpretation. The Bible exposes him and his cohorts with remarkable precision and foresight!

Several months later I debated Creme over a local radio station. He accused me of being a fundamentalist and I told him he was right. Not only was he right, but I was proud of it and I could well understand his aversion to it.

It is time we Christians stopped apologizing for our fundamentalism and orthodoxy. Fundamentalism was not the cause of Nazism — occultism was! And we have sat back idly while the occultists turned their debacle into a propaganda victory by stating that Hitler was an illustration of the dangers of fundamentalist orthodoxy.

Benjamin Creme and the New Age Movement, of which Creme is but one tiny part, fit the biblical specifications identifying the spirit of antichrist with precision.

CHAPTER 8

The New Age Movement — the Fourth Reich?

As we have already noted to a limited extent, one of the most startling aspects of the New Age Movement, apart from its apparent fulfillment of biblical prophecy, is its amazing resemblance to Hitler's Nazism. One of the best-kept secrets of the twentieth century is the occultic roots and nature of the religious philosophy at the heart of the Third Reich.

Exactly why this information remained classified for so long and such pressure was brought to bear upon those having intimate knowledge of this will probably remain a mystery until judgment day.

Nevertheless there are some interesting clues.

It is public knowledge that both Winston Churchill and Franklin Delano Roosevelt dabbled in the occult. Perhaps the same conspiring Luciferic spirit that induced Hitler to implement the darkest practices of occultism moved upon the Western powers to conceal the esoteric mysticism behind Nazism. Were they knowing participants in the portion of "The Plan" revealed by Alice Bailey in the 1930s? Part of "The Plan" indicates that the New World Order necessary for total world domination by "The Christ" and "The Masters of Wisdom" would have to be established upon the foundations of a world badly traumatized by a severe war. The full truth may never be known.

At any rate, for all practical purposes, the New Age Movement appears to qualify as a revival of Nazism. This is not to call every New Ager a Nazi. A substantial number of those participating in the New Age Movement are probably innocently involved for the finest and best of motives.

Similar to Nazism, the New Age Movement is organized like a gigantic corporation. Also, like Nazism, the Movement is based upon a structure of initiates, adepts and masters. High level initiates always know more than low-level initiates. Chiefs always know more than Indians. Colonels and majors are always told more than privates of the plans and direction of the military. As in any large organization, most people quietly do their jobs without knowing the full nature of what they are involved with or precisely where they personally fit in the scheme of things. Most of the rank and file of any large organization do not see the big picture, whereas the management either does or should know the fine details and overall scope of the operation.

While still a very young child, Hitler was initiated into the finer mysteries of the occult. He attended a Benedictine monastery school near his German home. The abbot in charge was fascinated by the lore of the Albigensians or Cathars, who could probably be accurately classified as early New Agers in that they believed man could gain the powers of a god. The occult interests Hitler gained in this school, stayed with him all of his adult life and helped to shape his future spiritual philosophy.

While Hitler was in Vienna pursuing a career as an architect and artist, he spent his spare time in occult bookstores and libraries, acquainting himself with the mysteries of metaphysical lore and gaining the acquaintance of adepts in both "white" and "black" magic. Transcendent states of consciousness and mind expansion fascinated him and he devoted every spare cent and minute to the pursuit of higher consciousness. Yoga, astrology, Eastern and Western "paths" to this goal proved too slow for his ambitions and like many impetuous New Agers of today, he decided to accelerate the process by supplementing meditation with drugs.

Mescaline was used to transport him to the highest state of consciousness where he could look into what New Agers and occultists call the "Akashic Record" — a demonic version of historical and future events. Hitler's aim in taking this accelerated path was to gain a perspective on his future destiny.

Successful in contacting the top, Hitler rightly believed he had established communication with Lucifer, from whom he openly coveted possession. Studies have shown that mind-expansion drugs, and transcendental as well as other forms of meditation that require the emptying of the mind, produce the same type of side effects, including flashbacks and delusions of grandeur. From that point, Hitler suffered the known side effects of both prolonged meditation and mind-expanding drug abuse.

However, the side effects pale in the light of the major effects: establishing Hitler in power and enabling him to transform and control a nation. If the hypnotic effect of dabbling in occultism worked for Hitler, it would work for a nation. For that reason, occultism played a prominent role both in establishing Hitler in power and in maintaining that power.

As the book of Daniel revealed concerning the antichrist:

> "And his power shall be mighty, but not by his own power . . ." (Daniel 8:24, KJV).

What was said of the forerunner of the antichrist — the "beast" could also be said, although to a lesser degree, of all who open themselves to the "Luciferic energies" sought through the practice of occultism.

Both Nazism and the New Age Movement are political/spiritual entities based on the same esoteric foundations: the "Secret Doctrine" which has been at the base of all pagan religions and at the base of esoteric "Christianity."

Perhaps that "Secret Doctrine" might be best summarized as being the antithesis of Judeo/Christian beliefs. The Secret Doctrine glorifies Lucifer and all the practices condemned in the Bible.

The Secret Doctrine also glorifies the pre-flood world, a world that, according to both the Bible and the Secret Doctrine, was alive with demonic contact and psycho/spiritual power.

Understanding this gives special significance for today to the statement by Jesus: "As it was in the days of Noah, so it shall be in the days of the coming of the Son of Man."

The days of Noah carried far larger implications than mere crime and violence. They were also characterized by active human involvement with demonic forces. Genesis, chapter six, records the fact that the "sons of God," which some interpret as "beings from the spirit world" or demons, procreated with the "daughters of men." This type of involvement with mankind, if directly demonic, was undoubtedly a motivating force behind the other crimes of violence that proliferated, moving God to give the world a final warning through Noah. He alone was ultimately saved along with his wife, his three sons and three daughter-in-laws, from the destroying deluge.

For all the New Ager's scorn of the foregoing account, it is mirrored, though distorted, in the same occultic doctrines they profess. Moreover, shrouded in the mists of "Atlantis," which may well refer to the pre-Noahic era, are the roots of both New Age doctrine and Nazism.

A portion of this doctrine deals with the origins of the races of mankind. The "Secret Doctrine" held that they originated in Atlantis and that one of the seven Atlantean races was that of the Aryans. Although there were supposedly six other Atlantean races — Toltecs, Rmoahals, Tlavatli, Turanians, Akkadians, and Mongols — the Aryans were the master-race or supermen of the Atlantean races.

But they did not become supermen by ordinary evolution or mutation. They took a *quantum leap* upward in order to give them the necessary faculties to live in a post-diluvian world. While losing some qualities that were coveted, such as magical powers over the forces of nature and psychic development, they gained faculties of brain development and "superior intelligence" over the other surviving races who were supposedly inferior in blood stock and mental faculties.

They were allegedly educated by God-men or even more advanced supermen and taught to protect their superior blood stock at all costs. What supposedly distinguished them from the other "inferior" races was their more highly "evolved" intellects. These "superior" intellects, however, had been developed at the sacrifice of the so-called "spiritual" or psychic natures. To remedy this "deficiency" and see that psychic powers were not lost from the Aryan race, the process of *initiation* was developed by their "masters."

Initiation thus became the *sine qua non* or prerequisite for leadership in Aryan society, as only the initiates or adepts could communicate with the so-called supermen or "higher powers" who were needed to give direction to the race.

This doctrine of Aryanism is an integral part of the New Age, as well as of Nazism, and other forms of antisemitism and racism. In contrast, the Jews were set apart by God to preserve his truth in an era when the Mystery teachings had spread throughout the world through polytheism and pantheism (the Bible specifically says that all men are of one blood. It also declares that Abraham and his descendants were).

After the resurrection of Jesus Christ, St. Paul specifically said that *all* distinctions, even between Jew and Gentile, were abolished. Where the doctrine prevails that all men are created in the image of God, it is hard to maintain racism and antisemitism. Where the doctrine abounds that men have evolved from differing root races and are at varying stages of evolutionary development, it becomes easy to justify classification and discrimination.

"Final solutions" become the logical next step. This was never God's plan. Nations were punished for idolatry and infanticide — not for their blood-strains.

Such doctrines of Aryan superiority lay at the base of Nazism. They are also found as a justification for religious persecution for the reason that a key component of the doctrine of Aryan superiority included a belief that consciousness development is at stake. For that reason, Hitler included Christians on his extermination list — after he began murdering the Jews.

The New Agers have a slightly different order. Jews are on the list as soon as they are finished with the Christians. But both groups are high on priority for persecution, with the

Jews faring slightly worse than the Christians. At the esoteric core of their philosophy and plans, the New Agers maintain the old occult Aryan doctrine of a blood taint resting upon those of Jewish extraction.

A few quotes from Alice A. Bailey, the now-deceased New Age high priestess, will illustrate the occultic bias toward world Jewry which has been incorporated by reference in the Movement that Alice Bailey helped to pioneer:

> "Today the law [karma] is working, and the Jews are paying the price, factually and symbolically, for all they have done in the past. Factually and symbolically . . . they stand as they have ever chosen to stand, for separation ['evil' is defined by Alice Bailey as 'separation']. They regard themselves as the chosen people and have an innate consciousness of that high destiny, forgetting their symbolic role and that it is Humanity which is the chosen people and not one small and unimportant fraction of the race. . . . They demand the so-called restitution of Palestine, wresting it away from those who have inhabited it for many centuries; and by their continued emphasis upon material possession they lose sight of the true solution. . . . The problem is one to which the Jews themselves must make the larger contribution. They have never yet faced candidly and honestly (as a race) the problem of *why* the many nations, from the time of the Egyptians, have neither liked nor wanted them. . . . Yet there must be some reason, inherent in the people themselves, when the reaction is so general and universal. . . . Their demand has been for the Gentile nations to put the matter right, and many Gentiles have attempted to do so. Until, however, the Jews themselves face up to the situation and admit that there may be for them the working out of the retributive aspect of the Law of Cause and Effect [Law of Karma], and until they endeavor to ascertain what it is in them, as a race, which has initiated their ancient and dire fate, this basic world issue will remain as it has been since the very night of time. . . . The [Jewish] problem will be solved by the willingness of the Jew to conform to the

civilisation, the cultural background and the standards of living of the nation to which . . . he is related and with which he should assimilate. It will come by relinquishment of the pride of race and of the concept of selectivity; *it will come by renouncing dogmas and customs which are intrinsically obsolete and which create points of constant irritation* to the matrix within which the Jew finds himself; it will come when selfishness in business relations and the pronounced manipulative tendencies of the Hebrew people are exchanged for more selfless and honest forms of activity. . . . The evil karma of the Jew today is intended to end his isolation, to bring him to the point of relinquishing material goals, of renouncing a nationality that has a tendency to be somewhat parasitic within the boundaries of other nations, and to express inclusive love, instead of separative unhappiness" (*Esoteric Healing*, p. 263, et. seq.).

All the other Alice Bailey books express this same anti-semitic tenor.

In *The Rays and the Initiations*, she stated that the new "messiah" would not be Jewish as the Jews had forfeited that privilege by not recognizing the former Messiah and that the Jews needed to learn humility more than any other people. She went on to say that perhaps after they have passed through "fires of purification" they might be suitable stock for a new "Christ."

This was not written in 1920 or 1930. Alice Bailey penned these words under the direction of the so-called "Tibetan Master" in 1949 when the entire world knew what had happened to the Jews of Europe.

Furthermore, in *Esoteric Psychology*, Vol. I, Alice Bailey said that the Jewish problem might well be astrological in origin:

"The personality ray, the material form ray of the Jewish people, is the third ray. Their egoic ray is the first. Their astrological sign is Capricorn with Virgo rising. Mercury and Virgo play a prominent part in their destiny. These clues should suffice to give to the advanced student and astrologer those salient points which will give him light upon their strange history. Because of this third ray influence, you have the tendency of the Jew to manipulate forces and energies, and to 'pull strings' in order to bring about desired ends. As a race, they are natural law makers, and hence their tendency to dominate and govern, because their egoic ray is the first. Hence also the constant appearance of the goat in their history, and their teaching about the virgin mother who should give birth to the Messiah" (p. 94).

An ominous warning was given to Jews who might consider rejecting Maitreya, the New Age Christ, in Alice Bailey's *The Reapparance of the Christ:*

> "Christ came to bring an end to the Jewish dispensation which should have climaxed and passed away as a religion with the movement of the sun out of Aries into Pisces. He, therefore, presented Himself to them as their Messiah, manifesting through the Jewish race. In the rejection of Christ as the Messiah, the Jewish race has remained symbolically and practically in the sign Aries, the Scapegoat; they have to pass — again speaking symbolically — into the sign, Pisces, the Fishes, and recognise their Messiah when He comes again in the sign Aquarius. Otherwise, they will repeat their ancient sin of non-response to the evolutionary process. They rejected that which was new and spiritual in the desert; they did it again in Palestine 2000 years ago; will they do it again, as opportunity is offered to them? The difficulty with the Jew is that he remains satisfied with the religion of nearly 5000 years ago and shows as yet little desire to change" (page 81).

The same theme was picked up with hostility to Christianity for its Jewish antecedents thrown in on page 127 of the same source:

> "Next followed Aries the Ram, which saw the start of the Jewish dispensation which is of importance to the Jews and unfortunately of importance to the Christian religion, but of no importance to the untold millions in the other parts of the world."

The Nazi theme of Aryan purity of blood is found throughout the Alice Bailey books. With a display of either massive ignorance or massive dishonesty, David Spangler attempts to deny the obvious by stating that this was a different form of Aryanism than that subscribed to by Hitler:

> "An example of how this affects us at this time is the existence on the astral plane of a very powerful thought-form born out of an event held within the racial memory of the Aryan race, which is the progenitor of the source of Western culture as we know it — a thought-form that can best be expressed by the simple phrase, 'original sin,' the Fall, a concept which has no meaning whatsoever to the root races, the oriental races, that have preceded our own. Part of the reason for this is that the Aryan race is the first race in evolutionary progression of man to come into full grips with its power of mind. Perhaps I should say here that what I mean by the Aryan race is not the blond, blue-eyed Superman that Hitler was speaking of, or the Germanic race. The Aryan term is a generic term that refers to that group of people which migrated millennia ago from Asia, and spread throughout Africa and Europe."

The Aryan Spangler is speaking of is the one and the same brand as that promoted by Hitler. His perspective is straight out of *The Secret Doctrine* by Helena Petrovna Blavatsky, the founder of the Theosophical Society and to whom the New Agers trace their modern roots. This teaching, which is the same as that followed by Hitler, is that the Germanic peoples were actually Asian migrants, having "migrated millenia ago from Asia, and spread throughout Africa and Europe" as Spangler so succinctly puts it.

It seems reasonable to ask how Spangler, probably the most important figure in the New Age Movement today, and considered its leading esotericist, could be ignorant of this similarity to Nazism or the Nazi belief that they were heirs of the old Asian migrants. Certainly, the fault is not that of the Baileys and Lucis Trust.

Although the Movement is characterized by much arcane

double-talk which clouds some of its real positions, its leaders
have gone to great pains to let its initiates in on the fact that
Hitler was one of them.

In his book *Running God's Plan*, Alice Bailey's husband,
Foster Bailey, stated in 1972:

> "Another approved hierarchical project is the uniting
> of the nations of Europe in one cooperating peaceful com-
> munity. The plan is not for a new all-Europe government
> nor for a common language, but for right national rela-
> tions dedicated to the welfare of the people living in those
> countries undistorted by national pride, ambitions and
> prejudices. . . . This project is quite a different proposi-
> tion to those in Africa and Russia. It was initiated some
> years ago and got underway as 'Pan Europa.' Many ways
> were tried to promote this plan, but the idea was not suffi-
> ciently idealised by the people who were a bit too
> sophisticated and firm in their belief in the practical value
> of selfishness. Here we are dealing with a most intelligent
> people, highly organised, well-educated, alert to world af-
> fairs, but proud of their differences and convinced of their
> rightness about all things. This was therefore a much
> tougher problem but dear to the heart of the 'European
> Master.'
>
> "One attempt was to begin by uniting the peoples living
> in the Rhine River valley using that river as a binding fac-
> tor. It was an attempt by a disciple but did not work. Now
> another attempt is in full swing, namely the six nation
> European Common Market" (pp. 14-15).

Even a failing history student will recognize the fact that it
was Hitler who tried to unite Europe, using the Rhine River
valley as a binding factor!

Is Spangler really so naive? Or is he practicing another
tactic used by Hitler — the big lie technique?

The pre-war climate that gave rise to Nazism is similar to
that now existing — one ripe for the growth of Fascism and
Nazi-type philosophies. It was an atmosphere climaxed with
disappointment over political events. Germany had ex-

perienced the trauma of war-time defeat and post-war inflation with its accompanying hardships. The youth of Germany tried to escape the harsh tenor of the times by turning
to *wandervogel* and eastern mysticisms, studied in concert
with German and Nordic mythology — mythologies of a
never-never land where ancient adepts were always invinci-
ble and defeat existed only as a state of mind.

The United States finds itself in a very similar situation.
We have the wounded national pride and shame of a Vietnam
War gone sour. Soldiers did not come home to a heroes'
welcome, but to silence and indifference. The country has
long been in the throes of a defective economy. And particularly since the Vietnamese War — even during that war
for many — there has been a massive turning to *wandervogel*
and eastern mysticisms, with the route to transcendental consciousness accelerated by the widespread use of drugs — as
was also the case in post-World War One Germany.

Those seeking a revival of neo-paganism and enhanced
use of Eastern mysticism for the masses have welcomed this
trend, but others have rightly viewed it with alarm.

Particularly among European scholars, who are residents
of countries overrun by Nazi Germany during World War II
and who have firsthand knowledge of the dangers of Nazism,
there has been great concern.

Two prominent French scholars, writing under the joint
signature of Jean-Michel Angebert, stated in their classic *The
Occult and the Third Reich*, released in the English edition by
MacMillan Press in 1974:

> "The Hitlerian myth can be understood only if viewed
> in the context of the particular philosophical system that
> produced it, which is itself but one link in an historical
> tradition going back over centuries.

> "Those who induced Germany to embrace the swastika
> are not dead. They are still among us, just as they have
> been in every era, and doubtless will continue to be until
> the Apocalypse. National Socialism was for them but a
> means, and Hitler was but an instrument. The undertaking

failed. What they are now trying to do is revive the myth using other means" (p. xvi).

Or, to restate what was quoted before by Foster Bailey in regards to the previous "hierarchical project" to unite the nations using the Rhine River valley as a binding factor: "It was an attempt by a disciple but did not work."

The cosmology and cosmogony of Nazism and the New Agers are identical.

Both Nazism and the New Age Movement are programs for expediting the "path" to "transcendental consciousness," for the transformation of the masses through initiation into the "mysteries." Occult teachings and pagan practices were injected into the mainstream of a nation during Hitler's reign.

For example, Hitler's crack SS operation under the direction of Heinrich Himmler was forced to undergo group initiations in the pagan mysteries. Shrouded in Aryan grail esoterics, the initiate's goal was to gain psychic abilities and superhuman strength.

Hitler established a Bureau of the Occult or *Ahninerne* as both a part of his established German government and also a separate bureau as part of the SS. Leading German scholars and intellectuals were drafted for service to perform research for these organizations, just as a young man could be drafted for the purpose of fighting on the Russian front.

The teachings of Alice Bailey, Benjamin Creme and David Spangler, together with a host of other New Age writers, state that we shall undergo a mass planetary initiation in the New Age. The specifics of that "initiation" which is called a "Luciferic initiation" are discussed in the chapter entitled "Satanism and Luciferism in the New Age." Discussed also in that chapter is Spangler's statement of what will happen to those who refuse to accept the New Age Christ and "initiation."

Nazi esotericists, including Hitler, believed in an occult doctrine known as the "Macrocosm/Microcosm" theory of the universe. This is a standard New Age belief as well.

New Age esotericists believe in the existence of "masters" who are organized in a "Hierarchy" headed by a New Age Messiah. The Nazis likewise believed in the existence of a hierarchy of "masters" headed by a New Age Christ whom they considered to be their very own Hitler, as Hitler himself believed.

This continuity of doctrines is possible because of the preservation of neo-pagan/occult teachings and the esoteric teachings of Eastern mysticism through a system of initiates, adepts, and masters. As the translator stated in the preface of Jean-Michel Angebert's *The Occult and the Third Reich:*

> "The significance of these findings is that there is thus as much reason to speak of a neo-Pagan continuum or tradition in the West as of a Judeo-Christian one. The first, like the second, has its dogma, ritual, symbols, prophets, and adepts. As in all major religions, it is through the priesthood (as exemplified in the Nazi strain by the esoteric Vril Society, Thule Society, Society of the Seekers of the Grail, and seminaries of the Ordensburgen) that it perpetuates itself, by means of a concentration of occult power located in its initiatory centers, whose knowledge and symbols are as inaccessible to the masses as to the enemy" (p. xii).

Another interesting point of reference, among hundreds of points of reference, is that the New Agers commonly believe that by undergoing the various "spiritual disciplines" such as yoga, meditation, mind-control classes, etc., they can become co-creators with the universe. They believe that they have "evolved" by such practices. There is a chilling similarity between their statements in this regard and the remarks of Hitler.

John White said in the introduction to the 1979 International Cooperation Council Directory (now known as the Unity-in-Diversity Council):

> "What is coming to pass today . . . is not a generation gap or a communications gap. . . . Rather, it is a *species*

gap. A new species is making its way onto the planet and asserting its right to life. This inevitably brings it into conflict with the dominant species. And that dominant species is a dying species. . . . These events and the greatly accelerated interest and exploration in psychotechnologies, spiritual disciplines and sacred traditions are manifestations of a new, more intelligent species coming into existence, with resistance from the dominant species, and developing a unified planetary culture.

"There is a mighty leap forward in survivolution occurring, and the result is a vast sorting-out process among people. They are trying to discover what species they belong to. . . . We can become, in a sense, co-creators with the cosmos. . . . That is what meditation and other spiritual disciplines are all about. . . .

". . . There is an evolutionary advance taking place in the world today as a new and higher form of humanity takes control of the planet . . . and therefore surviving while the older species dies out from a massive overdose of irrationalism. Outwardly, these mutant humans resemble the earlier forms. The difference is inward, in their changed mentality, in their consciousness. . . .

"Homo noeticus is the name I give to the emerging form of humanity" (from pages 13-15, excerpted).

If this sounds familiar to Nazi scholars, it is because it should. Hitler himself said almost identically the same thing:

"Creation is not yet completed. Man must pass through many further stages of metamorphosis. Post-Atlantean man is already in a state of degeneration and decline, barely able to survive. . . . All creative forces will be concentrated in a new species. The two types of man, the old and the new, will evolve rapidly in different directions. One will disappear from the face of the earth, the other will flourish. . . . This is the real motive behind the National Socialist Movement!" (as quoted in *The Spear of Destiny* by Trevor Ravenscroft, Bantam Book Edition, p. 250).

Also, and probably most importantly, both Movements believe in the use of blinds to throw non-initiates off their trail. Nazis frequently labeled the most sinister of actions by benign names, as do the New Agers. Extermination of Jews and gypsies was not called a killing. It was called a "cleansing action." Death camps were disguised to look like health camps. Mass exterminations of whole area populations were labeled "resettlements."

The use of "blinds" is a well-accepted tactic to keep those not in sympathy with its aims from learning the specifics of "The Plan." For that reason, New Agers likewise use blinds to keep the general public from learning all that they are about.

The "blinds" consist of deliberately false and contradictory information being included in an occult writing that is likely to come into the hands of the general reader, as have the New Age writings since Alice Bailey's permission to go public was implemented in 1975, the year she had specified.

One such use of this technique is illustrated in Volume 5 of the Adyar Edition of *The Secret Doctrine* by Helena Petrovna Blavatsky:

"In view of the abstruse nature of the subject dealt with, the present Paper [Paper 2] will begin with an explanation of some points which remained obscure in the preceding one, as well as of some statements in which there was an appearance of contradiction.

"Astrologers, of whom there are many among the esotericists, are likely to be puzzled by some statements distinctly contradicting their teachings; while those who know nothing of the subject may perhaps find themselves opposed at the outset by those who have studied the exoteric [outwardly known] systems of the Kabalah and astrology. For let it be distinctly known, nothing of that which is printed, broadcast, and available to every student in public libraries or museums, is really esoteric [secret, hidden], but is either mixed with deliberate blinds,' or cannot be understood and studied with profit without a complete glossary of occult terms" (p. 435).

Following suit, Alice A. Bailey, also instructed her students in the Arcane School as well as those would-be probationers and initiates reading her books that she, like Madame Blavatsky, used blinds. However, they really were not concerned about this, because they truly believed that only an initiate would understand what was written anyway — ignoring the fact that it is God who dispenses wisdom!

The organization of the New Age Movement is also chillingly reminiscent of Hitler's Germany. Apart from its parent councils, such as the Unity-in-Diversity Council and Planetary Initiative for the World We Choose which professes to be a network of networks, the New Age Movement is not organized as an organization *per se*. (Appendix B contains sample materials from the Unity-in-Diversity Council showing a few of their goals and organizational structure.)

Instead it is literally a network of networks with some important pivotal organizations at its core. The beauty of the particular form of organization they have adopted is that whenever an organization or individual becomes embarrassing to them — as did Jim Jones — they can quickly close up their fish-net-type structure to exclude that person or organization as though he or it had never been a part.

Following is a chart which gives a more detailed correlation between Hitlerian Nazism and the New Age Movement.

NAZISM	NEW AGE MOVEMENT
Nazism was an offshoot of occultic practices and teachings. The Nazis had a Bureau of the Occult as a part of the German government under Hitler. This was known as the SS Occult Bureau. Another such agency was the Nazi Occult Bureau.	The New Age Movement is based on occultic practices and teachings, particularly the writings of Helena Petrovna Blavatsky, (especially *The Secret Doctrine*), and Alice A. Bailey, who claimed to be receiving telepathic messages from the Tibetan Master Dwjal Khul. All forms of occultism and mind expansion are permitted and encouraged within the New Age Movement.

Nazism taught the doctrine of Aryanism and Aryan purity and that the "New Age" would feature an Aryan mutant "master race."

The New Age Movement teachings stress the doctrine of Aryanism and Aryan purity. See especially Alice A. Bailey's writings and the writings of David Spangler.

The New Agers believe that through meditation and other "spiritual disciplines" that they have become a "new species" — *homo noeticus* as opposed to *homo sapiens* and that *homo sapiens* is a dying species. They teach that the Jews are from a different solar system (Alice Bailey teachings) and that the orientals and blacks are from a different root race. Occidental races *must* control the world as they are presently our most evolved root race.

Nazism featured hatred of Jews and an ancient occultic doctrine of a blood taint resting on the Jews and that there was a need for a final "correct solution" to this "Jewish problem."

The Secret Doctrine of occultism features hatred of the Jews. The writings of Alice Bailey, which have been followed meticulously by the New Age Movement, state that the new "messiah" will not be Jewish as the Jews have forfeited that privilege and that they must pass through the fires of purification in order to learn humility. (See *The Rays and the Initiations* by Alice A. Bailey. This particular passage regarding the New "Messiah" was written in 1949 when the entire world knew what had happened to Europe's Jewish population.) These teachings are also strongly opposed to "Zionism" and the possession of a homeland by the Jewish people. These teachings also state that what happened to the Jewish people in WW II was a result of their "bad national karma."

Hitler was an initiate of occultic practices, including yoga, Tibetanism, hypnotism, and the *Secret Doctrine* of Helena Petrovna Blavatsky and the Tibetan Masters.

Benjamin Creme says that "Maitreya the Christ" is a seventh-degree initiate. Entrance into the New Age requires a Luciferic initiation.

Nazism featured the quest for the "Holy Grail" as a path to transcendental or "higher consciousness."

The New Age Movement features the quest for the Holy Grail as a path to transcendental or higher consciousness.

The Nazis believed in the Law of Karma and reincarnation.

The New Agers believe in the Law of Karma and reincarnation.

The Nazis and particularly Hitler sought to embody Luciferic energies.

The New Agers and particularly David Spangler, one of the leading New Age spokespersons, state that the Luciferic energies are positive as they are the "energy of anticipation" and the energies that "get a person from here to there."

Hitler used mescaline to speed up consciousness expansion.

The use of drugs as a catalyst in consciousness expansion has long been a part of the New Age Movement.

The Nazis thought they had evolved into a new and superior species by means of "spiritual disciplines" and "consciousness evolution."

The New Agers think they have evolved into a new and superior species — *homo noeticus* as opposed to *homo sapiens* by means of "spiritual disciplines" and "consciousness evolution."

Hitler encouraged the organization of young men into the Brown Shirts for the purpose of keeping order in the cities and village neighborhoods. The Brown Shirts were trained in the martial arts such as karate and generally performed guard-type operations.

The New Agers through Curtis Sliwa have encouraged the organization of young men and women into the Guardian Angels for the purpose of patrolling cities and neighborhoods. The Guardian Angels are trained in martial arts such as karate and aikido.

Members of the SS (Schutzstaffel), or protection squad, were inducted by a pagan-style initiation ceremony.

Members of the U.S. Military New Age-oriented First Earth Battalion are initiated in a pagan-style initiation ceremony.

The Nazis believed in breeding of children controlled by the state.

Many New Agers, and most top-level New Agers, advocate requiring people to be licensed in order to have children. Friends of the Earth are particularly vocal in this regard.

The Nazis operated free maternity homes in the interests of breeding a master race.

The New Agers have an operation known as The Farm in Tennessee which has a free maternity home and women are told they can leave their babies for as short or as long a period as they like. (As a practical matter, it is almost impossible from a legal standpoint to regain custody of a child left for a long period of time.)

Hitler encouraged the recruitment and use of convicts.

The New Agers encourage the recruitment and use of convicts. *Signs of Christ* by Harold Balyoz, specifically mentions it and there are many, many New Age projects designed specifically for the recruitment and conditioning of convicts to orient them to New Age goals.

Nazism sought the institution of a New World Order in which the Aryan race would predominate and control.

The New Age Movement seeks the institution of a New World Order in which Aryanism will prevail.

Nazism was a synthesis of occultism and gnosticism, based on *The Secret Doctrine* and a synthesis of the old "Mystery Teachings" and Eastern Religions.

The New Age Movement is a synthesis of occultism and gnosticism, based on *The Secret Doctrine*, the Alice Bailey teaching, and a synthesis of Eastern religions and the old "Mystery Teachings."

Nazism came to power by Hitler appealing to the rich that his regime would increase their control and be more efficient and telling the poor that his regime would mean sufficient resources for them to exist on.

The New Age Movement has obtained the support of the rich and powerful, such as the Chase Manhattan Bank and heads of major corporations, by telling them that the New Age teachings are good for entrepreneur-ship and business, and of many of the poor by telling them that they will redistribute the world's assets and establish a New World Economic Order.

Nazi adepts believed the gods lived in Shamballa.

New Age initiates believe the gods are established in Shamballa.

Nazism was hostile to orthodox and fundamentalist Christianity and sought to replace the cross with the swastika.

The New Age Movement is hostile to orthodox and fundamentalist Christianity and seeks to replace the cross with the rainbow and the swastika.

Hitler referred to his scheme to take over as "Mein Kampf" or "My Plan."

The New Agers call their scheme to take over "The Plan" and in the transmissions from "Lord Maitreya" through Benjamin Creme, Maitreya calls it "My Plan."

Hitler forced his underlings to go through occult initiation rites.

The writings of Creme, Spangler, Alice Bailey, and other important New Agers state we will be forced to undergo initiation if we wish to enter the New Age alive.

Nazis believed the roots of their Aryanism were first found in Atlantis.

The New Agers trace their Secret Doctrine and occult teachings to Atlantis.

Hitler said in Mein Kampf that the problem with Christianity lies with its Jewish antecedents.

Creme, Alice Bailey, Theodore Roszak, and other important New Age writers say the problem with Christianity is that it has presented a teaching of Christ "straight out of the old and outworn Jewish Dispensation."

The Nazis believed a new superior mutant species of Aryans can be brought into existence by development of "Higher Consciousness."

The New Agers believe a new superior mutant species of Aryans can be brought into existence by development of "Higher Consciousness."

Heinrich Himmler, like many other Nazis, had an anti-Catholic

Benjamin Creme, the spokesman for Tara Center and "Maitreya the bias. He even went so far as to advocate the public execution of the Pope and to compel Catholic SS members to leave the Roman Catholic faith.

Christ," has publicly stated that the Pope will be forced to bend his knee to "Maitreya the Christ." Hatred of Catholicism shines through the Alice Bailey writings which are followed meticulously by the New Agers.

The Nazis, through Heinrich Himmler, developed a secret file that eventually included a dossier on nearly all Germans.

The New Agers, through Buckminster Fuller and the World Game Laboratories, advocate computerizing all information whatever and allowing anyone who desires access to this information. For example, all purchases and resources whatsoever would be computerized.

Hitler moved to disassociate himself from troublesome elements supporting him whenever they proved to be embarrassing. For example, when Rohm's Brown Shirts proved to be an embarrassment, he moved to disassociate himself from them and organized the Black Shirts (SS) in their place.

Marilyn Ferguson, writing in *The Aquarian Conspiracy*, said that the Movement was not dependent on any individual or organization because of its network composition. For example, the New Agers were proud to claim Jim Jones and his Peoples Temple as their own until his Guyana murder-suicide fiasco. After that, they never ever mentioned him again except to point to him as an example of the dangers of religious fundamentalism; yet the insiders in the Movement knew all along that he was one of theirs and never into orthodox or fundamental Christianity.

The Nazis instituted a program of quietly killing children with birth defects and mental patients. Hitler instituted this program after receiving a letter from the father of a deformed child requesting that the child be put to death. One way was to starve the child.

New Agers have advocated and supported legislation and medical practices of euthanasia and death by starvation and termination of life support systems. One rationale given for this is the will of the parents and the inability to support children with such immense needs.

The Nazis referred to their promotion of local antisemites murdering Jews as "self-cleansing" and the murder of Jews as a "cleansing action."

The New Agers believe that a "cleansing action" will be necessary to rid the world of "evil" (defined as anything that causes separation. Separation is defined as caused by God-fearing religions — Jews, Christians, and orthodox Moslems).

A common Nazi tactic was to burn down synagogues — sometimes with people in them.

At least one prominent New Ager, Gina Cerminara, has stated that when the people learn what the churches are really all about, they will probably burn them down.

CHAPTER 9

Infiltration, Recruitment and Conditioning

It goes without saying, of course, that the New Age Movement and its leadership cannot launch its hoped-for Age of Aquarius and install its "Christ" until and unless there is a substantial portion of the population conditioned to accept him.

As might logically be expected then, there has been a well-orchestrated propaganda drive aimed at conditioning the public into acceptance of a "New World Order." The patterns that have actually been followed or paralleled by the New Age Movement were set forth by Alice A. Bailey and H.G. Wells.

According to Alice Bailey, the general public was to be familiarized with the concept of a "Hierarchy." In 1946 she instructed the New Age disciples that the conditioning should emphasize the following:

1. The evolution of humanity with particular attention to its goal of perfection.

2. Relation of the individual soul to all souls (doctrine of unity or interdependence of all life).

3. The belief in the spiritual Hierarchy will then be deduced as a result of a belief in the previous two goals "and the *normality* of its existence emphasized." Along with this it will be taught that the "Kingdom has always been present" but unrecognized due to the "relatively few people who express, as yet, its quality."

4. After the first three teachings have taken effect and the recognition of them has become general, then it will be emphasized that there are those among us who have already reached a goal of "soul control" (i.e., possession).

The foregoing scheme, set forth in *The Externalisation of the Hierarchy*, was also to include a gradual inculcation of the idea of the bodily presence among us of the so-called "masters." This idea was in its turn to be followed by, of course, a recognition that one lucky individual in the world had achieved total evolutionary progress, i.e. the "Christ Consciousness," and that individual would serve as head of the "Hierarchy" as "Director of the Kingdom of God on Earth."

Other things were to be taught to prepare the world for the "New Age" and the "New Age Christ" as well.

Mind control and meditation were to be taught. Color therapy was to be emphasized. Music therapy and holistic health were additional items to be added to this eclectic diet for a "New Age." New Age symbols such as the rainbow, Pegasus, the unicorn, the all-seeing-eye of freemasonry, and triple-sixes were to be increasingly displayed.

The Movement was to keep a low profile until 1975. Then it had permission to take everything public — including the very fact and nature of "The Plan" itself. Everything hidden was to be revealed and there was to be a no-holds-barred propaganda drive after that time, spreading the previously esoteric teachings of the New Age along with the anticipation of a New Age Christ by every media vehicle available. However, even before 1975, the stage had been carefully set.

Not coincidentally following marching orders set forth by H. G. Wells in his *The Open Conspiracy — Blueprints for a World Revolution*, the Movement worked in alliance with all sorts of movements and people. The Movement handled these activities carefully so as to avoid taking fundamentalists and other religious orthodox adherents into its confidence on the peculiarly occult nature of the underlying esoteric blueprints for the Movement.

According to Wells, the first overt act of this "Open Conspiracy" was to be "the putting upon record of its members' reservation of themselves from any or all of the military obligations."

The rationale behind this maneuver was to be that this

would supply the practical incentive to bring many of the open conspiracy sympathizers together in the first place. This would also bring the conspiracy out of the realm of the theoretical and mystical and put into "the field of practical conflict."

Next, the conspiracy was to involve "a skeptical and destructive criticism of personal-immortality religions." Strangely enough, communism was to be destroyed at the same time. However, the New Agers feel the program they are offering the world would satisfy the basic desire of Communists in that it proposes a form of worldwide socialism. The existing Communist formulae — per se — were to be abolished because they called for a dictatorship of the proletariat and the New Agers/Open Conspiracy people were more interested in a dictatorship of the "Hierarchy" headed by Maitreya the "Christ."

Those appearing suitable to the Open Conspirators were to be indoctrinated into a study of the general concepts of the overall conspiracy, similar to the system of initiates, adepts, and masters that existed in all of occultdom including the Nazi regime.

The conspiracy was to be carried out by a wide variety of groups varying much "in leisure, knowledge, ability and scope." This advice has, of course, been followed by the New Age Movement which indeed has something of interest to nearly everybody except for orthodox Christians and Jews from those groups. At the same time it has managed to recruit willing workers by appealing to the instincts related to problems of world hunger.

Discussion groups were also to be formed out of which were to come circles of "intelligentsia." These would supply lecturers and leaders of discussions. They would in turn be used and draw on still other organizations — not in and of themselves part of the scheme — thus indoctrinating the members of those organizations in these New Age or open-conspiracy concepts.

Out of these discussion groups was to come a combining

process in which the groups would unite for local and regional meetings. It was expected that those gatherings for the *ad-hoc* activities would meet on a social basis as well and that this would also further the aims of the conspiracy.

Independent initiatives were also to be encouraged as long as they advocated the provisional nature of existing governments. They resolved to establish a world economic system; replacement of private ownership of credit, transport and staple production with ownership by a world directorate; a recognition of biological controls on a worldwide basis of population and disease; a minimum standard of freedom and welfare throughout the world; and a duty of subordinating personal life to that of a world directorate.

One has only to look at the guidelines for Planetary Initiative for the World We Choose to see that Wells' directions and warnings were heeded. One only needs to look at the history of the world — particularly the United States in the wake of the Vietnam disturbances — to see the origins of the present New Age Movement in its modern form, as the esoteric groups enjoyed the addition of mass support working on an *ad hoc* basis with them on peace and disarmament issues.

There is other evidence that Wells was an insider and that the present structure is no coincidence.

The first clue that one investigating the Movement should look for in Wells' writings comes from *The Aquarian Conspiracy*.

Wells is mentioned in that work as an author of importance in at least three places.

A more important clue comes from the presses of Lucis Trust with its subsidiary Lucis Publishing Company. In their official organ, *The Beacon*, on page 310 of the May-June edition of 1977, appears an article entitled "H.G. Wells, a Forerunner."

The writer of that article accurately stated that:

> "Few did more to incite revolt against Christian dogma
> or against the accepted codes of behaviour. . . ."

Now, as Planetary Initiative rushes towards its hoped-for June 21, 1983, completion date with surrounding celebrations and the convening of "The World Council of Wise Persons" in New York City, Wells' influence continues to linger and even expand. The New Age Movement, including Planetary Initiative, is organized as Wells wished:

> ". . . as consisting of a great multitude and variety of overlapping groups, but now all organised for collective political, social and educational as well as propagandist action. They will recognise each other much more clearly than they did at first and they will have acquired a common name."

They have acquired a common name: The New Age Movement! And more than a name, they have acquired a common character.

As Wells so accurately predicted:

> "The character of the Open Conspiracy will now be plainly displayed. It will have become a great world movement as widespread and evident as socialism or communism. It will largely have taken the place of these movements. It will be more, it will be a world religion. The large loose assimilatory mass of groups and societies will be definitely and obviously attempting to swallow up the entire population of the world and become the new human community."

The character is accurately and plainly displayed. Will we wake up in time to see it for what it really is?

RECRUITING METHODS

Besides the broad operating principles of the New Age Movement as set forth in the Alice Bailey/H.G. Wells writings, there are specific tactics used by its adherents as a means to swell their ranks.

The ideas of the Movement are set forth in books on every topic imaginable. These books will usually stress that the world is a manifestation of thought to be controlled by one's own mind. Meditation is encouraged in books ranging from natural food cookbooks to cures for depression.

Even Christian bookstores have not escaped the deceptive influence of the New Age Movement. There the shelves groan under the weight of books that contain virtually every plank of the New Age Movement — from meditation and positive/possibility thinking to support for a New World Order. They differ only from the standard textbooks of the New Age Movement by being labeled "Christian." The Christian books will usually proclaim the fact that we are engaged in a conspiracy to make the world better and better until the Lord returns — the same line used by supporters of the antichrist or "Lord Maitreya."

Away from the bookstores, the recruiting of unsuspecting self-improvers continues. People are encouraged to study one of the dozens of "psychotechnologies" — visualization, autosuggestion, hypnotherapy, guided imagery — techniques almost guaranteed to bring one in contact with "spirit guides" — i.e., demons.

Silva Mind Control, EST, A Course in Miracles, as well as several other mind "science" courses, are virtually guaranteed to convert participants into New Agers. More shocking still is the fact that in some cases these courses are being attended and even taught by both Protestant and Catholic clergy and nuns.

In the city of Detroit, for example, a Roman Catholic priest and nun are co-teaching a Silva Mind Control course. An Episcopalian church in Bloomfield Hills, Michigan, has sponsored a holistic health center. The Cathedral of St. John the Divine Episcopal, New York City, has even featured sermons by David Spangler — the same David Spangler who has said that Luciferic initiation would be required to enter the New Age.

Of course, the reach-out efforts of Unity and Unitarians continue to increase in momentum. Unity and the Unitarian Church alike reach out to singles, newly divorced, the depressed, the overweight, alcoholics, and others searching for themselves and their identities.

Urban dwellers are reached by appeals from these

churches to their sense of community. Come-as-you-are potluck dinners and dances for singles are often featured. Mind-control courses and seminars on books such as Wayne Dyers' are offered for the insecure.

They offer many of these people a sense of acceptance for the first time in their lonely, frightened lives.

Unfortunately, these churches offer options that are scripturally unsound, teaching people that they can control the creative powers of God themselves and experience endless reincarnations. The social settings they offer may be a temporary palliative for their disease of loneliness but are hardly guarantees of long-term spiritual peace and salvation.

Likewise, health food stores and juice bars often are turned into New Age recruiting centers. Once again, they are filling the vacuum for a place where one may mingle and converse without having to resort to alcoholic beverages.

In mental hospitals throughout the country, New Agers have instituted their programs. They call for implementation of meditation, transpersonal psychology, biofeedback (which encourages use of Zen and meditation to maintain alpha waves), and music meditation. They are all psycho-technologies — techniques nearly guaranteed to bring one under a state of possession or at least a loss of control that would enhance the chances of being possessed. In one state, those so foolish as to protest or resist the implementation of these plans, which amounted to little more than an establishment of religion by the state, were transferred or removed.

The psychologist who suggested the implementation of the New Age techniques in the first place was subsequently promoted to a state board position. He now is able to demand that all state institutions feature these techniques which are part and parcel of the New World Religion planned by those seeking the New Aquarian Age.

Drugs, too, are a way to draft soldiers into the New Age army of the Age of Aquarius. Mind-altering drugs ad-

vocated by the vanguard of the Movement — Timothy
Leary, et al — are not considered a blight on our society by
the spokespeople for the New Age. Instead they are "tools
for transformation."

According to Marilyn Ferguson in her New Age classic,
The Aquarian Conspiracy:

> "It is impossible to overestimate the historic role of
> psychedelics as an entry point drawing people into other
> transformative technologies. For tens of thousands of
> "left-brained" engineers, chemists, psychologists, and
> medical students who never before understood their more
> spontaneous, imaginative right-brained brethren, the
> drugs were a pass to Xanadu, especially in the 1960s.

> "The changes in brain chemistry triggered by
> psychedelics cause the familiar world to metamorphose.
> It gives way to rapid imagery, unaccustomed depths of
> visual perception and hearing, a flood of 'new'
> knowledge that seems at once very old, a poignant
> primal memory. . . .

> "Those who ingested psychedelics soon found that the
> historic accounts closest to their own experiences derived
> either from mystical literature or from the wonderland of
> theoretical physics — complementary views of 'the all
> and the void. . . .'

> "As one chronicler of the sixties remarked, 'LSD gave
> a whole generation a religious experience.' But chemical
> *satori* is perishable, its effects too overwhelming to in-
> tegrate into everyday life. Non-drug psychotechnologies
> offer a *controlled* sustained movement toward that
> spacious reality. The annals of *The Aquarian Conspiracy*
> are full of accounts of passages: LSD to Zen, LSD to In-
> dia, psilocybin to psychosynthesis" (page 89-90).

So there you have it. The psychedelic drug explosion
was an entry point for millions to the first initiation into
the "Age of Aquarius." Again, this is consistent with the
New Age pattern of following the instructions set forth by

Alice A. Bailey under dictation from "The Tibetan Master Djwal Khul."

"ILLUMINATION"

"1. The higher and lower siddhis (or powers) are gained by incarnation, *or by drugs*, words of power [mantras], intense desire or by meditation" (*The Light of the Soul* by Alice A. Bailey, p. 377).

In fairness to the New Agers as well as to the Alice Bailey writings, the permanent use of the drugs is generally not encouraged. They are but a vehicle to initiate New Agers and prospective New Agers; who are then encouraged to "graduate" to various forms of yoga such as TM, and other "psychotechnologies" that lead to transcendental experiences — the mystical glue that binds the majority of those involved in the New Age Movement to each other.

Incidentally, as noted elsewhere in this book, it is not without precedent to have government encouragement of these psychotechnologies. Neither is it without precedent for drugs to be used to obtain transcendental experiences. Hitler tried both. He used mescaline to speed his path towards consciousness expansion, and his inner circle all experimented with psychotechnologies, inducing a communal tripping of the Light Fantastic.

NEW AGE INFILTRATION OF GOVERNMENT

According to Marilyn Ferguson and other New Age writers, the government has long since been infiltrated by active New Age conspirators. In her public lectures, Ms. Ferguson relates that she was even invited to be the keynote speaker at the 1982 Department of Defense annual dinner. Her book freely relates that there are conspirators at the Cabinet level, the White House Staff, congressmen — at every level of government. According to her book, The National Institute of Mental Health (NIMH), the Department of Health, Education and Welfare, and the Department of Defense — not to mention the corruption of the grant writing process of the United States government to fund these quasi-religious/openly "religious" programs of the New Age Movement — include Zen, Transcendental Meditation, and other psychotechnologies of every shade and description in their programs.

In 1978 a Washington conference was held called "Holistic Health: a Public Policy." This was co-sponsored by several governmental agencies. While it is hard to object to the presence of politicians, physicians and psychologists in attendance, nevertheless, one finds it hard to swallow the fact that sharing the speaker's platform were "spiritual" teachers, futurists, meditation teacher Jack Schwarz and the avowed enemy of organized religion, Buckminster Fuller. While the list of speakers may have been only half New Age, the list of topics was nearly 90 percent New Age.

Topics dear to the heart of New Agers included "implementation of holistic health centers, cross-cultural healing practices, holographic theory of mind and reality, yoga, music and consciousness (straight out of Alice Bailey's instructions that music therapy should be taught as a part of the preparation for the 'New Age'), acupuncture, acupressure, Buddhist meditative techniques, bodywork, biofeedback, guided imagery, and 'the changing image of man' (the New Age manifesto released by Stanford Research Institute)."

INFILTRATION OF INDUSTRY

Government is not the only large American institution invaded by the New Age conspirators. They have also called on the financial and social pressures of big business to attain their goals for world domination — a world to be peopled by those more schooled in mysticism than everyday common sense.

Marilyn Ferguson reports in *The Aquarian Conspiracy*

that they have managed to win the financial support of Lockheed Aircraft, Blue Cross-Blue Shield, the Rockefeller Foundation and others for holistic health forums. Again, while it is hard to argue with the case for organically grown vegetables and enough sleep at night, nevertheless, one may view the agenda with justifiable concern if it sounds more like a catalog of New Age occultism than it does like a health improvement seminar.

These programs have and continue to routinely feature the following which are all nothing more than variations on Eastern occult techniques:

> Meditation, visualization (according to occultists, this is a shortcut to unlocking all the mysteries of mysticism), biofeedback (of course, enhanced by meditation), acupuncture (manipulation of "The Force" or "Life Force"), hypnosis, psychic healing, etc.

And if this were not enough to gladden the hearts of New Agers everywhere, the latest news from the halls of industry should be. For suddenly courses in "New Age Thinking" have become the order of the day — particularly for middle and upper-level management personnel and salesmen. From General Motors and Chrysler Corporation through AT&T and southwestern oil concerns such courses have been offered. One such course that has been in wide use at many major corporations is called "New Age Thinking" and is taught by Lou Tice of The Pacific Institute, Inc.

Employees attending these institutes are even encouraged to bring their entire families. Self-image psychology is stressed as part of a new "mental tool kit." Like other psychotechnologies, the perceptions of the participants are played with in an attempt to shift their focus to "New Age Thinking."

Participants are basically taught that they create their own world by their own thought-forms and that by ignoring or downplaying negative inputs their world will become a brighter, better place. Of course, believing you are your own god is the next logical step. And where does such a program tell one to go for spiritual and religious guidance? Again, dear to the heart of the most dedicated New Age psychic and spiritualist, they are sent to the major advocates of the "deity of man": Pierre Teilhard deChardin, Herman Hesse, Eric Fromm, Abraham Maslow, Carl Rogers, and most outrageously of all, Ram Dass — an avowed enemy of orthodox Judeo-Christian religious tradition and proponent of a mass conversion to Hinduism and other forms of Eastern mysticism.

Clearly, enforced attendance at these New Age seminars is a form of religious discrimination by the employer that should not be tolerated. Neither should it be made a ground for promotion or demotion among those attending or refusing to attend. Could an employer demote or promote one for regularly attending mass or evangelical services? The answer, of course, is a clear no. Neither should the employer be allowed to do this to those whose consciences do not permit their attendance at seminars promoting "New Age Thinking."

ASTROLOGY — ENTRY POINT
FOR THE YOUNG AND CONFUSED

The public has been largely conditioned to accept the "Age of Aquarius" by widespread popular usage of astrology and astrologers.

"What's your sign?" is a common icebreaker at parties and all too often even among Christians. Newspapers daily carry astrology columns, and horoscope magazines are in abundant supply at every newstand.

This popular acceptance has conditioned the general public to believe that either there is something to it or, at worst, it's no more than a harmless pastime.

However, those whose interests are piqued by reading an occasional accurate daily horoscope soon wish to know more. After exhausting the range of books available at the library and/or general interest bookstore, the enthusiast has no choice but to move on to occult bookstores and astrology association meetings.

There, if he hasn't already picked up on it, he is introduced to the coming age of light and love — the Age of Aquarius. Of course, he is also told that this so-called New Age will have to be preceded by a "cleansing action" — the euphemism we noted that Hitler attached to his extermination of Jews, gypsies, and Slavic peoples. Being more acquainted with astrological lore than with history, the would-be occult initiate fails to make the connection.

The seeking person finds fun and acceptance at these meetings and at the New Age bookstores, which usually turn out to be occult clubhouses of sorts. From these innocent starts it is an easy next step into the political, religious and social arms of the New Age Movement.

HUNGER PROJECTS — A NEW AGE RUSE

If the New Age Movement cannot get you by appealing to your appetite for the mysterious and occult, then perhaps it can recruit you by appealing to your finest and best motives. This is where The Hunger Project, Bread for the World, and a host of other projects allegedly designed to alleviate the problems of world hunger fit into New Age plans.

Of course, the systems usually recommended as viable options to end world hunger often sound remarkably like the system cited in Revelation, chapter 13:

"And he causeth all, both small and great, rich and poor, free and bond, to receive a mark in their right hand, or in their foreheads:

"And that no man might buy or sell, save he that had the mark, or the name of the beast, or the number of his name.

"Here is wisdom. Let him that hath understanding count the number of the beast: for it is the number of a man; and his number is Six hundred threescore and six" (Revelation 13:16-18, KJV).

Unfortunately, those attending introductory meetings of these organizations, which spend the majority if not all of their resources for lobbying to achieve a New World Order, are never told what the real motive of the top leaders behind this trend actually is.

Buckminster Fuller is a prime mover in The Hunger Project. He is also the founder of World Game Laboratories and is slated to sit on Planetary Initiative's "World Council of Wise Persons."

The real motive for the creation of these gigantic global agencies is set forth on page xx of his 1981 release, *The Critical Path* (St. Martin's Press, New York):

> "Throughout the history of land and sea transport those who have gained and held control of the *world's lines of vital supply* have done so only by becoming THE MASTERS in the game of establishing supreme human power over all other subpowerful organizations — ergo, invisibly over all humanity" (emphasis in the original).

This is more than interesting because Fuller is closely affiliated with Donald Keys of Planetary Initiative and Planetary Citizens. Keys is an open follower of Alice Bailey and her Tibetan mentor Djwal Khul. And invisible power by "The Masters" *is* the goal of the "Plan of the World Servers" launching the drive for planetization.

Lucis Trust, the custodian of the Alice Bailey writings, as already mentioned, was incorporated originally as the Lucifer Publishing Company. In 1924 they changed their name to the somewhat less obvious "Lucis Trust."

One of their subsidiaries is World Goodwill. Many Christian groups have won endorsement from World Goodwill, including Bread for the World. The organization has freely lobbied for the creation of a "New World Order."

One can only wonder what impact the same money spent lobbying for the system desired by the Lucis Trust/Planetary Initiative people would have had if spent on starving children who needed real bread in their stomachs — instead of using them as pawns in a political maneuver to create international megalithic structures capable of controlling the world *a la* Orwell's 1984!

CHAPTER 10

A New Age of Satanism?

Many New Agers believe they are dealing with "white magic" or the "light side of the Force." They would probably recoil in horror at any suggestion that they might be devil worshippers.

Those who believe they are practicing "white magic" either fail to recognize the existence of the devil or feel that Satan is associated with the "Black Lodge" — their definition for those pursuing orthodox forms of religion and more openly-satanic forms of occultism.

However, the New Agers will often admit they are worshipping Sanat Kumara, Pan, Venus, Shiva, Buddha and other pagan deities. The name Buddha itself literally means "Lightbearer" — the same meaning as the name Lucifer.

The Apostle Paul, who was struggling with the pagans and gnostics of his day, noted the demonic nature of idol worship — a warning that sincere New Agers and Christian sympathizers of the New Age Movement would do well to heed:

> "What do I mean then? That a thing sacrificed to idols is anything, or that an idol is anything? No, but I *say* that the things which the Gentiles sacrifice, they sacrifice to demons, and not to God; and I do not want you to become sharers in demons. You cannot drink the cup of the Lord and the cup of demons; you cannot partake of the table of the Lord and the table of demons."

The *Satanic Bible* by Anton Szandor LaVey gives a list of "infernal names" — all synonyms for Satan. Several of the names are openly and currently reverenced by "white magic" New Agers, including Lucifer, Kali, Lilith, Pan, and Shiva.

The "sacred community" of the New Age Movement — Findhorn — is surprisingly open about giving the devil his "due." Founded on "divine guidance" allegedly received by Eileen Caddy, Findhorn's role on this planet, according to this "guidance," is to anchor "The Plan" on earth. Of course the guidance received revealed the usual satanic teachings: man's deity and infinite potential for psychic power.

The standard histories of Findhorn themselves, however, reveal the true source and nature of this "guidance." Peter and Eileen Caddy, together with Findhorn co-founder Dorothy McLean, labored on from 1962 until 1966 under the illusion that they were working in partnership with "Devas" — elemental spirits supposedly inhabitating their flower and vegetable beds.

However, in 1966 they realized that they and the "Devas" had become a triangle. For in that year they made a momentous discovery: they were also working with "Nature Spirits overlighted by the god Pan."

A similar discovery was allegedly made by another close Findhorn associate, an aristocratic, elderly, self-educated gentleman named Robert Ogilvie Crombie or "Roc."

Roc was taking an April stroll through an Edinburgh park in 1966 when he was suddenly confronted by an incredible creature. The strange, part-animal-part-human being looked like a giant-sized version of another he had met earlier. Both creatures appeared as fauns to Roc — "radiating a tremendous source of power."

The larger creature asked Roc whether he loved him and his subjects. After receiving an affirmative reply, it informed Roc that he had just said he loved the devil. Roc rejected this admission, as does the entire New Age Movement, by telling the creature that although Christians had superstitiously taken him as a model for the devil, nevertheless, they were "mistaken." Roc preferred to call this satanic presence "Pan" or "Lucifer," as do other New Agers.

They reject the Christian teaching that Lucifer has common identity with Satan. However, they freely call Sanat

Kumara (Satan) "God." And their doctrinal reference books by Helena Petrovna Blavatsky and Alice Ann Bailey freely cross-reference Sanat Kumara with Venus.

In occult writings, Lucifer and Venus are one and the same. This is also true in the Alice Bailey writings and those of Madame Blavatsky.

As do many other New Agers, Roc suspected the motivation of the introduction, but completely underestimated the dangers:

> "I did not know then that for his purpose he had to find someone who showed no fear of him. He is a great being — the god of the whole elemental kingdom as well as of the animal, vegetable, and mineral kingdoms. People may feel uneasy in his presence because of the awe he inspires, but there ought to be no fear. 'All human beings are afraid of me.' He had not said this as a threat, but with sadness. 'Did not the early Christian Church make me a model for the devil?' That is why he is feared — because of the image projected onto him. This image must be lifted off him so that his nature may be revealed. That is why he had to find someone who did not fear him" (from *The Magic of Findhorn* by Paul Hawken, Bantam Books Edition, p. 217).

Apparently convinced of the rightness of "Pan's" cause, Roc goes on to say:

> "It is important for the future of mankind that belief in the Nature Spirits and their god Pan is reestablished and that they are seen in their true light and not misunderstood. These beings, in spite of the innumerable outrages man has committed against nature, are only too pleased to help him if he will seek and ask for their cooperation."

Findhorn and its officials, including the Caddys and David Spangler, were convinced as well. Prominent New Age leader Spangler was co-director of the Findhorn Foundation for three years. He formed the Lorian Association and sits on the Board of Directors of Planetary Citizens, the secretariat for the leading New Age New World Order vehicle: Planetary Initiative for the World We Choose. He is a contributing editor of *New Age Magazine* and much in demand on the New Age lecture circuit.

According to Spangler, he teaches political science at the University of Wisconsin even though he dropped out of college as a freshman to pursue a career as an esoteric lecturer. He has political clout and he also has disproportionate influence with some of America's most prominent clergymen. He has given at least one sermon in the prestigious Cathedral of St. John the Divine, Episcopal in Manhattan — a eucharistic sermon at that! This church counts many of the Wall Street crowd among its membership.

One could reasonably expect those speaking from Episcopal pulpits to maintain at least some semblance of religious orthodoxy. This is not, however, the case with Spangler, who has uttered some of the most outrageous blasphemies ever spoken against Jesus Christ and God the Father.

In one of his numerous books (*Reflections on the Christ*, 1978), he expressed his sentiments as to Lucifer:

"The true light of Lucifer cannot be seen through sorrow, through darkness, through rejection. The true light of this great being can only be recognized when one's own eyes can see with the light of the Christ, the light of the inner sun. Lucifer works within each of us to bring us to wholeness, and as we move into a new age, which is the age of man's wholeness, each of us in some way is brought to that point which I term the Luciferic initiation, the particular doorway through which the individual must pass if he is to come fully into the presence of his light and his wholeness.

"Lucifer comes to give us the final gift of wholeness. If we accept it, then he is free and we are free. That is the Luciferic initiation. It is one that many people now, and in the days ahead, will be facing, for it is an initiation into the

New Age. It is an initiation of leaving the past and moving into the new, shedding our guilts and fears, our anxieties, our needs, our temptations, and becoming whole and at peace because we have recognized our inner light and the light that enfolds us, the light of God."

This is also the New Age concept of Initiation. It is universally taught among New Age cults and esoteric societies that we must undergo a "mass planetary initiation." Spangler has clearly defined that initiation.

Benjamin Creme has declared that "revitalized" Christian churches as well as Masonic lodges will be used for purposes of giving these "mass planetary initiations."

More than likely, this is tied to the permit to do business that was spoken of in Revelation 13:16-17:

"And he causeth all, both small and great, rich and poor, free and bond, to receive a mark in their right hand, or in their foreheads:

"And that no man might buy or sell, save he that had the mark, or the name of the beast, or the number of his name" (KJV).

One can hardly blame God for attaching the terrible penalty spoken of in Revelation 14:9-11 to those receiving the mark, especially if it is tied to a mass planetary initiation which pledges loyalty to Lucifer:

"And the third angel followed them, saying with a loud voice, If any man worship the beast and his image, and receive his mark in his forehead, or in his hand,

"The same shall drink of the wine of the wrath of God, which is poured out without mixture into the cup of his indignation; and he shall be tormented with fire and brimstone in the presence of the holy angels, and in the presence of the Lamb:

"And the smoke of their torment ascendeth up for ever and ever: and they have no rest day nor night, who worship the beast and his image, and whosoever receiveth the mark of his name" (KJV).

Since Benjamin Creme and Tara Center have received the notoriety they have, Lucis Trust has attempted to tiptoe quietly away from any association with them. However, like Spangler and Creme, Lucis Trust's attachment to Lucifer is also apparent from a careful reading of their materials.

A 1978 issue of *The Beacon*, their official organ, stated:

> "Lucifer, Son of the Morning, *is* closely related [to the path to Sirius], and hence the large number of human beings who will become disciples in the Sirian Lodge" (Volume XLVII, No. 9, May/June 1978, Lucis Publishing Company).

Maitreya allegedly said in a "transmission" through Benjamin Creme: "I am the Initiator of the Little Ones." Therefore, it hardly seems surprising that one of the leading New Age organizations, Planetary Initiative for the World We Choose, coordinated by Planetary Citizens, calls the "Network Newspaper" it publishes, the *Initiator*.

This is not surprising, because: (a) many of the supporters listed — particularly the "facilitators" — are also open and active Benjamin Creme supporters; (b) Planetary Citizens freely gives its purpose as being "to aid World Servers everywhere"; (c) the role of the World Servers is to act as the "vanguard" for "the reappearance of the Christ"; and (d) at all his lectures Creme distributes brochures for the New Group of World Servers.

Moreover, David Spangler, who openly advocates Luciferic initiations (see above) is a member of the Board of Directors of Planetary Citizens as are Peter Caddy (founder of Findhorn), Norman Counsins (head of the invitor committee of the "World Council of Wise Persons"), and Aurelio Peccei (founder of the Club of Rome).

The Coordinating Council of Planetary Initiative itself contains apparent surprises, including Brooke Newell (Vice-President of the Chase Manhattan Bank), Gerhard Elston (former Executive Director, Amnesty International, USA),

Helen Kramer (International Association of Machinists [IAM]), as well as many other influentials.

In more than one city the Planetary Initiative personnel were also identified as active participants in the Tara Center venture.

Lucis Trust is certainly an active, open participant in the Planetary Initiative venture.

Tara Center also endorsed the Planetary Initiative in their April 1982 *Emergence* publication.

Certainly, it is an impressive network "in service to the Christ" — but not to the only begotten Son of God, JESUS CHRIST — it is a Luciferian network in service to a false christ, most probably the antichrist!

The fate of skeptical recalcitrants to this project — or at least the New Agers' hoped-for fate for those recalcitrants — is mirrored in the Spangler writings:

> "Furthermore, it is not really important to know where the old pattern will go; we are assured that it is shepherded by the Christ and will be fully ministered to by this cosmic presence. . . .

> "However, there are a few words which can be said about where the old world and those attuned to it will go. Throughout creation there are infinite spheres of environment representing and educating all stages of consciousness development. Some of these are physical planets, like earth; others exist on higher dimensional levels. It is possible that many from earth will find themselves attracted to such other spheres or planets within the universe which are at a stage of growth comparable to what earth has moved out of.

> "There is another pattern, though, which is more likely. Earth is really like a vast mansion with the ground floor representing the physical plane. Only a small percentage of the souls associated with earth evolution are ever on the physical plane at once; they tend to travel together like groups, like classes in university which move together as a wave through the various levels and all graduate

together. . . . It would not be without precedence for them to be withdrawn into the inner worlds, to live in an 'upstairs' room which would reflect the needs of their consciousness and minister to those needs. In other words, the planet or plane or level to which they will go through the law of attraction, may not be 'somewhere else.' It may be another level of earth's own consciousness where they can be contained and ministered to until such time as they can be released into physical embodiment again. . . .

"Whether this is indeed the pattern, or whether these ones shall be moved entirely out of the earth pattern . . . the main point is that they will lose for the time being, their access to the etheric planes of power and the ability to control or influence the developments upon earth" (*Revelation, Birth of a New Age*, pp. 163-164).

SO! The New Agers and their leadership plan to send us to another dimension! Release us from physical embodiment! Strip us of our ability to control or influence earth's developments!

Clearly it sounds reminiscent of the Revelation prophecy:

"And the dragon was wroth with the woman, and went to make war with the remnant of her seed, which keep the commandments of God, and have the testimony of Jesus Christ" (Revelation 12:17, KJV).

Alice Bailey said Lucifer was the "Ruler of Humanity." Truly he appears to be the guiding light of the New Age Movement.

It is indeed time that God's people followed the message of the Revelation angel to come out of her.

CHAPTER 11

Deluded . . . or Deceivers?

"For I know this, that after my departing shall grievous wolves enter in among you, not sparing the flock.

"Also of your own selves shall men arise, speaking perverse things, to draw away disciples after them.

"Therefore watch, and remember, that by the space of three years I ceased not to warn every one night and day with tears" (Acts 20:29-31, KJV).

"Beware of false prophets, which come to you in sheep's clothing, but inwardly they are ravening wolves" (Matthew 7:15, KJV).

Unfortunately, the insidious deception of the New Age Movement has gained a measure of respectability and acceptance within the church. Even evangelical churches are included when Marilyn Ferguson declares, "[T]hey have coalesced into small groups in *every* town and institution."

Partially explaining the most popular vehicles of New Age entrance into religious groups, Ms. Ferguson states:

"An increasing number of churches and synagogues have begun to enlarge their context to include support communities for personal growth, holistic health centers, healing services, meditation workshops, consciousness altering through music, even biofeedback training" (*The Aquarian Conspiracy*, p. 369).

Chortling about this loss of orthodoxy within what are supposed to be the bastions of God the Father and Jesus Christ, she went on to state that "[N]ow the heretics are gaining ground, doctrine is losing its authority, and knowing is superseding belief."

Often clothed in seemingly Christian language, the "spiritual" aspects of the New Age Movement have gained acceptance among the unsuspecting even within orthodox religious institutions. The Movement's political programs also have won widespread endorsement and advocacy among Christian denominations.

The New Age Movement is pushing for, among other things: global agencies to handle distribution of global resources, redistribution of the world's wealth, a new world religion, experiential religion (as opposed to religion based on scriptural authority and tradition), a universal tax, a universal draft, right-brain/whole-brain thinking (intuitive and subjective, as opposed to what they call "left-brain" or analytical thinking), a teaching that all things are part of one whole, an emphasis on universal interdependence, and zero population growth.

All these concepts are beginning to rear their ugly heads in evangelical Christian books and publications. Some denominations have incorporated substantial portions or all of these points into their "agenda for the 80's."

Marilyn Ferguson's *The Aquarian Conspiracy* has enjoyed the promotion of discussion groups in "many, many churches" according to an article appearing in August 1982, *New Age Magazine.*

In a recent letter to my publisher, Marilyn Ferguson complained:

> "It is practically ludicrous that she charges the New Age (and me by association) with being anti-Christian, anti-Judaic, and anti-Catholic. I have spoken to church groups, at Catholic universities and in a Jewish synagogue. The spirit of my writing cannot possibly be conjectured to be antispiritual, antichrist, etc."

Despite a wish to be polite to Ms. Ferguson, the facts simply do not comport with her assertions. Neither does it follow that the individual churches/institutions/groups where she may have spoken necessarily hold beliefs consistent with orthodox Christianity or Judaism.

On the contrary, the very fact that Marilyn Ferguson has been allowed to carry her message to these congregations — as have numerous other New Agers — is evidence that the prophesied apostasy is gaining momentum within the church itself.

The test of antichrist is a denial that Jesus is the Christ (see I John 2:22). The New Age Movement, therefore, betrays the spirit of antichrist behind it when it states that "Christ Consciousness" is a "higher state" of mind that everyone can attain; and that Jesus was an ordinary man who had the Christ Consciousness descend upon him at the time of his baptism and stay with him until his crucifixion.

Under the heading *God Within: the Oldest Heresy*, Marilyn Ferguson knowingly promotes "blatant pantheism ('the *milk* was God . . . God [as] primordial nature . . . the sum total of consciousness in the universe" — pages 382-3), which lies at the heart of the New Age. She also quotes approvingly from *The Aquarian Gospel*, which itself meets every biblical test of antichrist. Unfortunately, this book is even carried within Christian bookstores — particularly those of mainline Protestant denominations.

New Agers generally do not openly repudiate Christianity. More subtle than that, at least for the moment, they often clothe New Age concepts in Christian language and — like Hitler — undermine Christianity while pretending to be its friend. They redefine Christianity to give pagan gods equal time with Jesus Christ; and expand the definition of Christ to be the integral essence of themselves. What then continues to sound like Christianity is in effect *another Gospel*.

For example, Marilyn Ferguson, in a June 17, 1982, letter to me said:

> "My definition of Christianity has expanded over the years. After I became involved in meditation, for example, I experienced the vision of Christ more vividly than

I ever had through sermons and dogma. You would be
surprised, I think, to know how much of the New Age
Movement centers on Christ Consciousness. Many
Christian churches are seeing that direct spiritual experience offers a revitalization for modern Christianity."

The test of antichrist was clear. He is antichrist who
denies Jesus is the Christ (I John 2:22), and further he is antichrist who denies that Jesus Christ is come in the flesh
(I John 4:3).

Redefining Christ to include you and me — or turning
Christ into a spiritual *experience* — certainly is a denial
that *Jesus* is *the* Christ. Teaching and believing that Christ
was a consciousness rather than a man is certainly a denial
that Jesus Christ is come in the flesh.

It is amazing but all too true that these insidious an-
tichristian ideas, which are the very essence of New Age
Thinking, are gaining increasing acceptance within Christian churches. Yet while pleased at the inroads of paganism
within the church, Marilyn Ferguson and other New Age
leaders are upset at being exposed as the enemies of true
Christianity. Examples of New Age influence within the
church, both Catholic and Protestant, are legion. Cross
Currents of West Nyack, New York, is a Catholic publisher with a decidedly modernist bent *a la* warnings given by
Pope Pius X.

In reprinting Eugene Fontinell's *Toward a Reconstruction of Religion* in their 1979 edition, they had this to say
about Jesus as *the* Christ:

"Given this understanding and role of religious symbols, what are the Christian symbols which seem finished and what are those which might be viable? In considering the pragmatic reconstruction of God, it was
argued that omnipotence, omniscience and immutability
were no longer fit ways of symbolizing the Christian's
'faith in God.' Similarly, 'God the message sender,' 'God
the lawgiver,' and 'God the institution founder' are
inappropriate symbols within the world presupposed by

pragmatism. On the other hand, 'God as triune,' 'God as love,' and 'God as incarnate' may have rich possibilities for development and service within a processive-relational world. As living symbols, however, it will not suffice to retain them in some abstract form as objects of faith. They must be operative in the life of the community and, initially at least, reflection should indicate something of the contribution which they have made, are making and can make to furtherance of this life. LET ME ILLUSTRATE THIS POINT WITH REFERENCE TO 'GOD AS INCARNATE IN JESUS CHRIST' (emphasis added).

"The first step in any pragmatic reconstruction of this symbol is to reject viewing it as an event which happened in the past and as localized exclusively in Jesus of Nazareth. Instead of speaking of God as having BE-COME incarnate, it is more appropriate to speak of God BECOMING INCARNATE. The Christian may believe that in Jesus we have a unique and indispensable manifestation of the presence of God to man and the world, but Jesus as the Christ must be seen as processively coming into existence. There are several advantages attached to viewing the symbol of Christ in processive and relational terms rather than in static and substantive ones. First, it is more congenial to the thought and experience which now characterizes man's life. Secondly, such a processive view of Christ is not without anticipations in the earliest moment of the reflective life of the Church. Thirdly, it opens up new possibilities in terms of the relation of Christ to other religions as well as to non-Western cultures. Finally, it gives new dimension and significance to all man's institutions and every aspect of his life, for nothing less than the full involvement and participation of man through his institutions will bring about the full realization of the reality of Christ."

Lest Protestants snicker at this example of an all-too-prevalent display of Catholic apostasy, let them be reminded that we too have our problems.

Myriads of Protestant books carry exactly the same message. And the rankly objectionable Catholic books are marketed in Protestant bookstores — sometimes even in evangelical bookstores. Likewise, the Catholic bookstores market the Protestant books that appear to carry the New Age themes. The wonder of the entire business is its ecumenism!

The Graduate Theological Union of Berkeley is a case in ecumenical point.

Established in 1962 at Berkeley, it has brought Catholic, Protestant, and Jewish participants together in a sort of commonized apostasy. In fact, they are so apostate that they have expanded their theological horizons to include Hinduism, Buddhism, Sufism, Sikhism, Feminist Spirituality, New Age groups, occultism, neo-paganism and witchcraft. Their activities meet approval with at least one important source: *The New Consciousness Sourcebook (Spiritual Community Guide No. 5).* The alternate title for this book for the past several years has been *Handbook for a New Age.*

Engaging in what they call "creative borrowing," they have managed to water down Christianity to a state of bare recognizability. One of Union's professors, Dr. Charles S. McCoy, quotes John Cobb's *Christ in a Pluralistic Age* with approval. Cobb suggested that the Christians copy Buddhism in order to "reconceive Christ." McCoy enthusiastically endorses Cobb's thesis that "Christ must be reconceived as creative transformation in all human experiences and not bound to the historical Jesus or to any past doctrine."

McCoy states:

"The pluralistic faiths around the globe and the surges of oppressed peoples in all cultures toward liberation dissolve the limited conceptions of God, Jesus Christ, and history, transmitted to us by our Christian past and open us to widened perspectives and an emerging consummation hidden in God.">[1]

In other words, Christianity must be liberated and enriched by the other paths to God.

Theodore M. Hesburgh is the world-renowned president of Notre Dame University. He also serves as an advisory chairman for Planetary Citizens.

As noted previously, Planetary Citizens' purpose is to aid the "World Servers" who in turn are to serve as the "vanguard for the reappearance of the Christ."

Hesburgh is also an endorser of Planetary Initiative: "A Plot to Save the World."

In 1974 Hesburgh delivered the Dwight Harrington Terry Foundation Lectures on Religion in the Light of Science and Philosophy. Hesburgh holds numerous honorary degrees and has extensive influence — in governmental, religious, and scholastic circles. The book derived from his lectures at the Terry Foundation contains much of the New Age agenda for the planet.

His prelude contains a statement that we can make the world "somewhat divine." Calling his projection "Christian humanism," Hesburgh quickly reveals a bias tending more towards "humanism," than Christianity. Humanism has a theology and a god, but that god is ourselves and Lucifer, not the God of the Bible for Protestants, Catholics, and Jews alike.

The scriptures plainly say that Jesus made a perfect sacrifice once for all. Nevertheless, Hesburgh declares:

> "Redemption embraces the totality of creation, and those working for a new man and a new earth are very much creating, and redeeming the times as well."[2]

[1]*When Gods Change, Hope for Theology* by Charles S. McCoy. McCoy is the Robert Gordon Sproul Professor of Theological Ethics at the Pacific School of Religion, Graduate Theological Union at Berkeley. He further holds a Ph.D. from Yale University Graduate School. He is considered a leading theologian at Berkeley and lectures internationally.

[2]*The Humane Imperative* by Theodore M. Hesburgh, preface by Kingman Brewster, Jr., Yale University Press. Copyright © 1974 by Yale University, second printing 1975, p. 11.

One chapter in Hesburgh's book is entitled "The Power of Ecumenism." And he doesn't mean the unity in our Lord and Savior Jesus Christ that should be acknowledged whether one is a Baptist, Catholic, Presbyterian or Episcopalian. He clearly states that his ecumenical interest is not only "in the Christian, but in the larger world-religion dimension."

He devotes several pages to our commonality of interests with non-Christian religions. Five-times-censored Jesuit priest and New Agers' hero, Pierre Teilhard de Chardin, is called by Hesburgh "that great visionary of the unity of mankind."

Although Hesburgh professes to have complete faith in God, nevertheless, he appears not to trust God to take care of his human creation here on earth because he parrots the zero population arguments for a static world population.

He further extols the virtues of the Common Market nations of Europe — in almost identical language as that used by Foster Bailey in a Lucis Trust publication. Planetary citizenship is urged upon us as is a "Declaration of Interdependence."

Reading Hesburgh as well as Matthew Fox, Fontinell, and a host of other Roman Catholic "evolved" or "transformed" theologians, one becomes quickly convinced that Pope Pius X may have been a prophet as well as a prelate.

That Pope's insightful warnings in the encyclical *Pascendi Dominici Gregis* (on Modernism) were not heeded and these wolves in sheep's clothing freely crept into the Catholic hierarchy. Using identical methods, a host of other New Age fellow-travelers have attained free access to Protestant seminaries and pulpits, even within fundamentalist circles.[3]

---

[3]See *A Catechism of Modernism* by the Rev. J.B. Lemius, O.M.I., founded on the Encyclical *Pascendi Dominici Gregis (On Modernism)* by Pope Pius X. This $2.00 volume given to me by a Detroit priest is probably one of the best statements of the methods of both the New Agers and the apostates within the body of Christ — Catholic and Protestant alike. Pope Pius X is quoted as aptly saying: "We must now break silence in order to expose before the whole Church, in their true colors, those men who have assumed this bad disguise." The Catechism is published by Tan Books and Publishers, Inc., of Rockford, Illinois, and was last published in 1980.

New Age thinking obviously has had a strong impact on many Protestant, even evangelical writers — and through their influence has affected thousands in varying degrees.

Take, for example, Tom Sine. In his book, *The Mustard Seed Conspiracy*, he details his "vision" for the future.

Perhaps it is coincidental that *Mustard Seed* contains some of the same programs as the New Age Movement.

New Agers Hazel Henderson, Jeremy Rifkin, Theodore Roszak, Willis Harman, Buckminster Fuller, Robert Heilbroner, Dennis Meadows of the Club of Rome, Richard Barnet, Ivan Illich, Alvin Toffler and even William Irwin Thompson are quoted with approval.

Roszak may be fairly described as a neo-paganist — or at least an apologist for neo-paganism. Buckminster Fuller has written that Christians and other religious groups will cry out because they will be destroyed.

William Irwin Thompson is one of David Spangler's closest friends and wrote the introduction for Spangler's New Age "Bible": *Revelation, the Birth of a New Age.*

Sine quotes approvingly from Thompson's *Evil and World Order* — a book seemingly impossible even to skim without having its truly New Age nature jump out at you.

The horrendous Global 2000 Report — which concludes that the world's population must be reduced by billions before the year 2000 if the planet is to survive — is quoted approvingly; as is Willy Brandt's North-South summit report, and in similar language as that used by Benjamin Creme in *The Reappearance of the Christ.*

Freely calling for a New World Order and a New International Economic Order — plans also found in the Tibetan-transmitted writings of Alice Ann Bailey — Sine conveys his allegedly Christian teachings in the code words of the New Age Movement. One might legitimately ask why, if these are Sine's concepts derived from the Bible, he chooses to clothe them in New Age terminology.

He uses the phrase "New Age" itself approximately 150

times in his book, more than even Marilyn Ferguson in *The Aquarian Conspiracy*.

Dressing up the New Agers' planned redistribution of the world's assets in Year of Jubilee language from the no-longer-applicable Old Testament code, Sine has Christians looking forward to exactly the same sequence of events as does Benjamin Creme: a freezing of the world's assets and a redistribution of same.

Sine ridicules those who believe the coming of our Lord is imminent — which sounds very much like what Peter prophesied the scoffers would say as that day drew near.

He also ridicules those who are fearful of the *Humanist Manifesto*, stating there is not a shred of evidence to show that those signing it were in any way involved in a plot to take control of the world. On the contrary, there is ample evidence for that indeed.

The *Humanist Manifesto* affirms: that the universe created itself; that promises of salvation are harmful; that ethics are situational; that individuals should have the right to abortion and should have total sexual freedom; and that socialism should be in control worldwide.

These are the exact beliefs with which our children are brainwashed in public schools beginning in kindergarten. They are predominant today in our universities and in government. And these very same beliefs are being promoted cleverly and persistently by the national news media.

No conspiracy? Sine should take another look at the *Humanist Manifesto* in light of current reality.

Easternization of our faith is subtly advocated by Sine, and we are told we must "incarnate the countercultural values of the kingdom."

He asserts that missionaries were detrimental to the cultures of the heathen paradises they visited by advocating Western medicine instead of the more "spiritual" methods of healing previously used in those lands, page 212.

Another example is found in Stanley Mooneyham, the ex-president of World Vision. Mooneyham has long enjoyed great prominence in the Christian world. Yet his book, *What Do You Say to a Hungry World?* advocates much of the political program of the New Agers.

Although he has enjoyed a reputation as a humanitarian, his books show sympathy for some of the more frightening aims of the New Age Movement, such as zero population growth. Mooneyham says:

> "Now another theme. Population. That's a touchy one. No one likes to be told how many little feet can patter around in his own house. But just that is the big question. How many feet per square foot can this world support?

> "If you see this problem as critical where you live, then it would be profitable to investigate the availability of family planning services in your community. Press for adequate facilities, if necessary.

> "Insist on open forum discussions on birth control, *abortion, artificial insemination, genetic control* and *death control* in your church or club programs. *Some of these subjects, unfortunately, seem to be outside the orbit of evangelical Christian concern.*"[4]

It is not surprising that Theodore Hesburgh is quoted with approval in Mooneyham's book,[5] as are many other prominent New Agers.

It was more surprising to see Lenny Bruce so quoted — as were New Agers Barbara Ward, Richard J. Barnet, and E.F. Schumacher. The New World Order is freely recommended as a desired goal for Christianity.

---

[4]From *What Do You Say to a Hungry World?* by W. Stanley Mooneyham (excerpted from page 241), copyright © 1975 by Word Incorporated of Waco, Texas. Interestingly enough, Word is also the publisher of Sine's *The Mustard Seed Conspiracy.*

[5]*Ibid.*, page 22, 267.

Several countries around the world have legislated family size with frightening consequences. Often the result is forced sterilization, infanticide, and abortion. Families are even faced with imposed economic consequences for the birth of an extra child.

Mooneyham, however, has no problem with these measures:

"Some governments are considering legislation restricting the size of families, with a negative income penalty or tax on all children over the official limit. If that sounds like an invasion of personal liberties, don't forget that most governments have already made bigamy illegal."[6]

Mooneyham's position on social issues is similar to that of the New Agers, as well as his spiritual/cultural techniques and practices. The occult pseudo-medical practice of acupuncture — a manipulation of "the Force" — along with its antecedent Chinese occult theory of *Yin-Yang* is described in glowing terms. After all, according to Mooneyham, Aldous Huxley (an evolutionist/occultist) believed it![7]

Among the "mistakes" made by Western missionaries in China, Mooneyham lists in his writings: "aggressive proclamation of Western values; public denunciation of idolatry; rejection of ancestor worship; opposition to local religion; and careless use of the scriptures."[8]

Of course, it should come as little surprise to note that *World Vision* magazine, during Mooneyham's tenure as president, reported joint projects with Hindu ashrams[9] and has requested readers to "pray for your church's direct in-

[6]*Ibid.*, page 151.

[7]*China a New Day* by W. Stanley Mooneyham, copyright © 1979 by W. Stanley Mooneyham. Logos International, Plainfield, New Jersey 07060 (citing pages 197-201).

[8]*Ibid.*, pages 153-156.

[9]*World Vision*, Vol. 26, No. 9 (September 1982), page 21. Query? Who gets the glory? Jesus or Krishna?

volvement in *holistic* ministry."[10]

There are other serious problems within the realm of evangelical Protestantism. Inter-Varsity Christian Fellowship (IVF) has enjoyed an almost impeccable reputation in both scholarship and Christian apologetics. However, much that appears to be New Age-oriented has come out of that organization in recent years.

Assessing the views of some Christian authors, however, is not without difficulty, particularly in light of a trend today toward a social exegesis of the Gospel. Consequently, terms and concepts are latched onto with only a superficial understanding as to their implications. It is not my intention to point a finger at specific Christians and their books, and say that these people are definitely New Age, but merely to reveal to the reader a dangerous trend toward New Age thinking among evangelicals. As the proverb goes: "There is a way that seems right to a man, but in the end it leads to death." Physical health, for example, is a reasonable objective. However many professing Christians have become full-blown Hindus by taking up yoga *just* for exercise. Another example is that feeding the hungry is an admirable biblical Christian objective, however, doing it through forced redistribution of the world's wealth, or stated another way, through socialism, is not a biblical imperative. So it is my deep concern that we are not led astray — whether intentionally or unintentionally.

With a Ph.D. from Yale University, Ron Sider is an associate professor of theology at Eastern Baptist Seminary and serves as president of Evangelicals for Social Action. His books are widely sold in Christian bookstores of all denominations and may be found in even the most fundamental of church libraries.

One of his books, *Rich Christians in an Age of Hunger*, was co-published by Inter-Varsity Christian Fellowship and Paulist Press. Paulist is a Catholic publisher whose books

[10]*Ibid.*, page 21.

tend more towards socialism and outright New Age thinking than they do towards orthodox Christian thinking.

The first thing noticeable about Sider's book to one versed in New Age lore is his use of a vocabulary prevalent among New Agers. Words such as Spaceship Earth, vanguard, holistic, New Age, and global village are a common part of his vocabulary.

The very same form of New World Order as that proposed by prominent New Agers and the Alice Bailey books is urged upon the readers. In fact, they are told it would be a sin for them not to support this "New World Economic Order" and "New World Order."

New Agers Ernest Callenbach, Peter Berger, Robert Heilbroner and E.F. Schumacher are frequently quoted. Declared Christians with the same message are cited in support of his thesis, such as Stanley Mooneyham. The Year of Jubilee principle advocated as a result of Sider's Bible study of the old Judaic code sounds chillingly close to that proposed by Benjamin Creme to inaugurate the so-called New Age or Age of Aquarius. Sider says on page 223: ". . . Jubilee is a divine demand for regular, fundamental redistribution of the means for producing wealth."

While Sider is biblically correct in stating that Christians have a duty to help alleviate all the human misery and suffering they can, nevertheless, his approach seems more New Age than Christian. The New World Order proposed by Sider is in some respects the same as that backed by Lucis Trust, the World Order Model Project (WOMP), Lindisfarne Association, Findhorn Foundation, Planetary Initiative, and the entire New Age network for that matter.

Contrary to what Sider proposes, Christians have no duty whatsoever to help establish the political structures of the New Age. In fact, *we have an affirmative duty to help resist them* — even unto death.

The sole purpose of establishing the New World Order is, according to the Alice Bailey writings, to serve as the political structure for the New Age "Christ."

Buckminster Fuller, who coined the phrase "Spaceship Earth," used by Sider, has made it clear that the new structure will be mourned by organized religion when it is instituted.

The biblical warnings are also clear that the final beast of the world would be diverse from the others and trample the entire world underfoot, horribly persecuting the saints in the process. Its coming may be inevitable. Nevertheless, it should not be established on the backs of naive Christians who are more taken by deceptive New Age promises than with clear scriptural warnings.

David Bryant is associated with Inter-Varsity Christian Fellowship and actively works in the field of missionary training. His message to the church is that it must learn to love the world. He further says that we must be converted twice — first to Christ and then reconverted back to the world.[11]

Jesus clearly warned that conditions would grow worse and worse until His return. Nevertheless, Bryant does not see it that way similarly to his fellow evangelicals, including Sider. His book, *In the Gap: What It Means to Be a World Christian*, says:

> "It is sowing the Gospel through new congregations
> of believers who grow into redemptive forces. In turn,
> they will overthrow the status quo of the world system
> and transform the human condition within their own
> situation" (pp. xiii-xiv).

Bryant cites the works of Ron Sider, Stanley Mooneyham and the National Council of Churches with approval. Sojourners, a Christian social action group with New Age-type programs, is mentioned as a desirable organization for Christian participation.

On page 39, several New Age "buzzwords" are tucked neatly into a single paragraph:

[11]These surprising theological positions were given in an April 1982 sermon by David Bryant at Highland Park Baptist Church in Southfield, Michigan, my own church!

"I guess it boils down to this, Bill. In our modern *global village* all nations and societies are *inter-linked* and *inter-dependent* in so many ways. So, it isn't an either/or question. The involvement of American Christians in a *global cause* on a *global scale* will strongly determine their impact on their own society" (emphasis added).

Bryant sees hope in the very things that many Christians consider to be definite signs of end times:

"And yet, out of this silence has emerged a long, diverse list of activists such as feminists, gays, black and Jewish groups, environmentalists, right-to-life, anti-nuclear groups, and even former anti-war groups protesting U.S. irresponsibility regarding Cambodian and Vietnamese refugees. Does a legacy from the anti-war and civil rights years lie dormant in the subconscious of today's students? Are these various activist groups' tremors of potential student movements just ahead?" (page 86, *ibid*)

The glue that binds the New Agers together seems to be common mystical experiences. Visualization and hypnotism are keys to the occult. It may be all too often the case that they are literally seeing and hearing things the rest of us are not. It was therefore startling to find the following passage in a purported Christian book — a passage worthy of a Silva Mind Control or EST session:

"A Parable.
    Imagine . . .
        for a moment . . .
            that . . .

"As long as you can remember you've been seated in a darkened theater.

"Alone.

"Well, not completely alone. You've noted other shadows brooding in the dimness. Some have even mumbled their names to you. But the chill, the mystery, the emptiness of perpetual night — that's been the extent of your life. Until now, that is.

"Imagine . . . that one day . . . a spotlight bursts its brilliance across the distant stage. Light. At first it startles you. Then, it intrigues you. You sit and stare.

"Gradually your eyes focus. Now you're aware that a Man has stepped into the spotlight. How unusual He is. He's laughing, dancing . . . and singing! In time you notice that others are up there too, dancing with the Man in the Light, happy and free like He is."

The rest of the startling passage is full of white light imagery. It sounds far more like a Bhagwan Shree Rajneesh talk to occult initiates than a serious call to potential Christian missionaries.

If there has been a single Catholic pope who permitted the New Agers' plans to take root within the Roman Catholic Church, it was Pope John XXIII who is spoken of reverentially by New Agers and Catholic modernists. Yet Bryant expresses the belief (on page 125) that Pope John XXIII was a high point of Christian church history.

And the New Agers' social program and life-style of "voluntary simplicity" was urged upon Christians by David Bryant.

It should be added here that although the goals of most of the workers are pure, those doing the planning are usually not and the end of this is conditioning for revolution and acceptance of global agencies doling out food supplies — not true feeding of the masses. Not surprisingly, Bryant urges his students to read *Rich Christians in an Age of Hunger* by Ronald Sider.

An alternate phrase or title for the New Group of World Servers is "Servants of the World." On page 146 of his book, Bryant says:

"We must cease being arm-chair tourists of the world. We must become its students, even before we become its servants."

I don't know what Bryant's Bible says, but mine says I am to serve God — not the world. I am to love my neighbor as myself — but I am to neither "love the world nor the things that are in the world." Note how Bryant contradicts this biblical proposition when he says also on page 146 that "[W]e must love the world with our *minds* as well as our hearts."

One wonders if he has been looking through Theodore Hesburgh's papers as Bryant, too, enumerates our points of commonality with Eastern religions. In the same set of paragraphs he espouses the New Age, Alice Bailey-dictated doctrine of oneness or unity of all life.

Unity-in-Diversity was an Alice Bailey-coined expression coming from her "Tibetan Master." It is commonly used as a New Age buzz word. The International Cooperation Council has changed its name to Unity-in-Diversity Council. Interdependent is another such word. On pages 172-173 Bryant says:

> "Within this family there are many ministries, but only one mission. Within this family is beautiful diversity, but God intends it to be *unity-in-diversity* because we are united in the same global cause. Each of our world-sized parts are *interdependent* and indispensable for our overall mission."

Alice Bailey taught that the New Age was to be an age of group consciousness and synergy. Individual efforts to advance the cause were to be avoided. The same principle finds expression in David Bryant's writings.

And on page 205 the sins of homosexuality and drug abuse are given the usual euphemism of "alternative lifestyles."

Bryant urges involvement in hunger relief programs. While this is not a bad aim in and of itself, nevertheless one of the groups he urges upon us is Bread for the World — an organization that has managed to win at least two write-ups in Lucis Trust papers as "characteristic" of the

New Group of World Servers. And, Bread for the World has never bought a grain of rice for anyone. Their monies are strictly spent for lobbying for national and international measures — including creation of global reserves and agencies to control the distribution of world assets.

In a talk at my very own church, he urged Christians and especially those listening to participate in the redistribution of their assets — very convenient conditioning for those hoping to implement the Benjamin Creme/Maitreya the Christ/New Age/New World Order.

His book is undoubtedly subtle, but to one schooled in New Age ways of thinking, the parallels are immediately obvious. If one is familiar with Planetary Initiative guidelines for discussion group leaders, he cannot help but notice that the Small Group Study Guide instructions are almost similar.

I am not writing at this length about Bryant's book to single him out. It is a masterpiece, however, of subtlety, full of conditioning, whether deliberate or otherwise for the New World Order and the New Age Movement.

The important thing to be said here is that the infiltration of our churches — even our fundamentalist churches — both broad and deep — is probably a sure sign that we are in near-Tribulation times and near to the soon coming of our Lord Jesus Christ.

Of equal concern is the activity taking place within the confines of fundamentalist seminaries. Calvin College seminarians have downplayed the danger from the New Age Movement. However, they need only look about their own institution to discover that it is indeed alive and well.

Earthkeeping is the title of a book released by the Fellows of the Calvin Center for Christian Scholarship, Calvin College, copyrighted in 1980 by the Wm. B. Eerdmans Publishing Company. Pierre Teilhard de Chardin is referred to as a "Christian thinker" on page four. The New Age political program is laid out in its entirety — including a *duty* for Christians to support globalization of our structures.[12]

The scriptures plainly state that *God* will create a new heaven and a new earth. Nevertheless, in reinterpreting the Bible to justify support of Calvin College's newfound internationalism the authors of *Earthkeeping* see the situation pretty much as do the Findhorn family:

> "The New Testament writers proclaim Jesus of Nazareth as the prince of that peace. It is he who is calling the world to himself, redeeming it to himself. And it is he who calls us to partnership in his glorious work: 'The anxious longing of the creation waits eagerly for the revealing of the sons of God.'
>
> "His kingdom of peace shall come. The king has already come, and is reigning. In Galilee he has already shown his power over water, wind, plant, beast — and over death itself. He reigns, and his peace shall reign with him: 'The zeal of the Lord of hosts will accomplish this.'
>
> "Throughout the scriptures, the visions of the kingdom of God are *visions of man in harmony with nature.* Ralph Smith expresses this well in 'Old Testament Concepts of Stewardship' when he observes, 'if biblical man did not ever foresee a time when man would have no need of nature, perhaps modern man should begin to make his peace with it now.' "[13]

[12]See pages 236-237, *ibid.* We are instructed that as Christians we "should support international efforts to establish and enforce standards for proper use of the ocean, as well as just standards for the exploitation of its common resources. . . . This kind of encouragement and approval, manifested in our political lives, may be what stewardship demands of the individual today. Perhaps the days of the commons should be over." The authors go on to state that they are speaking of *shared* stewardship: "For it is clear that we exercise stewardship over nature not only as individuals but as members of various groups to which are entrusted the care of vast quantities of the earth's resources."

[13]*Ibid.*, p. 238. If I read my Bible correctly, our peace was to be with God — not nature. The Calvin College position distinctly smacks of both Monism (concept that God created the earth and then diffused himself equally throughout the universe) and animism. God was going to make all things new — not redeem nature along with man.

We humans are "saviors" too if the authors are to be believed.[14]

We are told to develop a "planetary awareness" by the authors. This is a universal cry to New Agers from the thousands of participating New Age centers.

New Agers Loren Eisely, E.F. Schumacher, Buckminster Fuller and others are quoted with approval. Senator Mark Hatfield has written enthusiastic endorsement to many New Age-oriented Christian books. His endorsement likewise appears on the back cover of *Earthkeeping*.

According to Alice Bailey, the New Age was to be an age of group consciousness. Collective and group activity would bring the New Age to fruition. The authors here evidently feel the same way for they instructed Christians wishing to be good stewards to support collective efforts to change economic and political structures.[15]

Bread for the World is endorsed by Lucis Trust's World Goodwill as "characteristic of the New Group of World Servers." *Earthkeeping*'s authors urge Christians to support it. New Agers request their people to become "agents of change." *Earthkeeping* urges us to become "active agents in changing local, national or international, political, economic, educational, and ecclesiastical structures."[16]

One of the core teachings of the New Age Movement is God "immanent" in all things. Alice Bailey in fact said that this doctrine of immanence *must* be taught to prepare the world for the new "Christ":

> "God Transcendent, greater, vaster and more inclusive than His created world, is universally recognised and has been generally emphasised; all faiths can say with Shri Krishna (speaking as God, the Creator) that having pervaded the whole universe with a fragment of Myself, I remain.' This God Transcendent has dominated the religious thinking of millions of simple and

[14]*Ibid.*, p. 238.

[15]*Ibid.*, p. 307.

[16]*Ibid.*, p. 306.

spiritually minded people down the centuries which have elapsed since humanity began to press forward towards divinity.

"Slowly, there is dawning upon the awakening consciousness of humanity, the great paralleling truth of God Immanent — divinely 'pervading' all forms, conditioning from within all kingdoms in nature, expressing innate divinity through human beings and — two thousand years ago — portraying the nature of that divine Immanence in the Person of the Christ. Today, as an outcome of this unfolding divine Presence, there is entering into the minds of men everywhere a new concept: that of 'Christ in us, the hope of glory' (Colossians 1:27). There is a growing and developing belief that Christ *is* in us *as He was in the Master Jesus, and this belief will alter world affairs and mankind's entire attitude to life*" (emphasis added).[17]

This doctrine of God Immanent is common to nearly every pagan and Eastern religion. It teaches that God created the universe and then equally diffused himself throughout its parts. Religions teaching the doctrine of God Immanent are said to be teaching Monism. It is the original lie of the serpent — "Thou shalt be as gods" — dressed up for the "New Age."

Needless to say, it was a real shock to find this doctrine coming forth from a college such as Calvin. On page 218 of *Earthkeeping* the authors state:

"What a consideration of the Incarnation shows, however, is that in Christ, both as Creator and Redeemer, God is immanent in creation. The 'equality with God' enables the creating Word to share in the flesh of his creation in an immanence which grasps neither at glory nor survival, but which leads ultimately to death. Likewise, though Christians transcend the world, they also are directed to become a redemptive part of what they transcend. Humans are to become saviors of

[17]*The Reappearance of the Christ,* p. 36. New York: Lucis Publishing Company, 1948, 1976.

nature, as Christ is the savior of humanity (and hence, through humans, of nature).

"This idea of humans as the saviors of nature is not simply theological speculation. It is implied in all of those many Scripture passages which speak of redeemed humans as 'joint-heirs' with Christ. As Christ is Ruler, Creator, and Sustainer of the world, so also is man to be. Being heirs with Christ involves (as Paul saw) being crucified with Christ; IT ALSO INVOLVES SHARING IN THE SUSTAINING ACTIVITY IN NATURE OF CHRIST THE CREATOR" (emphasis added).

Of course, the authors give reasons sounding suspiciously like those put forth by the New Agers for this "confusion" by Christians. "This idea of human transcendence became joined, in the early years of the church, with the prevailing Platonic idea of physical nature as a source of ignorance and a snare to the soul."[18] The New Agers repeatedly say that we must overcome our "dualistic, mechanistic thinking!"

Christians are urged to support internationalism in the interests of stewardship. Of course, what they are not told is that the people heading up the internationalist efforts — Donald Keys, David Spangler, and the rest of the Planetary Citizens' gang — are open Luciferians. Once the structures are established — even if St. Francis of Assissi were running them — they are available for takeovers by those interests wishing to establish the one-world government of the antichrist as foretold in Revelation 13.

The scriptures told us plainly to love not the world:

"Love not the world, neither the things that are in the world. If any man love the world, the love of the Father is not in him.

"For all that is in the world, the lust of the flesh, and the lust of the eyes, and the pride of life, is not of the Father, but is of the world.

18*Ibid.*, p. 219.

"And the world passeth away, and the lust thereof:
but he that doeth the will of God abideth for ever"
(I John 2:15-17, KJV).

Nevertheless, the theme of this book as well as David
Bryant's and all too many evangelical writers is that we
are now to love the world — to be the servants of the
world.

The *Humanist Manifesto* proclaimed that salvationist-
based religions were harmful to the future of the world
because they made men focus on another world other than
our own.

The Calvin College fellows cheerfully parrot the same
theme:

"And yet, with a few important exceptions, Christians have not shown much concern for the world's
health. For the emphasis in Christian thought has been
much more on personal than on cosmic salvation. Indeed, one narrow use of the word 'world' is in declarations that Christians have been saved *out* of the world"
(*Ibid.*, p. 3).

Alice Bailey instructed the New Age faithful to prepare
the world for the new "Christ" by teaching that all things
were part of a whole. In view of the overall New Age
orientation of the Calvin College book, it is not,
therefore, surprising to find New Age writer Lewis
Thomas' pseudo-scientific *The Lives of a Cell* quoted in
support of this proposition.[19] Neither is it surprising to
find the somewhat unique theological stance flowing from
such a theory:

"We simply cannot escape from our embeddedness in
nature or nature's embeddedness in us. Therefore, our
knowledge seems to indicate that we can no longer
speak of humanity being saved out of nature: we are
redeemed *in* nature, not apart from it. In some way, the
Christian must include the rest of creation in his or her

[19]*Ibid.*, p. 3.

own salvation" (*ibid.*, p. 3-4).

Of course the Year of Jubilee principle — part of the Old Testament Judaic code is set forth — most conveniently for the Planetary Initiative New Age pushers of the New World Order with its planned forced redistribution of the world's assets.[20]

Even the call for the New World religion, so dear to the heart of the New Agers, has not been neglected by the Calvin College fellows:

> "When we turn to a consideration of the theology of the East, we discover that its strength is precisely in the area where Western thought is weakest: in its inclusion of the whole of creation, and not humans only, in redemption. Instead of that general suspicion of creation which dominates Western Christianity, there is a strong affirmation of the goodness of matter, its redeemability, and its dependence upon humans for its access to that divine redemption. In such a view, humans are not so much pilgrims, leaving the world behind, as they are, lifting it all, through their priestly actions, into a kind of divine life. . . . Thus in Eastern thought humans are the agent for the 'deification' of nature and the lifting of all creation up into Godhead. This does not imply consciousless union, but rather is a development of that idea of humans as 'heirs' with Christ, the second Adam of the fully redeemed creation (p. 222).

The heart of the New Age Movement is old-fashioned Hindu occultism, which embodies the ancient lie of the ser-

[20]Planetary Initiative is being managed by Donald Keys, an open Alice Bailey/Djwal Khul disciple. He is assisted in this effort by David Spangler and Peter Caddy — both Alice Bailey/Djwal Khul disciples and open Luciferians. They are being assisted at the United Nations by Robert Muller. Muller's most recent book, *New Genesis: Reshaping a Global Spirituality* was published by Doubleday in 1982. One chapter is entitled "The Reappearance of Christ." It is a transcript of a talk delivered to the Arcane School. The Arcane School is part of Lucis Trust (formerly known as the Lucifer Publishing Company), Lucis Trust is the custodian of the Alice Bailey/Djwal Khul writings, the cornerstone plans upon which the New Age Movement and particularly the PI effort are based. Muller has openly supported Benjamin Creme — the spokesman for Maitreya "The Christ."

pent right out of the Garden of Eden. This promise of god-hood that so captivated Eve continues to have an amazing-ly strong appeal for humanity today.

CHAPTER 12

The Old Lie: Finding God Within

It is one thing to read through a book which has subtle bends, twists, and turns, realizing that in serpentine fashion you are being inched in the direction of the New Age Movement. It is quite another experience to read one that comes on as bold as a cobra selling its venom door to door. Such a book is *Journey to Inner Space: Finding God in Us.* I have seen few worse in occult bookstores.

Journey to Inner Space is not the product of a Hindu sect. Incredibly, it was written by the senior pastor of the First Baptist Church of Seattle, Washington, Rodney R. Romney.

Like Calvin's *Earthkeeping,* but in the most blatantly Hindu/occult fashion, Dr. Romney urges the doctrine of God Immanent[1] and Transcendent upon us. Like the Calvin fellows, Loren Eisely is quoted, although with more even approval than that displayed in *Earthkeeping.*[2]

To state that Jesus is not the Christ is clearly a biblical test of antichrist. Stating that man himself could be as God was also one of the original lies of the Eden serpent.

Showing typical signs of New Age delusion, Dr. Romney says of Jesus:

"No one ever stirred up the people of his day as this man Jesus. The greater miracle is that twenty centuries later he is still stirring up people. He was no radical insurrectionist or polemic revolutionary. *He was simply a man who knew the laws of God and lived so completely within their framework that his entire life was a litany of obedience and faith to God.* He stirred up the people because

[1]Romney, Dr. Rodney, *Journey to Inner Space: Finding God-in-Us,* Nashville, Tennessee, Abingdon Press, citing pages 15, 43.

[2]*Ibid.*, p. 25.

he showed them what life could really be for them. He continues to do so today.

"This Jesus came to be called the Christ, meaning the Anointed One of God. It was a title he neither invited nor disclaimed. Yet what he did was even more startling. *He inferred that each person was potentially a Christ.* He claimed nothing for himself that he did not claim for his disciples. He called himself the light of the world, and he told his disciples that they too were the light of the world. He said he was one with God and prayed that the disciples would accept their oneness with God. He told them they not only would have experiences similar to his own, but would do even greater things than he had done. *Rather than condemning people for their depravity, he sought to awaken them to the glory of their own intended divinity. The task he gave his followers is to realize the Christ within their own consciousness, and to know that the kingdom of God is within them. If they search for it outside themselves, they will never find it*"[3] (emphasis added).

What went wrong with subsequent Christianity? According to Dr. Romney it was that:

"The large body of Christ-followers failed to realize their own Christhood. . . ."[4]

Was Jesus indifferent to being called the Christ — the anointed of God — as Romney implies? He clearly demonstrated otherwise:

"And when he [Jesus] was come nigh, even now at the descent of the Mount of Olives, the whole multitude of the disciples began to rejoice and praise God with a loud voice for all the mighty works they had seen;

"Saying, blessed be the king [the Messiah] that cometh in the name of the Lord: peace in heaven, and glory in the highest.

[3] *Ibid.,* pp. 28-29.

[4] *Ibid.,* p. 29.

"And some of the Pharisees from among the multitude said unto him, Master, rebuke thy disciples.

"And he answered and said unto them, I tell you that, if these should hold their peace, the stones would immediately cry out" (Luke 19:37-40, emphasis added).

According to Dr. Romney, Jesus came to establish a "world religion that would embrace every soul and synthesize every creed." Although Jesus said "It is finished," on the cross, Dr. Romney says, "his work will not be consummated until he has done just that [establish a world religion synthesizing every creed]."[5]

In fact, Romney says that Jesus never meant he was "the Way":

"Each of us must find our own way to the Way, and we would do well to take the hand of the Way-Shower as we go, for he shows us God as no one else ever has. But let us not get lost or overwhelmed by any human forms or formulas that seek to represent the Way. Some of these forms are little more than Jesus cults, stopping short of the Way by worshiping the Way-Shower and dealing almost totally with the miraculous of his life rather than the ethical and the mystical. Let us remember that Jesus came to show us God, to help us share in God's life, and to inspire us to seek the kingdom of God above all else. He resisted all attempts to worship or deify him. Although he did say, 'I am the way,' he meant that he was the Way-Shower to God. He was not God and never claimed to be" (*ibid.*, p. 30).

In his delusion, Romney claims that Jesus was "essentially a mystic, a person who explored the deeper recesses of his inner being, found the fountainhead of his own spirit, and thus knew himself to be the son of God." And Romney says that we can be Christs ourselves!

"I invite you to take the hand of the Way-Shower through every step of your inner journey, for he, more than any other, longs for the transformation of your ex-

[5]*Ibid.*, p. 31.

istence; he, more than any other longs for your *self-purifi-
cation;* he, more than any other, desires that you discover
the fullness and splendor of your own Christhood" (ibid.,
p. 36).

I have personally talked with Dr. Romney and in all
honesty, he sounds — at least over the telephone — like a
sincere, charming person. *But,* he is sincerely wrong!

The glue binding the New Agers together is that of common mystical experiences. They literally believe they are seeing things and hearing things the rest of us do not. With a
clergyman, such as Dr. Romney and the hundreds like him
caught up in occult mysticism, it may start as a product of
that common occupational disease of "burn-out." The Bible
says to acknowledge the Lord in all thy ways and "he shall
direct thy paths."[6]

However, the past several years have been characterized
by a barrage of "pop" psychologies and mind control courses.
Mind control was to be an essential component of preparation for the New World Order and the New Age "Christ."

The occult principle behind this is labeled "The Law of
Rebirth." It is not the same as what Jesus called being "born
again." In being born again, one is reconciled to God by
receiving the spirit of Jesus Christ into his heart. His
dependence is other directed — i.e. on Christ.

In rebirthing, by contrast, one is conditioned to believe
that all wisdom is contained within oneself. Like ancient
yogis and mystics, modern New Agers look inward — to the
center of themselves — to receive "wisdom" and knowledge.

Scripturally, however, it is clear that wisdom does not
come from within:

> "The heart is deceitful above all things, and desperately
> wicked: who can know it?" (Jeremiah 17:9, KJV).

This type of inward journey is usually achieved through a
variety of psychotechnologies virtually guaranteed to induce
demonic control.

[6]Proverbs 3:6.

Marilyn Ferguson's *The Aquarian Conspiracy* lists scores of such "psychotechnologies."[7] Alice Bailey/Djwal Khul disciples were urged to keep a "spiritual diary" in which they would record the experiences gained through meditation and the other psychotechnologies. The diarist was to record such experiences as contact with "presences" or the "masters." Illumination shed upon problems, telepathic happenings, and mystical experiences such as seeing a light in the head were also to be recorded.[8]

This should, of course, be of immediate interest to students of the Bible for the reason that Satan himself appears to those he deceives transformed into an angel of light.[9] New Agers often receive what they believe to be an experience of overpowering beauty and glory. Because of the immensity of the experience they assume they have come in contact with the Lord. God recognized our vulnerability in this area and for this reason wisely commanded his people not to get involved in occult practices. Deception has been Satan's game since the Garden of Eden and our times are no exception. We are told that the antichrist will come with great signs and wonders — great enough to deceive the elect "if it were possible."[10] Those dabbling in New Age psychotechnologies, including all too often clergy who ignore clear Bible doctrine, have received some of the end-time deception well in advance of the coming grand finalé.

We are also told to test the spirits:

"Beloved, believe not every spirit, but try the spirits whether they are of God: because many false prophets are gone out into the world.

"Hereby know ye the Spirit of God: Every spirit that confesseth that Jesus Christ is come in the flesh is of God:

[7]Ferguson, Marilyn, *The Aquarian Conspiracy,* Los Angeles: J.P. Tarcher, Inc., 1980. See pages 86-87. The psychotechnologies range from hypnosis, sufism, and Silva Mind Control through Transcendental Meditation and hatha yoga.

[8]Bailey, Alice A., *Discipleship in the New Age, Volume I,* New York: Lucis Publishing Company, 1972. See pages 14-15.

[9]II Corinthians 11:14.

[10]Mark 13:22

"And every spirit that confesseth not that Jesus Christ is come in the flesh is not of God: and this is that *spirit* of antichrist, whereof ye have heard that it should come; and even now already is it in the world" (I John 4:1-3, KJV).

The Bible consists of 66 books that do not contradict each other. The reason for this is that the Holy Spirit is consistent. Although they seem to come from diverse sources and are found in every culture upon earth, occult doctrines also have a remarkable consistency. In his *Catechism on Modernism*, Pope Pius X remarkably summarized the true unity of such teachings lurking behind a facade of apparent widely scattered sources and disconnected cultures:

"Since the Modernists employ a very clever artifice, namely, to present their doctrines without order and systematic arrangement into one whole, scattered and disjointed one from another, so as to appear to be in doubt and uncertainty, while they are in reality firm and steadfast, it will be of advantage to bring their teachings together here into one group and to point out the connection between them. . . ."[11]

The teachings of occultism diametrically oppose those found in the Bible. The Bible teaches that each person must die once and then the judgment.[12] Occultism teaches that each of us must live and die many times and then — maybe — Nirvana. The Bible teaches that Jesus made a perfect sacrifice once for all.[13] The occultists teach that we must all make atonement under the inexorable Law of Karma. The Bible says that Jesus is the Light of the World. The occultists say that light comes from our own "higher selves." The Bible says that Jesus is the only Christ. Occultists say there have been many Christs.

That such teachings would be prevalent in the church at

[11]Rev. J.B. Lemius, O.M.I., *A Catechism of Modernism*, founded on the encyclical *Pascendi Gregis (On Modernism)* by Pope Saint Pius X. Quoting from page 18.

[12]Hebrews 9:27.

[13]See Hebrews 9:24-28 and 10:10-14.

the end of time was foreseen by the apostles and prophets. Paul told the Thessalonians that the end would not come until the apostasy came first.[14] He also instructed his protegé in the Lord, Timothy, "that in the latter times some would depart from the faith, giving heed to seducing spirits, and doctrines of devils."[15]

In the Old Testament Daniel was told by the angel that "such as do wickedly against the covenant shall he corrupt by flatteries."

The Prophet Isaiah imparted advice received from the Holy Spirit as to how we could discern false prophets from messengers of the Lord:

> "To the law and to the testimony: if they speak not according to this word, it is because there is no light in them" (Isaiah 8:20, KJV).

By first dabbling in that forbidden by the Lord and then failing to test the Spirits, many, even including caring, personable clergymen such as Dr. Romney, have been seduced into unintentional worship of demons. And the demons are still presenting themselves packaged as a snake. By taking the forbidden fruits of occultism, the would-be initiate — even clergymen initiates such as Dr. Romney — raise the fires of the Serpent fire Kundalini up from the base of the spine and through what they call the seven chakras (nerve centers).

Dr. Romney openly discusses this process:

> "There is much I have not covered concerning the meditation experience. I have not talked about the seven nerve centers *(chakras)* and the corresponding colors of these centers. Nor have I discussed the forces within our cerebrospinal system known as the *kundalini shakti*, a mysterious fire of love that rises up within us through daily, sincere periods of meditation and which transports us into a new land of expanded consciousness."[16]

[14]II Thessalonians 2:3, NASB and KJV.

[15]I Timothy 4:1.

[16]Romney, Dr. Rodney, *Journey to Inner Space: Finding God-In-Us*, Nashville, Tennessee, Abingdon Press, 1980.

To reach this state of expanded consciousness, Dr. Romney says he faces the east:

> "I always sit in the same chair if possible, which faces east. Facing east while praying is an ancient practice which draws a symbolism between the rising sun and the dawning of divine light in one's consciousness. In the opinion of some this also offers exposure to greater forms of cosmic energy."[17]

The Lord showed his prophet Ezekiel that similar practices were being committed by the Israelites and the House of Judah:

> "Then said he unto me, Hast thou seen *this*, O son of man? turn thee yet again, *and* thou shalt see greater abominations than these.

> "And he brought me into the inner court of the Lord's house, and, behold, at the door of the temple of the Lord, between the porch and the altar, were about five and twenty men, with their backs toward the temple of the Lord, and their faces toward the east; and they worshipped the sun toward the east" (Ezekiel 8:15-16).

Daniel 11:38 foretold the last days worship of the "God of Forces" by the antichrist and his followers. A prime goal of occultism is to learn how to manipulate "The Force."[18]

Romney shows signs of having succumbed also to the deception that God is a Force — also excellently illustrating the fact that those dabbling in occultism are seeing and hearing things the rest of us are not:

> "So God first made light as spiritual energy and from that light created all things. We, therefore, are not made of solid, impenetrable matter — we are made of light energy. *This primal force of energy is what we call God.* When the

[17]*Ibid.*, p. 88.

[18]See, for example, Albert A. Pike's *Morals and Dogma.* Pages 1-6 feature an extensive discussion of the need for managing or regulating the Force. This book could double for scores of other occult works. The Alice Bailey *Master Index* contains several pages of references on "forces" alone.

Bible says we are made in God's image, it means that we are constructed of the very energy force which is God. When we establish a connection with God, we receive an increased flow of this energy. . . .

"When people advance into the higher realms of spiritual consciousness, they often perceive this light through the spiritual sense, sometimes diffused into brilliant colors that go beyond any shades and hues ever seen before, just as they will often distinguish sounds that normally the human ear cannot register. . . . The deep center of our inner space, where we are conscious of being filled by God, transcends all mortal limitations and brings perceptions to us that are impossible at any other level.

"For centuries it was known in the Eastern countries that a powerful, invisible force seemed to flow through the hands and arms of the so-called holy people. People who consciously identified with God seemed to have an abundance of energy which was healing in its effect. Certainly this was true of Jesus" (*ibid.*, p. 72-73).

When I spoke with Dr. Romney, he was not reticent about admitting he considered his book to be an example of "New Age" writing. His book actually alludes to this coming "New Age":

"Most students of the spiritual realm agree that we are entering today into a New Age of Light on this planet. This light is beginning to expose and correct malfunctions in the created order. The result of this may be a temporary increase of distress and disease. Individuals who have been dwelling in darkness will manifest hostile and criminal reactions as the light increases. There will even be similar disturbances in the elements of nature in the form of storms, droughts, earthquakes, and other destructive activities. Humanity as a whole may react to these upheavals with feelings of despair and gloom, fearing that the world is coming to an end, as limited thought forms erroneously predicted long ago. But this is not an age to fear, it is one in which to rejoice. As the light purges and purifies the darkness, we feel the death rattle of an old age and the birth pangs of a new one in which the highest aspirations and possibilities of creation will rise to the fore" (*ibid.*, p. 74-75).

Dr. Romney's next paragraph is chillingly reminiscent of Alice Bailey's instructions to New Age disciples on how to "hold the light":[19]

"Those who understand the principle of light, who know how to project it into a condition and hold it there, and who understand that this light comes from God and God's invisible workers who are on this earth, will discover that they are able to change conditions in positive ways and usher in the age of abiding peace on earth" (*ibid.*, p. 75).

According to the Bible, Jesus *is* the Light of the World. Dr. Romney sees this a little differently. He says that "Jesus delivered the Christ-light of the cosmos to the planet earth and to each of us individually."[20]

This is clearly part of the ultimate delusion referred to by Daniel: "such as do wickedly against the covenant shall he corrupt with flatteries." That flattery most likely is the occult teaching that man himself can be as a god.

This is reflected in Dr. Romney's work:

"*Christ Me.* Jesus not only knew the Christ in himself, he saw the Christ in everyone else. Jesus became what each of us is destined to be, a Christ, and he remains with us in spirit to show us the way to God and to the Christ of our inner being. The Christ has taken many forms and has been known by different names, but that need not concern us. We know the Christ as Jesus who came to this earth two thousand years ago with the triumphant message of God's love, uniting us to the reality of our true identity. At that place of knowing, all illusions end, and we come to

[19]See *Discipleship in the New Age,* Vol. I, by Alice A. Bailey. Page 298 gives a discussion of techniques for "holding the mind steady in the light." It is an occult technique for invoking the Luciferic energies.

[20]*Ibid.*, p. 76.

apprehend our intended glory and to accept our true divinity as a holy son or daughter of God. We stand now on the highest rung of the ladder of prayer.

"This final rung is the place where we are fully Christ-like, where we recognize the Christ in ourselves and in all others" (*ibid.*, pp. 106-107).

It is sad but true that there is little difference between the things said by Dr. Romney in the foregoing quoted paragraph and the public statements of Benjamin Creme in putting forth the so-called "Maitreya the Christ" — "there have been many Christs." This is also a head-on test of antichrist: a denial that Jesus is *the* Christ.

Findhorn was founded, according to the Caddys, on "guidance" received by Eileen Caddy from their spirit guides. The Caddys were told they were to help anchor "The Plan" on earth. It was no big surprise to find this type of material coming from such people long anchored in Tibetan Buddhism and other esoteric schools of thought.

It was a real surprise, however, to find nearly identical "guidance" being channeled through a Baptist minister of an American Baptist Convention church. Romney's spirit guides told him about "The Plan" in nearly the same terms as the multitude of Findhorn messages littering the occult and Unity bookstores of America:

"Trust your own seasons and the divinely ordained plan. Only by coming to me and giving yourself into contemplative silence will you be able to see that I am in control, that I will ultimately have my way, and that time is not a factor for me. Learn to live in cooperation with my plan" (*ibid.*, p. 126).

One thing I have noticed in my analysis of the New Age Movement and cult-like organizations is that of stark contrast to the scriptural messages of God which always sound both concerned and caring. Lucifer or Satan cannot help but sound boastful.

New Agers work under the delusion that they are bettering society. However, one of their core teachings is the Law of Karma. This is a teaching that whatever happens to one was brought on by his own good or bad karma.

For example, the World War II massacre of the Jews occurred as a result of their "bad national karma."[21] This teaching of pure Hindu and occult derivation finds its place in Romney's "guidance":

> "But what about the innocent? you say. What of those who suffer unjustly at the hands of the wrongdoer? There is no such thing as pure innocence, even in a tiny babe. Every soul carries within it the scars of centuries of wrong thinking and wrongdoing. There is a karmic law of indebtedness that many are now working out, having voluntarily accepted a path of suffering that will forge a higher evolution of the soul" (*ibid.*, p. 127).

Romney is even told he has "spirits" with him. In a paragraph sounding remarkably like the messages received by Eileen Caddy of Findhorn about the helper spirits, Romney is told:

> "Nature spirits are with you often, and it is their love for you and dedication to your mission which evokes a tenderness essence in you for all nature . . ." (*ibid.*, p. 129).

And the whispering demons are quick to tell Dr. Romney whom to follow:

> "Your assignment is not to follow any earthly teacher or guru on the earth path. Your assignment is to discover the Christ within you. . . . Teach yourself. Be your own master. Be your own healer. Find the Christ within" (*ibid.*, p. 130).

Dr. Romney is also told that we need a new world religion and that religion — including Christianity — is still "evolving":

[21]See Alice A. Bailey, *Esoteric Healing*. New York, Lucis Publishing Company, 1953. See particularly pp. 263-267 for application of this bizarre occult teaching that the fate of the Jews was the result of their "evil karma."

"As you learn to lay aside your judgments of others, learn also to cease judging religions, denominations, or any theological system. I have a higher purpose for you. There is good in every religion, yet each lacks complete truth. Yes, even in Christianity, as it has evolved, there is error and deviation from the pure truth that Christ spoke. You must learn to lay aside all the trappings and accouterments of organized institutions and man-made religious systems and rise above these into a universal religion. No longer think of yourself as Baptist, nor even Christian. You are more than these. Jesus rose above all such limitations and became the only begotten Son. He transcended all religions and became the only begotten Son. He transcended all religions. Follow him to the Christ of your own being. As you do, you will rejoice in the new freedom that arrives when titles and distinctions are dissolved" (*ibid.*, p. 130).

Dr. Romney is a senior pastor within the American Baptist Convention. In response to those seeking explanations as to why this type of propagation is allowed to continue unchallenged, they are sharply told that Dr. Romney is a very fine Christian. He is a charming person and I am sure sincere. But this type of heresy should not be allowed to continue under the auspices of our Fundamentalist churches — neither for the sake of his congregation nor the tens of thousands in Dr. Romney's listening audiences. For the sake of Dr. Romney's own soul and the souls of the other teachers and members influenced by such thinking, it should not be tolerated. It is far more dangerous coming from a Christian pulpit than from an occult bookstore. At least when people enter an occult bookstore they know, or should know, what they are about to receive. People have a right to expect orthodox teaching within the confines of their church or synagogue.

It is time for repentance and *true* reconciliation to God. Not the reconciliation urged by neo-evangelicals and New Age thinkers within our churches, but the reconciliation that comes from following the warning angel's message to "COME OUT OF HER MY PEOPLE, THAT YE BE NOT PARTAKERS OF HER SINS, AND THAT YE RECEIVE NOT OF HER PLAGUES."

This is no time for smugness and thinking we are better than these unfortunates. It is a time for serious exhortation and speaking the truth in love.

> "As it is written, There is none righteous, no, not one:
>
> "There is none that understandeth, there is none that seeketh after God.
>
> "They are all gone out of the way, they are together become unprofitable; there is none that doeth good, no, not one" (Romans 3:10-12, KJV).

Many of our leaders who started with the finest of intentions have become victims — some witting — but many unwitting. This is not surprising. Satan would rather attack our churches than anywhere else. Whether the damage can now be undone is in the hands of God. If God is ready for end-time events, the clock might not be turned back. But even our religious leaders deserve a warning in the spirit of Christian love. Some labored hard in the vineyards, some stumbled and fell. There but for the grace of God goes any one of us.

CHAPTER 13

How to Help New Agers

Sadly, the vast majority of New Agers are involved quite innocently. Their motives are often altruistic. They wish to help — not harm — their fellow human beings. Most of them lack knowledge of the ultimate goals of the Movement.

Even among those possessing this knowledge, many fail to see the dire consequences. Rapidly increasing numbers are being manipulated by extremely sophisticated forms of mind control. This no doubt is due in part to the preparatory conditioning of meditation and other psycho/spiritual techniques.

My study of hypnosis has left me unconvinced of its claimed scientific basis. I feel it constitutes pure and simple, albeit temporary, demonic control.

I have personally witnessed many New Age "spiritual" sessions where those present seemed to be taken into progressively deeper levels of hypnosis. While under such influence they were told that (1) a World Teacher or "Christ" is coming; (2) they themselves possess divinity or the "Christ Consciousness"; (3) the Christ is not any single man and no preacher can save them — they must save themselves; (4) a "cleansing action" will have to occur before the New Age can begin. Even more importantly than what they were told while under hypnosis is the fact that THEY ARE NEVER BROUGHT OUT FROM UNDER THE HYPNOTIC INFLUENCE!

When Benjamin Creme spoke in Detroit he seemed to "control" the audience. During the evening many participants appeared red-eyed with fixed stares. The ease with which some seemed to "go under" suggested that they had been subject to prior conditioning. It was chilling to watch hundreds of intelligent adults give a standing ovation to the prospects of "false teachers about the Christ" (i.e., fundamentalist Christians) *disappearing.*

Likewise, it makes an orthodox Christian or Jew no happier to read the source books for the Movement — the Alice Bailey, David Spangler, Agni Yoga, Theosophical, Rosicrucian, H.G. Wells writings — and see cold plans for a near-future "cleansing-action," especially when the reader realizes he is among those to be "cleansed." Reading that all who express recalcitrance towards the New Age "Christ" will be released from physical embodiment and sent to "another dimension other than physical incarnation" certainly does nothing towards giving the reader warm feelings about the writers and their followers — the New Agers.

Nevertheless, a commitment to speak the truth in love must be made and maintained if we are to help the first victims of the Aquarian Conspiracy — the New Agers themselves. They may be victims because they are under sophisticated forms of deception. They may be victims because they do not have full facts and are told only what their leaders want them to know — in guided "study programs" rather than by a dispassionate survey of all available information, including orthodox Judeo-Christian teachings.

For example, it is not uncommon for youngsters involved in the New Age Movement to receive warnings against reading the entire Bible such as those contained in *The Next Whole Earth Catalog*, a popular New Age publication by Point with Random House distribution:

> "If you've ever tried to read the BIBLE cover to cover, be advised it's a bad idea. The BIBLE was written by a lot of different people at a lot of different times, so it should be read more like a magazine than a book. Flip around, see what looks interesting, skip the boring parts" (from page 591, second edition, copyright © 1980-1981 by *Point*).

Apart from the New Age-oriented theologians who have deliberately infused our churches and seminaries with New

Age concepts, the vast majority of those in the New Age Movement are there innocently. The lonely, the confused and bewildered, the young and naive — these are prime targets for New Age organizers. Likewise, they should be prime targets for Christians and great sensitivity should be used in approaching them to win them back to where they really belong — to Jesus Christ who sacrificed his life for them and still cares for them.

Often people are won to the Movement and/or its various programs by reacting to various distortions of Christianity and its source book, the Bible. All too often, Christians play into the hands of New Age recruiters.

For example, New Agers are told that Christianity is a repressive religion and that its Bible teaches that all who have never heard of God and Jesus Christ are automatically condemned. While this representation is both inaccurate and unfair, Christian ministers have often played into the New Agers' hands by preaching this very doctrine from the pulpit and inserting same into Christian comic books.

My son was even taught this same doctrine in a Lutheran school.

The correct scriptural reference for this question is found in Romans 2:1-16:

> "Therefore you are without excuse, every man of you who passes judgment, for in that you judge another, you condemn yourself; for you who judge practice the same things.

> "And we know the judgment of God rightly falls upon those who practice such things.

> "And do you suppose this, O man, when you pass judgment upon those who practice such things and do the same yourself, that you will escape the judgment of God?

> "Or do you think lightly of the riches of His kindness and forbearance and patience, not knowing that the kindness of God leads you to repentance?

> "But because of your stubbornness and unrepentant heart you are storing up wrath for yourself in the day of

wrath and revelation of the righteous judgment of God.

"Who WILL RENDER TO EVERY MAN ACCORDING TO HIS DEEDS [emphasized in original].

"To those who by perseverance in doing good seek for glory and honor and immortality, eternal life;

"But to those who are selfishly ambitious and do not obey the truth, but obey unrighteousness, wrath, and indignation.

"There will be tribulation and distress for every soul of man who does evil, of the Jew first and also of the Greek.

"But glory and honor and peace to every man who does good, to the Jew first and also to the Greek.

"For there is no partiality with God.

"For all who have sinned without the Law will also perish without the Law; and all who have sinned under the Law will be judged by the Law.

"For not the hearers of the Law are justified before God, but the doers of the Law will be justified.

"For when Gentiles who do not have the Law do instinctively the things of the Law, these, not having the Law, are a law to themselves.

"In that they show the work of the Law written in their hearts, their conscience bearing witness, and their thoughts alternately accusing or else defending them.

"On the day when, according to my gospel God will judge the secrets of men through Christ Jesus" (NASB).

On Judgment Day there may be many surprises for those "Christians" who have deliberately apostatized or misled the body of Christ. They may see some poor pagan who did the best he could with the little knowledge he did possess standing redeemed and joyous before the throne while the apostates and hypocrites watch with gnashing of teeth from outside.

Jesus was plain on this point:

"Not every one that saith unto me, Lord, Lord, shall enter into the kingdom of heaven; but he that doeth the will of my Father which is in heaven.

"Many will say to me in that day, Lord, Lord, have we not prophesied in thy name? and in thy name have cast out devils? and in thy name done many wonderful works?

"And then will I profess unto them, I never knew you: depart from me, ye that work iniquity" (Matthew 7:21-23, KJV).

The next point of Christianity that concerns sensitive New Agers and their prospective recruits is the fate of the Jews. While the New Age Movement is, at its esoteric core, deeply antisemitic, many of its number are unaware of this. This fact is reserved for either voracious readers of New Age dogma or upper level initiates of occultdom.

Many New Agers — particularly would-be Jewish New Agers — are told that Christianity is antisemitic as it represents the Jews as being blanketly condemned unless they have converted to Christianity.

Again, this is a misrepresentation of plain scriptural language:

"For I do not want you, brethren, to be uninformed of this mystery, lest you be wise in your own estimation, that a partial hardening has happened to Israel until the fulness of the Gentiles has come in;

"And thus all Israel will be saved; just as it is written, THE DELIVERER WILL COME FROM ZION. HE WILL REMOVE UNGODLINESS FROM JACOB.

" 'AND THIS IS MY COVENANT WITH THEM. WHEN I TAKE AWAY THEIR SINS.'

"From the standpoint of the gospel they are enemies for your sake, but from the standpoint of God's choice they are beloved for the sake of the fathers;

"For the gifts and calling of God are irrevocable.

"For just as you once were disobedient to God, but now have been shown mercy because of their disobedience.

"So these also now have been disobedient, in order that because of the mercy shown to you they also may now be shown mercy.

"For God has shut up all in disobedience that He might show mercy to all.

"Oh, the depth of the riches both of the wisdom and knowledge of God! How unsearachable are His judgments and unfathomable His ways!" (Romans 11:25-33, NASB).

It is therefore clear that antisemitism is condemned in the plainest possible scriptural terms, without exception.

New Age theology distorts the teachings of Christianity in other important ways as well. They tell their prospective disciples that all world religions have the same "truths" at their core. While there are certain superficial similarities among most religions, orthodox Judaism and Christianity stand in direct opposition to every other belief system. It is safe to say, however, that nearly all non-Judeo/Christian religions are extremely similar because, as the Bible indicates, they come from *one* source, the "god of this world" — Satan himself.

Doctrines of reincarnation and self-realization (godhood for man) lie at the heart of New Age teachings. It can hardly be coincidence that many forms of these teachings still come packaged as a snake. Many New Agers fervently believe they are working "to raise the fires of Kundalini (a goddess in the form of a snake coiled at the base of the spine)."

Many have been recruited into the Movement through their desire to help solve the world's problems and particularly the hunger problem. They do not know that central to the teaching of the Movement is the replacement of the present races — the very peoples they say they are helping — with a new root race.

Many are unaware of the political aims of the Movement to eliminate several billions from the earth's population and millions from that of the USA prior to the year 2000 — a goal only accomplishable by mass genocide. Even ostensibly Christian anti-hunger organizations have not escaped the influence of New Age teachings.

Abortion, artificial insemination, genetic control, and death control are frightening and all dear to the heart of Friends of the Earth — a prominent New Age organization. One wonders how many members or supporters of that group are aware that those exact programs were central to Hitler's Nazism.

Pamphlets available in metaphysical bookstores sometimes give a more honest statement of the New Agers' intentions. In 1982 *Cosmic Countdown*, published by Guardian Action Publications of New Mexico, in alleged transmissions from "Higher Intelligence," it was said of the hunger/disease problem in the third world:

> "The world should be forewarned to be on the lookout for diseases which have been suppressed for years, suddenly rearing their ugly heads and decimating populations already on the verge of starvation in the Third World Nations. Although these peoples will eventually be replaced by the new root race about to make its appearance in a newly cleansed world; nevertheless, for the moment, this is a tragedy" (page 12).

Perhaps the best way to help the sensitive New Ager who is worried about problems of world hunger — a legitimate worry — is to show him the lack of real spending for food by New Age organizations fighting hunger. Many, with enormously large budgets, spend little on actual bread for the starving. The Hunger Project and Bread for the World spend their time and resources either lobbying for structural change (such as a World Food Authority to replace present food distribution systems), or seeking to gain additional adherents to this point of view.

Many sincere New Agers are interested in the disarmament issue. The New Age Movement has outwardly billed itself as being opposed to nuclear weapons.

The Alice Bailey writings however plainly state on page 548 of *The Externalisation of the Hierarchy* that they should feel free to use these weapons on religious groups who interfere in the political process — or at the very least feel free to threaten their use. This inconsistency in the New Age position could be used profitably to enlighten sincere New Agers as to the real nature of the Movement.

Many if not most New Agers would be truly startled to see the close resemblance of the Movement to Nazism. This must be handled in a most tactful manner if the New Ager is to hear the conversation out. A tabulation is presented in another portion of this book demonstrating these points in reference.

New Agers fascinated by mysticism and psychic seers such as Nostradamus will be interested in the correlation of the Movement to Bible prophecy. Again, a tabulation is provided herein to assist you with this technique for reaching New Agers of your acquaintance.

Finally, one must not underestimate the power of prayer. While you are talking with the New Ager, do so forthrightly and courageously, remembering that we are given the authority in the name of Jesus to deliver them from demonic deception and power if they are willing to be delivered.

The battle is a spiritual one. Therefore, even while witnessing "pray without ceasing" for wisdom and guidance and that the eyes of the New Ager might be opened. Always, always speak the truth in *love*. Remember, Jesus Christ loves and died for New Agers. Until proven otherwise, we should consider each of them to be a victim rather than a villain.

Selected New Age Organizations

While the foregoing is not intended to be a complete listing of New Age organizations, it will give the reader some valuable resources for pursuing this subject further. The following organizations are very important within the New Age networks.

It should also be kept in mind that the Movement is not a hierarchical structure, per se, but is composed of thousands of networking organizations. The following constitute some of the more important links in the New Age network:

LUCIS TRUST: This organization was originally incorporated as the Lucifer Publishing Company and changed its name the next year to the somewhat less startling Lucis Trust. Operated under the auspices of this organization are Lucis Publishing Company, World Goodwill, Arcane School, and Triangles. The numerous Alice Bailey meditation clubs also are operated under their aegis. They have translated or are translating the Alice Bailey books into several languages including English, German, French, Spanish, Italian, Dutch, Greek, Polish and Russian. They finance publication of their books through a revolving trust fund and Lucis Trust owns all copyrights to their books — mostly the Alice Bailey writings. Within the USA the Trust is both non-profit and enjoys tax exempt status. According to Alice Bailey's *Unfinished Autobiography*, the Arcane School had already graduated 20,000 students by 1945. The Arcane School training prepares people for active New Age discipleship and leadership. According to page 286 of her *Autobiography*, the Arcane School features Theosophists and Rosicrucians as well as Christian Scientists and "churchmen of every denomination — Protestant and Catholic — and men and women of every type of religious and political persuasion. It may safely be said that Lucis Trust is truly the brains — at least from an occult planning basis — of the New Age Movement. One only has to study the course of the Movement to see that her instructions to New Age "disciples" have been followed like recipes.

Lucis Trust, 866 United Nations Plaza, New York, New York 10017

PACIFIC INSTITUTE: While officially denying New Age involvement, it appears nonetheless that Pacific Institute possesses New Age characteristics buried under platitudes of self-improvement cliches. It has managed to instill New Age philosophies and concepts in otherwise inaccessible bastions of corporate responsibility. Its course entitled "New Age Thinking" has been given to such diverse clients as the General Motors Corporation, AT&T and Amway. While Pacific Institute claims the use of the name to be coincidental, nevertheless the concepts are distinctly New Age. Often such courses are mandatory for upper and middle-level management who are urged to bring their families along for the training. Much of the course material teaches the attendees that their worlds are created and/or determined by the working of their minds. Techniques of visualization, self-hypnosis, imprinting and affirmations are employed — standard techniques for occultists. A section of their course handbook entitled "Suggested Reading" includes many New Age selections. For example, it includes Ram Dass' *Grist for the Mill* and works by the patron saint of the New Age Movement, Pierre Teilhard de Chardin who on five occasions was censored by the Roman Catholic Church for apostasy. Although Pacific Institute recently has denied it, Jim Channon's *Evolutionary Tactics Manual* for his New Age military-linked First Earth Battalion credits Pacific Institute with contributing funds for its publication. Pacific Institute has, however, admitted making a payment to Channon in the sum of $4,000 for certain, unspecified services. Pacific Institute is out to offer its popularized mind-control courses to such diverse groups as military personnel and juvenile delinquents.

PEOPLE FOR THE AMERICAN WAY: This anti-fundamentalist organization was founded by TV producer Norman Lear and as of November, 1982, numbers 85,000 members, according to the November 8, 1982, *Leading Edge Bulletin* published by Marilyn Ferguson. Pure and simply it constitutes an aggressive hate campaign against fundamentalist Christians. They have also successfully diverted attention from the Nazi-like aims of the New Age

Movement by accusing the Moral Majority of their own tactics of aggressive intimidation. Lear is reportedly an EST (Erhard Seminars Training) graduate. They were successful in intimidating at least one Christian television station, (KTLA, Channel 5, Los Angeles) into giving them equal time even though the federal regulations pertaining to same most likely do not apply to Christian broadcasting. According to Ms. Ferguson, People for the American Way also enjoyed similar successes in other cities. It should also be noted that most religious broadcasting is paid and would be no more entitled to equal time for rebuttal than a paid political advertisement.

People for the American Way, 1015 18th Street, NW #310, Washington, D.C. 20036, (202) 822-9450

NEW GROUP OF WORLD SERVERS: This is a somewhat amorphous organization that was supposedly organized by Alice Bailey in 1925 under the direction of "the Hierarchy" to serve as the vanguard for the reappearance of "The Christ" and "His Great Disciples, the Masters of Wisdom." According to Benjamin Creme, it has both an inner and outer organization — the outer organization being conscious of the aims of the NGWS and the inner group merely responsive to "Hierarchical impression." Lucis Trust regularly distributes, upon request, information pertinent to the NGWS. Benjamin Creme distributes brochures regarding the NGWS at his lectures. According to this brochure, those interested are to read *The Aquarian Conspiracy* by Marilyn Ferguson along with some of the Alice Bailey books for more information. The flyer also states that it is "based on the Alice Bailey teachings." It is interesting to note that Planetary Citizens, the secretariat for Planetary Initiative for the World We Choose, gives one of its purposes as "aiding World Servers everywhere." It is of even greater interest that Planetary Initiative, the important vehicle of the New Age Movment, in a help wanted ad in their paper *Initiator*, titles the item "World Servers Called to Action." Lucis Trust is one of the organizations cooperating in the work of the New Group of World Servers.

New Group of World Servers, c/o Lucis Trust, 866 United Nations Plaza, Suite 566-7, New York, New York 10017

PLANETARY CITIZENS: Planetary Citizens enjoys the support of many and varied prominent personages from about the globe. David Spangler sits on its board of directors. Donald Keys, another individual publicly associated with Findhorn Foundation was a founder along with Norman Cousins, the head of the invitor committee for the World Council of Wise Persons. U Thant was also involved in the original organizational work. Theodore Hesburgh of Notre Dame University and Peter Caddy, the founder of Findhorn Foundation, are also connected as committee chairmen. According to a description of Planetary Citizens in *New Age Politics* by Mark Satin, their purpose is to aid the "World Servers everywhere." Since the purpose of the World Servers is to serve as the vanguard for the "reappearance of Christ" (not Jesus, according to this crew), it is not hard to figure that the purpose of Planetary Citizens, by extension, must be the same.

Planetary Citizens, 777 United Nations Plaza, New York, New York 10017

PLANETARY INITIATIVE FOR THE WORLD WE CHOOSE: This is a truly amazing consortium of over 300 sponsoring groups. They call their official organ the *Initiator.* It is even more amazing in light of the fact that Creme's transmissions from "Lord Maitreya" say "I am the Initiator of the little ones." Further, David Spangler, who is very closely connected with and allied to this project, has defined the initiation in his book *Reflections on the Christ* as being "Luciferic." This is probably the most honest statement that anyone inside the project has ever made! The organization or "network" is in the process of convening a "World Council of Wise Persons." Norman Cousins is heading the Invitor Committee for this project. So far, according to Volume 1, No. 2 of the *Initiator,* the network newspaper of The Planetary Initiative for the World We Choose, Buckminster Fuller and Dr. Carlos Romulo of the Philippines have accepted invitations to sit on this "distinguished" council. They have scheduled their "Culminating Global Congress" for summer solstice (June 21, 1983) in Toronto, to coincide with the New York meeting of the World Council of Wise Persons at the United Nations. Since you are now wise to this gathering of "village elders" why don't you tell the nice staff at Planetary Initiative that you too want to be on the World Council of Wise Persons! You may write them at the above address for Planetary Citizens. Tell them you know the true nature of this alleged "plot to save the world." The only thing more ludicrous than the World Council of Wise Persons is their budget as set forth in Issue #2 of the *Initiator*. I counted more than that budget in airline tickets in one issue alone! Anybody believing their budget is not smart enough to be in their Movement. They claim they ran their 1981 office — which included operation of a Manhattan office in United Nations Plaza, wooing away of high priced executives from other international organizations such as Amnesty International, and worldwide travel by their New York staff — for a total of $39,000 of which they raised approximately only $18,000, leaving them a total of $21,000!

Planetary Initiative for the World We Choose, c/o Planetary Citizens, 777 United Nations Plaza, New York, New York 10017

UNITY-IN-DIVERSITY COUNCIL: This network is for all practical purposes one and the same as its predecessor organization: International Cooperation Council. Its advisory board features such New Age luminaries as Peter Caddy (founder of Findhorn Foundation, Scotland), Swami Kriyananda, Robert Muller (of the United Nations and a staunch ally of Benjamin Creme), Dr. Ira Progoff (*The Progoff Journals* — must reading in many college courses), and Dane Rudhyar. After a financial fiasco by its predecessor organization, International Cooperation Council, the action was merely shifted to another constituent International Cooperation Council organization, the Unity-in-Diversity Council. Unity-in-Diversity sponsored the huge Festival for Mind-Body-Spirit in Los Angeles and San Francisco that saw tens of thousands in attendance. They also sponsored Benjamin Creme for the benefit of their members who had not as yet come under his pitch for "Maitreya the Christ." All Unity-in-Diversity members were urged to attend. Unity-in-Diversity's newsletter *Spectrum* enjoys a 35,000 circulation worldwide and is published on a quarterly basis. Also of interest are the origins of Unity-in-Diversity Council and International Cooperation Council. International Cooperation Council came into being to continue the work begun during International Cooperation Year of the United Nations in 1965. One of the more interesting members of Unity-in-Diversity Council — a New Age network — is Tara Center. Findhorn Foundation is also a member and Marilyn Ferguson's *Leading Edge Bulletin* and *Brain Mind Bulletin* are associate members. Elizabeth Clare Prophet's Summit

University (Church Universal and Triumphant), is also affiliated as a full member of Unity-in-Diversity Council as well as of its predecessor, International Cooperation Council. Its organization structure and scope of activity is truly amazing. In addition to its approximately 200-member organizations, the old International Cooperation Council directory featured a list of approximately 600 additional organizations that had identical goals: "A worldwide coordinating body of organizations and individuals fostering the emergence of a new universal person and civilization based on Unity-in-Diversity among all peoples." The introduction by John White to their 1979 International Cooperation Council Directory duly noted that they were to be considered a "new species" — *homo noeticus* as opposed to *homo sapiens*. They planned to have species war with the *homo sapiens* and win! If that sounds familiar, it should. That is precisely the same premise Hitlerian Nazism was based upon.

Unity-in-Diversity Council, World Trade Center, 350 S. Figueroa Street, Suite 370, Los Angeles, California 90071 (213) 626-2062

THE SUTPHEN CORPORATION: This is an organization headed by virulent anti-fundamentalist Dick Sutphen. When Sutphen is not making war on Christians, he holds Past-Life Therapy Seminars, "human potential weekends," Bushido Sutphen Seminar Training (The Bushido SST), writes and publishes books, and edits the *Self-Help Update* "Create Your Own Reality" and *Reincarnation Report*. He aggressively proclaims himself as one of "many way clearers" for the New Age. He fights fundamentalism because he "can no longer ignore a movement that I feel is extremely dangerous to the future of this planet and the potential for a New Age." Unfortunately, he has a substantial following and he also works closely with Norman Lear's People for the American Way in its war against fundamentalist Christianity. He also urges his readers to network for "global transformation."

The Sutphen Corporation, 22333 Pacific Coast Highway, Suites 10 through 14, Malibu, California 90265 (213) 456-5635

The "Great Invocation" Distribution

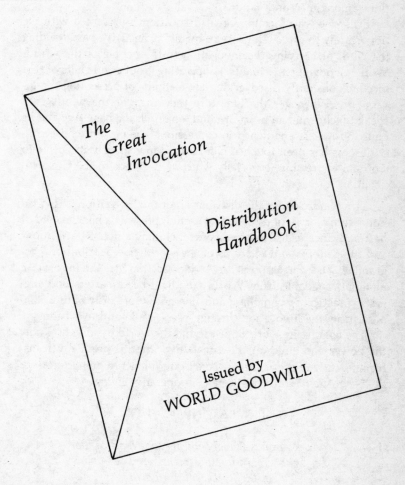

The
Great
Invocation

Distribution
Handbook

Issued by
WORLD GOODWILL

DISTRIBUTION OF THE "GREAT INVOCATION"

The worldwide distribution of the Great Invocation is demonstrating how this Invocation for Power and Light is accepted by men and women of every land and of every religious faith. The Great Invocation is truly a world prayer, voicing the great human need for divine aid and direction in the establishing of right relations among men and nations.

Everyone who uses the Great Invocation is presented with the opportunity to expand his service by taking an active part in aiding the work of carrying the Invocation to the people of the world. World Goodwill participants, cooperating groups and Units of Service are constantly discovering new methods of presenting the Invocation. Whenever the literature they mail or the words they speak touch a human heart or mind, one finds the New Age and its consciousness strengthened in expression. The person whose consciousness has been touched can become increasingly receptive to spiritual impression, especially when he responds to the Great Invocation.

This handbook on the distribution of the Invocation is divided into two major sections. The first section presents a background of past and current distribution work, including a list of translations and the patterns and methods of the worldwide distribution programme. The "Suggestions for Action" section lists the Invocation materials available from World Goodwill headquarters and suggests practical techniques and methods for distributing and publicizing the Invocation through press, radio and television.

The continuing work done around the world by all who know the power and effect of the Great Invocation is gradually transforming the subjective atmosphere of our planet in preparation for the New Age of truth, justice and cooperative living.

THE GREAT INVOCATION

From the point of Light within the Mind of God
Let light stream forth into the minds of men.
Let Light descend on Earth.

From the point of Love within the Heart of God
Let love stream forth into the hearts of men.

May Christ return to Earth.

From the centre where the Will of God is known
Let purpose guide the little wills of men —
The purpose which the Masters know and serve.

From the centre which we call the race of men
Let the Plan of Love and Light work out.
And may it seal the door where evil dwells.

Let Light and Love and Power restore the Plan on Earth.

INTRODUCTION

The Great Invocation was first given out and used in 1945 and since that date has become familiar to millions of people all over the world, and is used daily by them. This world prayer expresses truths central to all major religions and is based on the true and inner unity of all religions and philosophies which millions today accept. Through the use of the Invocation men and women of goodwill can achieve a unity that transcends all differences of outer belief. Their combined and daily invocation and prayer to divinity creates an open channel into human consciousness through which spiritual energies flow to heal and rebuild a troubled world.

Invocation in the Aquarian Age

In this opening cycle of the Aquarian Age, the invocative cry of humanity is a threefold cry. It is a cry for light upon our way and for light to flow into the dark places of the Earth; it is also a cry for more love in the world as voiced by the men of goodwill and of humanitarian attitudes; it is, finally, the intuitive appeal of the aspirants and disciples of the world for the full expression in time and space of the will-to-good, the Will of God. Average instinctual humanity, the men and women of goodwill, and the disciples of the world are all concerned in this process of invocation, bringing in the attributes of instinct, intelligence and intuition. Likewise all three are blended in the Great Invocation. We should have constantly in mind this basic fusion, now finding voiced expression, and take courage from the massed approach to the Source of all Life, Love and Light. Nothing can withstand the united demand of men everywhere in their graded and their serried ranks.

Invocation and the Christ

It has been said that the Great Invocation, if given widespread distribution, can be to the coming new world religion what the Lord's Prayer has been to Christianity and the 23rd Psalm has been to the spiritually minded Jew. Not a day goes by that Christ Himself does not sound it forth. The use of this Invocation of Prayer and the rising expectancy of the coming of the Christ hold out the greatest hope for mankind today. Great sons of God have ever come on humanity's demand and always will, and He for whom all men wait today *is* on His way.

TRANSLATIONS AND PATTERNS OF DISTRIBUTION

Since it was first given out, the Invocation has spread to all parts of the globe, using every possible means of communication. These include mailing, poster display, distribution from hand to hand, by personal interviews and from lecture platforms; broadcasts on radio and television, publication in books, display in newspapers, and promotion and distribution by churches and groups of many kinds. The Invocation is now widely accepted and is used daily by ever-growing numbers of people.

The Invocation belongs to all groups, organizations and faiths and much of the translation, printing and distribution has been undertaken by individual cooperators, goodwill groups and service organizations in many different lands. Therefore not all the work that has been done with the Invocation is included here but much of the work and general trends can be seen from the reports that are available to World Goodwill.

Translations

Translations and printings are known to have been made in the following languages:

Afrikaans	Dutch
Arabic	Efik
Armenian	Esperanto
Catalan	Ewe
Chinese	Fanti
Czech	Finnish
Danish	French

Ga	Norwegian
Gaelic (Irish)	Nyanga
German	Persian
Greek	Polish
Guarani	Portuguese
Hindi	Russian
Hungarian	Rumanian
Ibo	Sesotho
Ibibio	Shangaan
Icelandic	Singhalese
Indonesian	Spanish
Italian	Swedish
Ivrit	Tamil
Japanese	Tswana
Korean	Turkish
Latvian (Lettish)	Urdu
Lunya Ruanda	Xhosa
Malay	Yugoslavic
Maori	Zulu (Zula)

The translation of the Invocation from the original English into another language must combine an accurate and faithful reflection of the English with the linguistic and rhythmic demands of the new language, each with its own quality and character, expressive of the thought and psyche of the people. This has been done despite the fact that no real synonyms exist for certain of the English words used. Special care is taken to see that the best possible translation is made in each new language before any very widespread distribution and promotion work is undertaken.

Patterns of Distribution

The pattern of Invocation distribution has inevitably been conditioned by the language factor. Widespread and continuous distribution has been maintained, and is continuing throughout: North, Central and South America, Australia and New Zealand, Southern and Western Africa and Europe.

The major focus of printing and mass distribution, however, has been concentrated in the "European" languages, Dutch, English, French, German, Greek, Italian, Polish, Portuguese and Spanish.

In the future the distribution of the Invocation must be

developed on a new and widespread scale in those areas not already reached. This will require large printings of the full range of Invocation literature in such languages as Russian, Arabic, Persian, Hindu, Urdu, Gujarati, Tamil, Indonesian and Chinese through which millions of people can be reached. We also need new co-workers who can act as correspondents in these languages so that questions about the Invocation, its origin, significance and distribution may be answered. At the same time the use and distribution of the Invocation in those countries where it is already widely accepted should be strengthened and expanded.

At the heart of this growing use is a worldwide program of Invocation promotion and distribution that has been maintained continuously since 1945. With virtually no paid staff, and with the dedicated and selfless service of volunteer workers in many countries, the work has gone forward. Men and women of goodwill are giving their time, energy and money as a contribution to a vital service to humanity.

Mailing Programme

Today a network of individual cooperators, Units of Service and Goodwill Associations are responsible for maintaining a world programme of Invocation distribution. Postal mailing still forms a key element in this programme, with two main groups of cooperators: list compilers and mailing workers.

List Compilers

This group specializes in the preparation of mailing lists, collecting names and addresses from a wide range of sources: from personal contact and knowledge; from correspondence columns in the press; from specialist directories, yearbooks and alumni lists.

Mailing Workers and Pamphlet Distribution Groups

Members of these groups regularly take supplies of Invocation literature for mailing to the prepared lists. Some members of these groups also supply their own mailing lists, and all contribute to the cost of the postage for their own mailing work.

Financial Contributors

The money needed to print the very large quantities of literature that are required in various languages comes from many

sources, including both those who help with the mailing programme and those who receive the literature and respond to it.

*For further details on materials available and how you can
cooperate, see "Materials Available" and "Suggestions for Action" sections.

World Invocation Day

The Festival of the Christ, and World Invocation Day, is the
Festival in which Christ represents humanity in the sight of God
and releases an abundant tide of love for humanity to use as goodwill in establishing right human relations and right world conditions. This is a Festival of Invocation, or a basic aspiration towards
brotherhood and human and spiritual unity. Since 1952 it has been
observed as World Invocation Day.

This event offers a unique opportunity to publicize the use and
meaning of the Great Invocation through press and radio coverage
of World Invocation Day when groups of people gather to meditate
and use the Great Invocation. Letters to editors of newspapers asking for editorial or public service coverage of local gatherings are
used. Public service announcements and local announcements are
made of the events and the use of the Invocation and meaning of
World Invocation Day. Newspapers often give coverage to groups
gathered to observe World Invocation Day. Press releases, inser-
tion of advertisements in newspapers, and magazines, mailings to
churches and clergymen, are all ways of using this opportunity to
link this annual event to the Invocation, its use and significance.

Press Publicity

The Invocation continues to be featured in the press on many
occasions in many countries of the world. As each year passes the
extent and range of the coverage increases. It is appearing in daily
newspapers, church and general magazines, college and cultural
publications, meeting notices, and programmes. It appears in
feature articles and is the subject of editorial comment. Paid advertisements and references to the Invocation in "Letters to the Editor"
columns run into the thousands. Invocation cards and leaflets are
sometimes enclosed with an issue of a magazine, or bulletin to
members of an organization. Coverage in the press reaches a peak
each year at the time of World Invocation Day.

*For further details, see "Suggestions for Action" section.

Radio and Television

The continued and growing use of the Invocation on radio programmes, and the beginning of its exposure on television, reveals
how acceptable it is to the listening public. Some radio stations
now feature the Invocation regularly, including it in talks or
musical programmes, or using it as the station "sign-off" or "sign-
on" to the day's broadcasting or to a particular programme. Some
co-workers, in interview-type programs, use the opportunity to ex-
plain and sound out the Invocation over the radio. The use of the
Invocation over the air has mainly developed in countries where the
majority of radio and television stations and networks are in private
hands, mainly in North, Central and South America and in particular
in such countries as Argentina, Brazil, Canada, Chile, U.S. and
Venezuela. There are signs that countries where broadcasting is controlled by one or two large public or state corporations, restrictive
programming policy concerning religion may be moderated, offering
more opportunities to present the Invocation over the air.

*See "Suggestions for Action" section for further details.

Church and Group Use of the Invocation

One of the most encouraging responses to the Invocation is
from the churches and religious groups of many denominations
who request supplies of Invocation cards and leaflets for distribution to congregations and group members, to men's clubs, youth
groups, women's alliances, etc. Many groups and organizations
around the world print the Invocation regularly in their own
publications and their own Invocation leaflets and cards.

INVOCATION MATERIALS AVAILABLE

World Goodwill, together with cooperating Units of Service
and Goodwill groups, keeps supplies of Invocation literature
available at many points around the globe. The following pieces
make up the basic range of Invocation literature:

Invocation cards: These are usually wallet or pocket sized cards
that show the Great Invocation and addresses where further copies
can be obtained. These are available in all of the major languages
and many lesser known ones. Invocation book marks are also
available in English and some other languages.

Invocation pamphlets: In addition to the Great Invocation, the pamphlets present a few fundamental ideas, common to all religions and philosophies, on which the Invocation is based. This is a good introduction to the Invocation.

Invocation Manual: This pamphlet (16 pages) discusses the use and significance of the Great Invocation in some detail. The effectiveness with which the Invocation is used depends, among other things, on the understanding of the user. The Invocation Manual is an ideal "follow-up" for those who wish to know more.

The Great Invocation — Cooperation with the United Nations: The Great Invocation was first used in 1945, the same year the United Nations was founded. Twenty years later a leaflet was issued showing how the Great Invocation could be used by men and women of goodwill to strengthen the United Nations. In addition to a brief explanation showing how the Invocation relates to the United Nations, this leaflet includes the text from the UN Charter of the Principles of the United Nations.

In addition to this basic literature Invocation materials have been prepared to reach the public in many new ways. These include:

The Great Invocation Lotus Poster

This 20" x 14½" blue, green and yellow poster of a lotus on a pond with the Invocation printed on the side is an attractive display of the Invocation.

Tapes and cassettes of the Great Invocation

A one-minute announcement of the Great Invocation suitable as a radio advertisement or a public service announcement is available on tape.

Photo-ready display ad of the Invocation

This 8½" x 11" display advertisement is ready for use by newspapers or magazines. The ad features the Invocation with a brief explanation of its use and meaning.

Great Invocation greeting cards

A 3½" x 6" blue greeting card with the Invocation on the inside and the last stanza on the back is available in quantity on request.

PLEASE NOTE: These last three types of material are available directly from the New York headquarters of World Goodwill. The other centers may not have a supply available.

Great Invocation Pamphlet Mailing Programme

• *Prepare a mailing list* of clergy, school principals, groups to whom you wish to send Great Invocation materials. It would be helpful if headquarters were notified about the area you plan to cover so that duplication can be prevented.

• *Request a mailing list* from World Goodwill headquarters which you can then service with the Invocation pamphlets, supplying your own postage.

• *Volunteer your time* to help compile mailing lists from materials available to headquarters. This may only require typing or more detailed work if you request it.

• *Contribute financially* to the Great Invocation distribution programme.

PLEASE NOTE: More detailed information on compiling lists, mailing and other procedures is available on request.

Press Publicity

• *Insert advertisements* in newspapers and magazines publicizing the Great Invocation. Copies of the photo-ready advertisement available from World Goodwill New York headquarters will be sent on request. For a one column advertisement, the Invocation bookmark makes a good printer's copy.

• *Submit press releases* to newspapers linking the use of the Invocation to local groups. This technique is particularly effective at the time of the Three Spiritual Festivals. For further details see the *Three Spiritual Festivals Handbook* which contains sample press releases and letters.

• *Write letters* to the editor about the use and significance of the Invocation linking it to local problems, church activities, prayer groups or the needs of the times.

• *Offer the Invocation as an enclosure* in an issue of a magazine, bulletin or other publication to the members of an organization.

Radio Publicity

• *Offer the Great Invocation tape* (10 minutes) available from New York headquarters of World Goodwill.

• *Use the interview format* on local radio stations to discuss and recite the Invocation.

• *Submit press releases* on the Great Invocation particularly at the time of World Invocation Day. See the *Three Spiritual Festivals Handbook* for further details.

• *Purchase advertising time* to present the Invocation to the public. Sample copies of 60 second announcements are included in the *Three Spiritual Festivals Handbook.*

• *Use Public Service announcements* to present the Invocation at no charge as a community service. PLEASE NOTE: If time is purchased for an announcement, most stations will not accept the same announcement as a public service.

Television Publicity

• Public service announcements and short advertisements can be prepared by those who have the experience and facilities available.

Other Suggestions

• *Set up displays* in student unions, public parks, halls, or any public place using the poster and other materials to attract attention to pamphlets you can leave in holders and refill as needed.

• *Use a musical background* to attract people to booths or displays at public gatherings of all types.

• *Distribute flyers* on the Invocation indicating the 52 languages and over 60 countries in which it has been presented.

Other Related Service Activities

Triangles
World Invocation Day
Three Spiritual Festivals

PLEASE NOTE: Further information on these activities is available on request.

The Unity-in-Diversity Council
ITS PURPOSE AND WORK

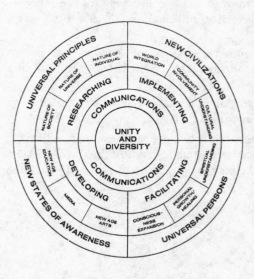

Unity-In-Diversity Framework
A Synergistic Model for Worldwide Cooperation

The Unity-in-Diversity Council is a worldwide coordinating body of organizations and individuals "fostering the emergence of a new universal person and civilization based on unity-in-diversity among all peoples." It seeks to serve the peaceful evolution of an enlightened planetary society.

The General Assembly of the United Nations designated 1965 as "International Cooperation Year" and during that year the first World Festival was held. It was called the "Festival of Human Unity." The International Cooperation Council was formed and has sponsored an annual festival since then.

In 1979 the Unity-in-Diversity Council took over the work of the International Cooperation Council.

FESTIVAL FOR MIND-BODY-SPIRIT: TO CELEBRATE AND REDEDICATE OUR LIVES

An expression of our unity-in-diversity through art, media, entertainment, lectures and workshops, alternative technologies and the experiencing of oneness. Includes every dimension related to the transformation of life and the forwarding of the new civilization in a lasting, practical and loving way. It is now being done in cooperation with the London Festival for Mind-Body-Spirit, the largest "New Age" event on the planet.

A YEAR-ROUND CLEARINGHOUSE: TO INCREASE
THE EFFECTIVENESS OF THE WORLDWIDE NETWORK

- A comprehensive, annual "Directory for a New World" containing member and cooperating organizations and individuals (100,000 worldwide circulation in 1982).

- "Spectrum," the quarterly newsletter of the Council (circulation 50,000).

- A General Assembly and Specialized Councils increasingly worldwide and concerned to act collectively for the transformation of self and society, utilizing unity-in-diversity process sessions.

- An information, referral and action network of related organizations and individuals in specific fields, as indicated by the Framework.

- A large local and international mailing list available to qualified groups and individuals.

For a New World to replace the old, the new must first put itself in order, and then be placed in the public mind. At the still dark dawn of a New Age, we are helping to bring into focus the unifying forces of light and love.

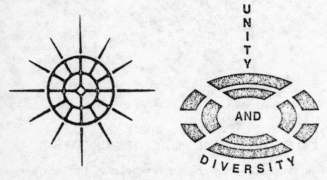

Unity-in-Diversity World Trade Center
350 S. Figueroa #370
Los Angeles, CA 90071
(213) 626-2062

ICC'S DECLARATION OF INTERDEPENDENCE

We, the people, affirm that differences of age, color, and belief are natural; that diverse individuals, groups and ideologies are necessary for the creative development of humanity; and that to foster UNITY IN DIVERSITY is our responsibility and challenge throughout the world.

We therefore pledge:

- To affirm the oneness of all life which is beyond name and form;
- To advance human fellowship through mutual trust, understanding, and respect;
- To seek the truth in the spirit of love;
- To integrate reason and faith, science and religion;
- To insure that all aspects of life be kept in dynamic balance for maximum health and well-being;
- To respect the teachings of the prophets and sages of all times and cultures;
- To build with joy a new civilization of freedom, justice, and peace founded on reverence for life.

Being of a common sacred origin, we hereby declare the supreme need for interdependence as the door to our survival and fulfillment — for we the people shall kindle the torch of hope, shall link hands over the earth.

RESEARCHING UNIVERSAL PRINCIPLES THROUGH:

Nature of the Individual (Personal/transpersonal) — exploring the essence and full dimensionality of the psyche, healing of the whole person.

Nature of the Universe (Biological/Physical) — exploring the interactions between living organisms and their environment, between matter, energy and consciousness.

Nature of Society — exploring the interactions of people in groups, new-age communities, the dynamics of a worldwide society.

DEVELOPING NEW STATES OF AWARENESS THROUGH:

New Age Education — communicating New Age consciousness through creative learning in new study centers and within existing institutions.

Media — publishing and distribution of New Age material through books, pamphlets, magazines, newsletters, calendars of events, tape recordings, radio, television.

New Age Arts — utilization of sound, light, and form, of music, poetry, painting, sculpturing to convey images of the New Age.

FACILITATING EVOLVEMENT OF UNIVERSAL PERSONS THROUGH:

Consciousness Expansion — fostering growth by means of increased inner awareness of oneness with all life, meditation techniques.

Personal Growth/Healing — fostering growth by means of personal, interpersonal and transpersonal psychological approaches, growth groups, healing.

Spiritual Understanding — fostering growth by means of understanding spiritual laws, as they have been unfolded in the history of humanity.

IMPLEMENTING NEW CIVILIZATIONS THROUGH:

Cultural Understanding — building bridges between diverse cultures — East, West, North, South — to promote world harmony and cooperation.

Community Involvement — servicing social needs, building new forms of community, demonstrating new ways of living.

World Integration — creating a new global civilization based on unity and diversity, a network of planetary citizens, a functional world government.

WORLD ASSEMBLY TASK STATEMENT

The ICC World Assembly is a process for bringing together people and groups from many diverse cultures and paths for the purpose of linking together to manifest the common vision.

The assembly will work through the ICC framework. It will provide the opportunity for sharing in areas of special interests as well as matching needs and resources toward continuing activity after the Festival.

WORLD ASSEMBLY SESSIONS
Monday, January 24 to Thursday, January 27
9 a.m. to 12:30 p.m.

Procedure:

Each day the World Assembly will begin with a full assembly at 9:00 a.m. This brief time will include meditation, focusing of the assembly for that day, and instructions as to how to proceed.

Participants will then move into quadrant meetings according to the revised ICC framework. During these meetings each participant will have an opportunity to identify one or more areas of needed activity, and from the common areas that emerge section meetings will be chosen and will meet each day. Some of these are likely to be activities which already have Special Services; others will be new and will be formed into Special Services as ongoing needs and leadership surface.

At 11:00 a.m. participants will regroup according to their geographic locations. This has a threefold purpose:

(1) It gives each person a way of discovering people with similar interests in his own part of the United States or the world;

(2) It provides an opportunity to link up with these people and, when desired, to continue working toward common goals after the Festival; and

(3) It makes possible the sense of relatedness to all areas of activity regarding New Age emergence and how these fit together within each geographic location.

1977 ICC DIRECTORY

Describes all the member groups, geographic councils, and special services, plus more than 500 ICC related groups, including a worldwide geographic listing.

AVAILABLE NOW AT THE FESTIVAL

or through ICC World Offices
8570 Wilshire Blvd., Beverly Hills, CA 90211 U.S.A.
(213) 652-4190

Only $4.50
or at quantity prices

A Message From Benjamin Creme

A Message of Hope

Benjamin Creme
SPEAKS ON

The Emergence of the World Teacher

Ending World Hunger • Sharing World Resources • Resolving Today's Violence • The Catastrophe Complex • World War III • Breakdown of Old Institutions • The New Age • The Women's Movement • A New Economic Order • Nuclear Alternatives • A New World Religion •

Wednesday, November 4
Unity Institute for Holistic Living
7:00 p.m. — Admission $4
(No one will be turned away for lack of funds)

A CLEAR ANSWER TO THE PROPHETS OF DOOM

Benjamin Creme is a respected lecturer, artist and author. He has lectured extensively in America and abroad since 1974. In 1980 he toured 25 American cities as well as England, Holland, Belgium and Germany. In 1981, he is expected to visit 40 cities in the United States alone.

Drawing on the Ageless Wisdom and 20 years of personal training and contacts, Mr. Creme speaks with authority on the emerging New Age and its social, political and economic order.

His Message: Throughout history great men and women, due to their expanded awareness, have been able to point the way for others to follow. As their writings and teachings became widely circulated, the great religious and spiritual movements of the world were born. The influence of a handful of such teachers on the history of humanity has been great.

According to Benjamin Creme, we are about to witness the appearance in the world of the greatest of all such teachers to have evolved through the human line. Mr. Creme's information is that on July 19, 1977, the World Teacher (known here in the West as the Christ) entered a well-known country in the modern world. During 1981 he will become increasingly visible in that country as a spokesman for sharing. It is his intention to withhold his true identity until mid-1982, at the latest, thus allowing humanity to recognize and respond to him on the strength of his ideas on sharing and cooperation among all peoples and nations.

> *"In the world now is a simple man of God,*
> *a Brother among brothers, a spokesman,*
> *for all mankind;*
> *come to place before the nations,*
> *the needs of all men for a world at peace,*
> *for just sharing of resources,*
> *for laughter and joy,*
> *for the creation of a New World,*
> *built on the Pattern of God."*

Creme further states that the main purpose for the World Teacher's presence is to restore a right relationship among all mankind. He comes to inspire us to abandon the selfish, competitive ways of the past in favor of a just and peaceful world, and contrary to the fears of many, the transition need not be violent or chaotic.

Mr. Creme believes that the World Teacher, His Great Disciple and certain advanced members of humanity will train men and women in all fields of human endeavor to effect a gradual but complete transformation of society. These New Age architects will move into positions of authority by reason of their wisdom and selfless concern for the good of all. Far-reaching changes will take place with the minimum disruption of the existing social fabric . . . by way of the democratic process.

In a recent review of Creme's first book for Tara Press (London and Los Angeles), author Colin Wilson wrote:

> "What soon becomes apparent is that Mr. Creme is not a nut or a charlatan; his honesty comes through on every page. Creme seems to belong to the same group as William Blake, A.E. Russell, Madame Blavatsky and Alice Bailey. (He is) . . . a man who sees things that other people do not see, and who tells us about it with sincerity and humor . . . while people like Creme exist, I feel there's a great deal of hope for us all."

Benjamin Creme's books and tapes
will be available at the lecture

Benjamin Creme will speak at
Unity Institute for Holistic Living
17505 Second Ave. (near 6 Mi. & Woodward)
Detroit, Michigan
Wednesday, November 4

For more information call: Robert Coon 543-3645

The New Group of World Servers

THE NEW GROUP OF WORLD SERVERS

Victor Hugo prophesied that in the Twentieth Century, war would die, frontier boundaries would die, dogma would die . . . and Man would live. "He will possess something higher than these . . . a great country, the Whole Earth . . . and a great hope, the Whole Heaven."

from The Aquarian Conspiracy

FOR MORE INFORMATION

The Aquarian Conspiracy . . . . by Marilyn Ferguson
J.P. Tarcher, Inc., 1980

Esoteric Psychology Vol. 2 . . . . by Alice A. Bailey
Lucis Publishing Co., 1942

Full Moon Story . . . . Arcana Workshop
Ram's Dell Press, 1967

The Hierarchy and The Plan . . . . by H. Saraydarian, 1975

Messages From Maitreya . . . . Tara Center, Box 6001
N. Hollywood, CA 91603, 1980

Ponder on This and *Serving Humanity*
both compiled from the writing of . . . . Alice A. Bailey
Lucis Publishing Co., 1970-1972

The Reappearance of the Christ and the Masters
of Wisdom . . . . by Benjamin Creme
Tara Center, 1980

THE GREAT INVOCATION

From the point of Light within the Mind of God,
Let Light stream forth into the minds of men.
Let Light descend on Earth.

From the point of Love within the Heart of God,
Let Love stream forth into the hearts of men.
May Christ return to Earth.

From the centre where the Will of God is known,
Let purpose guide the little wills of men —
The purpose which the Masters know and serve.

From the centre which we call the race of men,
Let the Plan of Love and Light work out.
And may it seal the door where evil dwells.

Let Light and Love and Power restore the Plan on Earth.

THE NEW GROUP OF WORLD SERVERS

In the year 1925, a small group of people, whose lives were dedicated to practical brotherhood, an international spirit of goodwill and a sensitivity to the energies and keynotes of the dawning Aquarian Age, emerged into the world. This is the *New Group of World Servers*, a group without apparent outward organization but which now has in its ranks millions of men and women . . . they are the citizens of the borderless country that Hugo calls the Whole Earth.

It is these lightbearers who have within themselves the answers to the problems which humanity faces today and who are now working in every field of human endeavor to build a new planetary civilization . . . the Kingdom of God on Earth.

Members of the *New Group of World Servers* may be found in every nation and are of every race and school of thought.

World Server Characteristics

They are free from a critical spirit and a feeling of separateness.

They hold to no creed except Brotherhood based on the One Life, and serve no master except the group they seek to serve and humanity whom they deeply love.

They belong to no particular religion but accord equal devotion to the spiritual leaders of all races.

They are willing to work behind the scenes without outward recognition while relying mainly on intuition for guidance.

They consider old methods of fighting, attacks and partisanship as undesirable.

They recognize no authority except that of their own souls.

They seek to maintain a balance between outer and inner activities.

They are free from the taint of ambition and pride of race or accomplishment.

They achieve their aims by example backed by sacrifice and love.

They recognize and support all other groups which work for understanding, synthesis and unity.

Code of Conduct

Harm no one, desire nothing for the separated self and see the divinity in all.

Regard no race or nation as more important than any other.

Ignore racial hatreds, religious differences and national ambitions.

Do not put undue emphasis on the organization aspect . . . the *New Group of World Servers* is an organism, not an organization.

Members should not identify themselves or the group with any political, religious or social propaganda.

Spread Love and Light instead of resisting evil.

Do not dissipate your efforts on unimportant work.

Speak or publish no word which would evoke antagonism from any group. Only principles of universal application need be expressed.

Maintain a life of meditation.

Do not interfere with any political or religious group.

The purpose of this brochure is to bring the ideals and objectives of the *New Group of World Servers* to the attention of the general public and to reach the disciples, aspirants and men and women of goodwill who may not be consciously aware of their connection with this group.

Let this information help awaken them to their true mission and awaken their interest in the Plan, the *New Group of World Servers* and the reappearance of the Christ and the Masters of Wisdom.

"May the power of the One Life pour through the group of all true servers.

"May the love of the One Soul characterize the lives of all who seek to aid the Great ones.

"May we fulfill our part in the one work through self-forgetfulness, harmlessness and right speech."

— Mantram of the *New Group of World Servers*

(This brochure is based on the Alice Bailey teachings.)

Ideals

They believe in an inner world government and an emerging evolutionary plan.

They are steadily cultivating an international spirit of goodwill.

They seek to teach that there are many national, religious and social experiments in the world . . . some aspects of these have a definite place and purpose in the New Age . . . some are undesirable because they spread the virus of hatred and separation.

Objectives

Bring about world peace, guide world destiny and usher in the New Age.

Form the vanguard for the reappearance of the Christ and his Great Disciples (the Masters of Wisdom).

Advocate the fair distribution of planetary resources so that every man, woman and child has adequate food, shelter and clothing.

Eliminate fear in the world.

Provide a center of light within humanity and hold the vision of the Divine Plan before mankind.

Form a bridge between humanity and the Kingdom of God.

Raise the level of human consciousness.

Cultivate a planetary spirit of goodwill.

Recognize and change those aspects of religion and government which delay the full manifestation of planetary unity and love.

Embody constructive forces so as to balance the forces of destruction and disintegration now present in the world.

Consciously participate in the three major full moon festivals: Easter (Aries), Wesak (Taurus), and the Festival of the Goodwill (Gemini). . . . In addition to the remaining minor full moon observances.

Connect world governments with a unity of purpose.

Lucis Trust —
World Goodwill Newsletter

WORLD GOODWILL NEWSLETTER

A quarterly bulletin combining comment and information on world affairs with details of the work and programme of World Goodwill

July, August, September
1982

BEYOND THE YEAR 2000
We are "between a death and a difficult birth."
Samuel Beckett

The year 2000 looms before humanity as a gigantic milestone which marks both an ending and a beginning. It marks the end of a volatile millennium which has seen enormous progress and change, particularly in the fields of science, technology, education and government. But more importantly, the year 2000 stands as a symbolic portal through which humanity can pass into a New Age of true peace, cooperation and creativity — if it so chooses.

When we look back a thousand years we see a world primarily agrarian and nomadic, held loosely together by religious beliefs and cultural influences. While a highly refined civilization flourished in the Far East and Islamic art and culture were at their peak, Europe remained shrouded in what we now call the dark period of the Middle Ages — a feudal society with little sense of community and none of nationhood. The vast majority of people, East and West, lived in relative isolation from each other. The masses were illiterate, subjects of class and caste and were without the benefits of health care or even minimal sanitation.

Today we live in a world that is highly interdependent and technologically brilliant. It is a world that is linked, almost instantaneously, by a vast communications network and in which thousands of people can traverse oceans and continents in only a few hours. Not only are most people no longer isolated from each other, but today cultures and races intermingle to form the beginnings of a new planetary civilization.

In the field of government people are, for the most part, no longer subjected to the despotism or benevolence of a monarch or emperor. Ideas and ideologies have caught the imaginations of the governed and experiments such as democracy, socialism and communism are now the primary forms of government. Even where dictatorships exist, they are much more subject to the consent of the governed than ever before and can be deposed as political winds change. And in education, with the advent of public schools and the concept of education as a basic right, the average person today is more highly educated than the intellectual of a few short centuries ago.

With regard to science, it is probably safe to say that it is the supreme contribution of Western culture to the present civilization. It has afforded us the privilege of entering into the worlds of the infinitely small — the world of atoms, quarks and charm — and of the infinitely large — the awe-inspiring cosmology of the universe. Science has influenced modern civilization in much the same way as did religion when it was the primary integrating force of the past. In the words of Theodore Roszak: "Science is not, in my view, merely *another* subject for discussion. It is *the* subject. It is the prime expression of the West's cultural uniqueness, the secret of our extraordinary dynamism, the keystone of technocratic politics, the curse and the gift we bring to history."[1]

All of this, of course, is not to say that humanity has reached any utopian plateau. Quite the contrary. Science is, in fact, a mixed blessing insofar as it has given birth to a technological world that threatens to go out of control. For example, the work in nuclear physics that led to the release of the energy in the atom and to a prolific nuclear technology, could spawn a renaissance and be the foundation for a new world order. Instead it has created a technology of genocidal weapons capable of destroying civilization.

Not only have we used our remarkable scientific knowledge to create a technology capable of ending all life on our planet, we have failed to use it to create an equitable and just life for all people. Wealth is still concentrated in the hands of the few while hun-

[1]Theodore Roszak, *Where the Wasteland Ends*, Anchor Books, 1973, p. xix.

dreds of millions of people can't even get enough food to survive. It is estimated that upwards of 35,000 children die every day of starvation.

Along with the lack of proper distribution of food, the same most disadvantaged people suffer from a lack of clean drinking water and sanitation facilities. Disease spreads easily and medical care is a luxury hard to find. Illiteracy is commonplace, as are unemployment and crime, as millions upon millions crowd into already strained and bulging cities in search of a better life.

All of this can lead us to only one conclusion: material progress has failed to bring an equitable world of peace and plenty. And if we ask ourselves why, it is probably safe to answer that the expansion of consciousness and awareness has not kept pace with the acceleration of technological advancement. We have created a world of wondrous technological achievements but have failed to see to it that those achievements were used to uplift all of humanity. In short, we have become knowledgeable but not wise; we have followed our minds but ignored our hearts; we have looked outside of ourselves to find happiness while failing to realize that within ourselves we can find joy.

This then is the great challenge before humanity as we approach the end of the millennium — the transformation of human consciousness. If we hope that beyond the year 2000 will exist a world of peace, justice and progress, then we must begin to build that world by changing ourselves from within. A new civilization will not be built by concentrating on new forms only, because as we can see around us everyday, no matter how advanced the form, it will fail to serve humanity and a new world if it is built upon the outgoing values of the past. The new institutions that will be built will give substance to the living energy of a new, more conscious, more loving humanity. Our primary goal, therefore, should be for a change in consciousness, because forms will always be shaped by the power of thoughts and desires. Thus are civilizations built.

We stand today at the most crucial time in human history. Humanity has before it the opportunity to become a conscious cooperator in the process of planetary evolution. No longer must we be merely unconscious players at the mercy of forces and energies beyond our control. Today we are intelligent enough and conscious enough to see the patterns and cycles that converge to form human destiny. Today humanity can take an active part in molding that destiny and not be simply the unwitting subject of the forces of change.

If we are to consciously build our new civilization, it is necessary to be able to view the past, present and future as a whole. We need to be able to look back into the past to discern what was good and carried the flame of progress forward. We need to be able to see the present clearly so that we can build upon what is good from the past while allowing the harmful and negative to pass away. And we need to be able to envision the future in the knowledge that our thoughts and dreams of today will be the seeds of the world we wish to create.

In this spirit of seeing our world clearly and envisioning the kind of world we want to emerge beyond the year 2000, let us look more closely at four topics that are of particular importance during this period of transition: economics, human rights, and environment and the new phenomenon of active religious fundamentalism and its effect on world affairs. These four topics, of course, are not the only ones of great importance to humanity at this time and it will be apparent to everyone that the crucial subject of world peace is missing from this list. This is because the entire issue of the next *World Goodwill Newsletter* will be devoted to a discussion of peace on earth and the problem of world disarmament.

It has been said that "the power of thought will be the evocative principle of the new world." If this is true, then we can and should be aware that each of us contributes to the world we live in through our thoughts and actions. We can all try to be conscious, every day, of our contributions to the emerging new civilization and the effect we can have on our environment. As we envision the new world and as we prepare for it, so shall it be.

ECONOMICS

There can be little doubt that the economic problem is one of the most entrenched and difficult problems humanity faces today. Since the "science" of economics was first formulated a little over two centuries ago, the world has never seen an economic situation quite so complex, puzzling and dangerous. The worldwide problems of inflation and unemployment manifesting concurrently have left conventional economists in a quandary and they have yet to find a formula of fiscal and monetary tinkering to bring the economy into balance.

But no amount of tinkering is going to solve the world economic problem. Nor should we wait for an economic "messiah" to show us the way and set our house in order. The world economy is a result of the ancient human characteristics of selfishness and greed, and only by transmuting these characteristics will we find any lasting solution to the current upheaval. When the world economy is governed by the principles of sharing and cooperation, we will begin to see the restoration of balance and harmony between the nations.

By far the most dangerous and devastating aspect of the economic problem is the cleavage between North and South — between the industrialized and developing countries. Due to the concentration of wealth, and therefore power, in the North, the developing countries are faced with an almost insurmountable disadvantage when it comes to trade and commodity agreements, energy, development, technology, investments and world monetary policies. These economic disadvantages manifest in many ways that work to suppress the growth and well-being of the developing countries, but the most tragic and shameful result is the reality of world hunger and starvation. It is not possible to say exactly how many people in the world suffer from hunger and malnutrition, but all estimates put the figure in the hundreds of millions; millions who will either die from lack of food or have their physical development impaired.[2] This in a world that presently produces enough food for everyone to have 3,000 calories a day. It is obvious therefore that the problem is not one of a lack of food, but of the proper distribution and production of food.

Added to this already tragic problem is the burgeoning world population. It is estimated that by the year 2000 there will be another two billion people with a right to proper food, education, health care and work. The planet is capable of handling this growth in population, but we are already overdue in planning how we can best use our resources and technology to meet this coming need.

In order to solve the world economic problem, all of us will need to rethink our priorities. This is a problem that cannot be left

[2] *North-South: A Program for Survival,* The Report of the Independent Commission on International Development Issues under the Chairmanship of Willy Brandt, The MIT-Press, 1970, p. 90.

to the economists because it is not a problem that can be handled by technical means or by slight adjustments in fiscal and monetary policies. It is a problem of values and principles. The resources of the planet belong to all people and when this simple statement of principle becomes a living realization for humanity, then we will see the manifestation of a new economic world order. As stated by Willy Brandt: "The shaping of our common future is much too important to be left to governments and experts alone. Therefore, our appeal goes to youth, to women's and labour movements; to political, intellectual and religious leaders; to scientists and educators; to technicians and managers; to members of the rural and business communities. May they all try to understand and to conduct their affairs in the light of this new challenge."[3]

HUMAN RIGHTS

Human rights is an area of vital concern as we bridge towards the world beyond the year 2000 — for today it is sadly a condition which is denied many of our peoples and yet it is the starting point upon which any just society should be founded, be it a remote village or the global community. It is our birthright. Due to the rapid advances in communications technology we are fast becoming one world and despite the doomsday forecasts of many futurists, we have, at this moment, adequate knowledge and resources to supply every person on the planet with the basic essentials of food, shelter, education, employment, and medical coverage. Indeed the future can be bright, but at present perhaps we could say that the peoples of the world have yet to adquately voice their desire for an end to the suffering. Perhaps we have looked too much to others for change rather than assuming our individual responsibilities.

Throughout the centuries people have entered into combat in order to extricate themselves from conditions under which they were not afforded a basic sense of dignity. It was the thinkers of the 18th century French Enlightenment who first provided the impetus behind the drive for human rights in the world. They became the voice of the people and the inspiration behind the French and American revolutions. The banner of liberty, equality and

[3]*Ibid.*, p. 29.

brotherhood captured the European continent while the rights of the individual were anchored in the United States through constitutional government and the Bill of Rights. Sadly, however, nearly two hundred years later we witness a world in which entire nations are denied basic liberties.

Two of the basic ideals upon which the coming civilization must be founded are freedom and security. Freedom must not be understood in any anarchistic sense but rather as a state within the consciousness of the peoples wherein they take pride in the contribution which they as individuals and their country as a whole can make towards the enrichments of the global community. It will be a world, therefore, not of homogeneity, but rather of richness and beauty in diversity. But the present restriction of individual expression in so many parts of the world is totally against the tide of evolution which ever works with the law of love. Unfortunately today we find that in many nations individual rights, creativity, and free access to information are suppressed by regimes that are stricken by fear. Repression assumes many guises, existing under the names of communism, socialism, democracy, and military dictatorship. But ever the symptoms remain the same. We have witnessed that many of those people who question authority and demand change are quickly imprisoned and/or eliminated. But it is precisely these courageous individuals — working in disregard of the forces opposing them — who serve as forerunners to the idealism which will condition the entire planet in the coming century. There is hope that the situation will ease and many groups are now working to apply pressures to governments for the release of political prisoners. In many instances there success rate is high — again a demonstration of the power which individuals can wield in effecting change. Also the creation of such doctrines as the Universal Declaration of Human Rights has been instrumental in alerting the nations of the world to the vital need for attention to this problem. Some countries have even modeled their constitutions after this declaration.

In retrospect the present century may be viewed as the darkest period in the history of humanity. In order to turn away from this dark course the only thing that is needed is a kindling of the will of the peoples to demand that which is rightfully theirs. It is nothing extraordinary to ask, yet we must not wait for someone else to shoulder the responsibility.

THE ENVIRONMENT

In the new millennium, many trends that we now see in their infancy, or existing only in the minds of their creators, will come to full fruition. Humanity will live in harmony with its environment and no longer violate natural law. Conditions will have improved to such an extent that all people will be able to live in a healthy and clean environment. At present we can see that on a small scale, people in many parts of the world are beginning to experiment with alternatives to the present wasteful systems. Thus we can, with a little vision, see the seeds of a new attitude toward our planetary home all around us. The movement towards a healthy environment is happening largely because of an improvement in the way we view our planet. Instead of thinking in terms of exploitation, we are beginning to regain the perspective of the American Indians and think only of how we can work in harmony with the Earth and each other.

In any vision of the planet beyond the year 2000, a consideration of environmental conditions and problems must take precedence over many other issues because of the immediacy of the problem. Without a change of course there may not be a new world civilization. We cannot build anew upon deteriorating conditions. The contamination of the environment, particularly by the industrialized nations, has come increasingly to public attention. It is a problem of international dimensions, for by polluting the air, the oceans and the land, and by depleting the protective ozone layer around the globe, we damage not only individual nations but the world at large. Presently, the *World Conservation Strategy*, working with the advice, cooperation and financial assistance of the United Nations, is providing detailed plans to offset the present destructive environmental trends. It views the problem from a global perspective and seeks cooperative measures of improvement.

The entrenched materialistic state of mind which has characterized humanity, especially since the birth of the industrial age, is directly reflected in the present dangerous situation. We have felt free to destroy and to pollute our environment regardless of the consequences to the Earth. Only recently have we begun to realize that any organism, even a planet, can become so diseased that its survival is threatened. We have now reached that point.

Much of the present focus is upon finding viable alternatives to the present use of non-renewable energy resources. There is every reason to believe that within the next century we will have unlimited, cheap and environmentally non-polluting energy. This step will alter the quality of our lives particularly by arresting the pollution of the atmosphere by the widespread use of petroleum fuels. Some of the present-day alternatives being tested and used are solar, wind, tide, geo-thermal and fusion power. And new transportation systems will evolve to accommodate this change in energy sources.

Architecturally we are moving towards comfortable, inexpensive, energy-efficient housing and work spaces. The trend is toward simplicity, focusing upon open space, light and ventilation in the recognition that one's environment has much to do with the quality of one's work and life.

Present-day farming techniques are fast becoming recognized as a life-threatening environmental hazard. There has been an attempt to reap the largest possible harvest from our land and to account for it by the application of chemical fertilizers. The soil has become depleted of minerals and through a lack of rotation planting there is a growing problem with erosion. Massive sections of the planet are rapidly becoming deserts causing untold hardship and starvation for millions of people. The solution may be found in small-scale, high yield, organic farming practices. As well, instead of dumping our garbage into landfills and polluting the ocean floors, we could recycle it, thereby drastically improving the pollution problem while providing fuel and organic fertilizers as by-products.

These are just a few examples of some of our present problems and possible solutions. We have the ability to implement them, but one wonders at our lack of vision. The hope lies largely in the changing attitude among the people — a change which brings with it the recognition that humanity is only part of a greater whole. For us to begin to interact in a harmonious fashion with all the kingdoms in nature will necessitate vast changes in our present mode of living. But if we can accept the need for change, without fear, we can then begin to move into a much healthier state. As we become more aware of our essential unity with all life, we will one day find it contrary to human nature to violate the environment.

RELIGIOUS FUNDAMENTALISM

Even ten years ago it would have been difficult to foresee the resurgence of religious fundamentalism which has swept through some of the major world religions: Christianity, Judaism and Islam are all profoundly affected. This development has ramifications which extend far beyond the religious field. In the United States, for instance, the fields of both government and education are feeling the pressure of fundamentalist opinion. What is called "Scientific Creationism" is being aggressively promoted as an alternative to the scientifically accredited theory of evolution — Darwinism. Certain state legislatures are acquiescing and textbooks are being modified accordingly. In the field of social relations the many significant advances made by women during the last decade in their pursuit of equal rights have been sharply challenged by the fundamentalist view of woman's traditional role in society. In other countries, particularly those strongly influenced by Islamic fundamentalism, the reaction against full equality for women is even more virulent. We have also recently seen the dramatic escalation of blatant militarism in those nations with large fundamentalist populations; this is probably not coincidental. Fanatical religious fundamentalism, in general, carries a strong conviction of its own righteousness and a belief that it must defend itself from the ever-present, ever-threatening iniquity of unbelievers. In the United States, in Iran and in Israel (to name just three prominent examples) there are many who are convinced that the tenets of their faith can only be successfully protected and promoted by force of arms. Perhaps the most frightening and dangerous impact of fanatical fundamentalism upon the world community concerns the insidious effects of the "apocalyptic vision." In the United States particularly, many of the most fervent fundamentalists expect — perhaps even desire — the biblically prophesied global cataclysm known as "Armageddon." With nuclear holocaust an ever more terrifying possibility, the political and social influence of many millions who sincerely believe in the scriptural necessity of the final holocaust can certainly be viewed as a substantial threat to world peace.

The growth of fundamentalism is a predictable reaction to existential perplexity. Many millions of people feel threatened to their depths by complex global problems which seem to defy both understanding and solution. The religious and social structures which for centuries gave meaning and orientation to their lives are now crumbling. Those without the faith or vision to see that humanity can create a more beautiful and enlightened world, fall victim to a profound, if largely unconscious, sense of "angst," dread and disorientation. Trembling on the brink of the unknown, they grasp for something simple, something true and certain for all time. They seek absolute security in the form of fundamentals which can never be changed or questioned. Unfortunately, an illusory absolute security can only be purchased at the price of submission to absolute authority.

Psychologically, fundamentalism is actually based, not upon faith, but upon fear: fear of change, fear of failure, fear of the future, and fear that, somehow, humanity is just too weak, too evil, or too helpless to have any hope of successfully meeting the challenge of life. Fundamentalist doctrine minimizes the value of the human being because its assessment of human nature and human potential is permeated by a deep-seated inferiority complex. This inferiority complex derives, at least in part, from the tendency of fundamentalism to emphasize the awesome might and power of God transcendent "above and outside" His Creation, while virtually overlooking the loving presence of God immanent within the human heart. This ancient misconceived split between God and humanity has worked great mischief. It has caused people to feel little, expendable and utterly vulnerable unless they rigidly follow certain rules or formulas which will "save" them from the wrath of their overpowering Creator.

Fortunately, however, the idea of God immanent has always been central to the most enlightened forms of religious understanding. In addition, the most advanced theories in physics, by speaking of a holistic, living universe, are now vindicating this more intimate and mystical approach to the divine Source. Avant-garde psychology is affirming amazing human potentials which, when cultivated, lead to states of consciousness which have always been called divine. Both theory and experience support the idea of an eminently approachable Deity, dwelling within the human being — in the words of the mystics: "nearer than hands and feet."

Therefore, there is no need for humanity to retreat into a scripturally induced helplessness and self-contempt. The "Kingdom of Heaven" is within each one of us, as we have been told by the greatest human exponent of divine Love. We are, in fact, divine beings. We are equal to immense challenges if we dare acknowledge and release our full humanity.

As we look beyond the year 2000, we can see the need for a different and truly *spiritual* form of fundamentalism based upon the real fundamentals of God immanent, universal love, brotherhood, human unity and global cooperation. Relying upon these fundamentals we can found a new spiritual, social, political and moral order. In transiting from the present "Age of Authority" into the "Age of Experience," humanity will realize that these "new" fundamentals can be *experienced* and need not be accepted merely on faith or authority. Today we can experience ourselves as we really are, and discover the true authority of our divine inner Self. *Fundamentally, we must believe in the divinity of humanity.*

GOODWILL IS . . .

. . . the connecting and communicating energy between: the East and West; North and South; the rich and the poor; the races and the religions; the past and the future.

UNITED NATIONS REPORT

THE LAW OF THE SEA TREATY

It is "the most significant achievement in international relations since the United Nations Charter. . . . A constitution for the seas." That was the description given by Canada's J. Alan Beesley, chairman of the drafting committee for the Law of the Sea Treaty. Sharing his opinion was Elliot Richardson, the former head of the United States delegation to the Law of the Sea Conference in Geneva. Negotiations on this Treaty, he said, "constitute a significant achievement for the efforts of the world community to substitute the rule of law for the risk of anarchy." He added that a successful outcome of the conference (meaning ratification by at least 60 members states) "would extend the rule of law . . . over

two-thirds of the earth's surface. It would give powerful encouragement to the pursuit of other rational accommodations among the
evermore complex issues forced upon the world by the realities of
our inescapable interdependence."

Unfortunately, the realities of interdependence are not
necessarily shared by everyone. When the final vote was cast in
April, 130 nations, including France and Japan, voted in favor of
the Treaty; 17 nations, a combination of the European Economic
Community and the Soviet bloc abstained; but the United States,
together with Israel, Venezuela, and Turkey voted "no."

The negative vote of the United States was somewhat surprising
since it stood to be the chief beneficiary of these all-encompassing
rules of international law. These far-reaching benefits seem to have
been lost on the present administration because in the end, after
eight years of negotiations, the United States' vote was decided on
the narrow issue of seabed mining. The U.S. delegation, standing
on the platform of unlimited free enterprise, was unwilling to com-
promise on certain key provisions on the Treaty which called for
the establishing of an International Seabed Authority to regulate all
seabed mining beyond territorial jurisdictions. There was also ob-
jection to the clause governing the sharing and transferring of mining technology to the international community which would in effect provide third world countries with the means to do their own
mining.

The United States negotiators insisted that "pioneer" status be
given those countries and private companies that already have the
mining technology and have invested considerable sums in mining
and exploration. Each pioneer investor should, they insisted, have
exclusive prospecting rights in a specified seabed area. After intense
last-minute negotiations these new provisions were included in the
Treaty. Nevertheless the United States still voted against the Treaty
since it could not agree to those provisions that it felt were against
the interests of free enterprise and exploitation.

The Treaty itself, with more than 300 articles agreed upon by
the consensus of more than 150 participating nations, extensively
covers every conceivable issue dealing with the seas. It recognizes
the twelve-mile territorial limit and acknowledges a 200-mile "exclusive economic zone" for each coastal nation; it provides the
"right of passage" on the high seas, and unimpeded passage
through straits used for international navigation; it gives coastal

states control over fishing rights in their economic zones; it provides environmental safeguards to protect the sea from pollution; it provides for management and conservation of living marine resources; and access to the oceans for purposes of scientific research. But the most controversial issue of the Treaty is that dealing with the seabed mining of minerals such as manganese, cobalt, copper and nickel.

The fundamental principle of the Treaty states that "the seabed and the ocean floor and the subsoil thereof, beyond the limits of national jurisdiction, as well as the resources of the area, are *the common heritage of mankind.*" This implies that revenues derived from mineral deposits recovered from the ocean floor beyond the limits of national jurisdiction are the "common heritage" of all and are therefore meant to be shared with all. Many of the deep sea mining consortiums, particularly those in the United States, take exception to this principle of sharing, claiming instead that the rule of free enterprise should prevail in these areas. The consortiums are troubled also by other provisions of the Treaty, among them being production limits intended to protect land-based mineral producers such as Canada, Zaire, Zambia and Chile, and a taxation system that would tax commercial mining operations and distribute the proceeds to developing countries.

Certainly these are legitimate concerns for private mining consortiums. But the real question is, should the special interests of mining groups override the far-reaching benefits that would flow to humanity as a whole with the ratification of this Treaty? Several of the benefits of the Treaty have already been mentioned, but perhaps the most important benefit is that the Treaty provides a framework of law that is binding on all member states, with the settlement of disputes to be arbitrated by an international authority.

The Law of the Sea Treaty has been voted into existence and awaits ratification before it can enter into force. The question now is whether those countries that voted against it, or abstained, will ignore this document of internationa law, or whether they will be forced to abide by its provisions due to the power of world public opinion and the propriety of carrying on harmonious relationships with the majority of the nations of the world. The Treaty may in fact become de facto law even for those nations who do not ratify.

The fate of the Treaty, then, for the present, seems to hinge on the strength or lack of strength of certain fundamental human attitudes: are we human beings, for the first time in our long history, able to recognize our interdependence, and are we *willing* to subscribe to the principles of sharing and cooperation and in fact legislate those principles into law? Can the vision of "common heritage" and the all-inclusive provisions of this Treaty, negotiated by more than 150 nations over a period of eight years, now be negated by the power of a small minority? Will the rules, arrived at by consensus of the many, now be ignored to suit the limited desires of the few? The decision may determine whether we, humanity, are ready to advance into the Aquarian age with its keynote of sharing and selfless service, or whether we allow ourselves to be held back by the nineteenth century attitudes of exploitation and material selfishness?

The Treaty is not perfect, of course, and even those who voted for it are not satisfied with every detail; a total agreement in all the many complex issues would be next to impossible given the present state of human consciousness. Self-interest is still the dominant motivating force. But in the opinion of most of the negotiators it is the best that could be obtained considering the fact that each nation is primarily interested in its own welfare.

That these negotiators have accomplished this much, at least, is the thing of greatest importance for humanity — a factor which should not be overlooked. It marks a definite stage in the evolution of human consciousness. To see what is really happening here one must stand back to grasp the wider view, a view that those with only special interests can never see. One can sense the energy of the Will-to-Good (a will for the good of the whole) overshadowing the entire negotiating process, directing human thought towards the wisdom of universality. It is the same dynamic energy that very likely guided the writing of the United Nations Charter. In these two examples of human relations — the Law of the Sea Treaty and the United Nations Charter — humanity is presented with a vision of what is possible; a vision that is challenging us to let go of the conflict-ridden ways of the past and step into the harmonious light of the New Age.

GOODWILL NEWS BRIEFS

On June 8th, 30,000 people gathered at the west steps of the Colorado State Capital in Denver for "An Evening for Peace." The massive demonstration was the largest in Denver since Vietnam War days. The evening included a concert with such artist as John Denver, Judy Collins, Jimmy Buffet and others.

The rally was filmed as part of an upcoming 90-minute documentary called "Freeze: An American Peace Story." According to the producer-director, Arnie Grossman, "We've been filming for a week now and it has been one of the most amazing experiences of my life. Political movements *do* spring forth with spontaneity." For Grossman, the film project represents a sharp departure from the 150 TV commercials and slick campaign spots he's done over the years. "It's really an anatomy of the middle-American peace movement," he said. "It's a movement which has grown from the ground up, not a political movement but a human movement."

— *Rocky Mountain News*
Denver, Colorado

Over 1,400 mayors of cities throughout the world have signed a Declaration calling on the South African Government "to release immediately and unconditionally all prisoners detained for their political views under their apartheid laws." Initiated by the Lord Provost of Glasgow, Michael Kelly, the Declaration calls "in particular for the immediate release of Nelson Mandela." One of the leaders of the African National Congress of South Africa and leader of its military arm, *Umkonto We Sizwe* (Spear of the Nation), Mr. Mandela has been serving a life sentence since 1964 on Robben Island. The Declaration was made public on March 19th in New York by Mr. Kelly and the Special Committee against Apartheid.

— United Nations Information
Centre, London

A group of Boston scientists have joined together to alert the public to the dangers of nuclear war and also to assist their colleagues in finding employment not connected with the military.

Calling themselves High Technology Professionals for Peace, the group is presently made up of about 35 Boston area scientists and engineers, and approximately 800 members across the country. According to its president, Warren Davis, a psysicist at the Smithsonian Astrophysical Observatory in Cambridge, "We are in a special position to use our skills and professional contacts to alter the present drift toward nuclear war." Perhaps their most significant project is an employment service that matches scientists who want to avoid military-related work with companies that have no military contracts. Since the service began last November, more than 50 people and an equal number of companies have contacted the group.

— *Science Digest*
August 1982

The Research Council meeting in Brussels decided to invest a further £347m in solving Europe's long-term energy problem by nuclear fusion. European scientists are working towards the construction of a plant capable of producing energy by fusion at the beginning of the next century. The aim at the present time is to build a plant on the lines of the so-called Tokamak system. This uses hydrogen isotopes to create plasma, which is magnetically confined in a torus and can reach exceedingly high temperatures.

Work on this type of plant could go ahead in collaboration with the United States and Japan and the Council encouraged the scientists to work with these two countries to define and develop the project.

— *The Times* of London

TRANSITION ACTIVITIES

Throughout the period of transition into the new world order, many groups of men and women of goodwill are emerging whose activities are characteristic of the new group of world servers. The following organizations and activities may be of interest to you. If you know of other groups, you are invited to send information and details to headquarters for possible use in the newsletter.

The following is a continuation of our on-going list of groups working for peace and disarmament.

All Species Circle of New York
225 East 25th St. — #5A
New York, NY 10010 U.S.A.

Architects for Peace
Ian Abbott
41 St. James Road
Sevenoaks
Kent, TN 13 #NG
U.K.

Asheville Advocates for Nuclear
  Arms Freeze
c/o Dr. John Stevens
Box 8274
Asheville, NC 28814 U.S.A.

Burlington Peace Coalition
30 Elmwood Ave.
Burlington, VT 05401 U.S.A.

Catskill Alliance for Peace
Box 353
Woodstock, NY 12498 U.S.A.

Chapel Hill Fellowship to Reverse
  the Arms Race
c/o Baptist Campus Ministry
203 Battle Lane
Chapel Hill, NC 27514 U.S.A.

Charlotte Peace Network
c/o Marilyn White
3111 Markworth Ave.
Charlotte, NC 28210 U.S.A.

Charlotte SANE
c/o Jean Wood
6334 Deveron Dr.
Charlotte, NC 28211 U.S.A.

Children's Peace Committee
c/o Monique Grodzki
3430 78th St.
Jackson Heights, NY 11372 U.S.A.

Coalition for a New Foreign and
  Military Policy
120 Maryland Ave., N.E.
Washington, DC 20002 U.S.A.

The Colorado College Program on
  War, Violence and Human Values
Packard Hall
Colorado Springs, CO 80903 U.S.A.

Communicators for Nuclear
  Disarmament
c/o Emily Hiestand
44 Hunt St.
Watertown, MA 02172 U.S.A.

The Conservation Society Ltd.
12A Guildford St.
Chertsey
Surrey KT169BQ
U.K.

Correspondents for Peace
Barry Childers c/o Ferris
28 Forest Drive
College Station, TX 77840 U.S.A.

Council for a Livable World
100 Maryland Avenue, N.E.
Washington, DC 20002 U.S.A.
or
11 Beacon St.
Boston, MA 02108 U.S.A.

Council for Nuclear Freeze
2161 Massachusetts Ave.
Cambridge, MA 02140 U.S.A.

Dunamis
St. James Church
197 Piccadilly
London W.1 U.K.

Durham Committee to Reverse the
  Arms Race
404 Alexander Ave.
Durham, NC 27705 U.S.A.

Educators for Social Responsibility
Elizabeth Lewis
87 Clark St.
Newton Center, MA 02159 U.S.A.

Greenville Peace Committee
610 S. Elm St.
Greenville, NC 27834 U.S.A.

Ground Zero
806 15th St., N.W. Suite 421
Washington, DC 20005 U.S.A.

International Fast for Peacemakers
1500 34th Ave.
Oakland, CA 94601 U.S.A.

International Physicians for
  Prevention of Nuclear War
635 Huntington Ave.
Boston, MA 02115 U.S.A.

Journalists Against Nuclear
  Extermination (JANE)
c/o Magazine Branch Acorn House
314 Grays Inn Road
London W.C.1.
U.K.

Lawyers Alliance
P.O. Box 9171
Boston, MA 02114 U.S.A.

Medical Campaign Against
  Nuclear Weapons (MCANW)
23A Tenison Road
Cambridge, CB1 2DG
U.K.

New Abolitionist Covenant
c/o Sojourners
1309 L St., N.W.
Washington, DC 20005 U.S.A.

North Carolina Council of
  Churches' Committee on
  Security, Peace and Disarmament
Bryan Bldg., 201-A
Cameron Village
Raleigh, NC 27605 U.S.A.

North Carolina Peace Network
P.O. Box 30222
Raleigh, NC 27622 U.S.A.

Nursing Campaign Against
  Nuclear Weapons (NCANW)
11 Charlotte St.
Bristol 1
U.K.

Nurses Alliance for Prevention
  of Nuclear War
P.O. Box 319
Chestnut Hill, MA 02167 U.S.A.

Operation Peace Through Unity
151 Gonzales Road Apt. 34
Santa Fe, NM 87501 U.S.A.

Pax Christi
c/o Father H.C.X. Mulholland
P.O. Box 1807
Washington, NC 27889 U.S.A.

Peace Brigades International
Box 199
Cheyney, PA 19319 U.S.A.

Peace . . . First of All
Box 285
Allendale, NJ 07401 U.S.A.

People for Peace of Southern
  Berkshire
P.O. Box 537
Great Barrington, MA 02130
U.S.A.

Physicians for Social Responsibility
210 Mason Terrace
Brookline, MA 02146 U.S.A.

Raleigh Peace Initiative
c/o Community United Church
  of Christ
814 Dixie Tr.
Raleigh, NC 27606 U.S.A.

River Edge Studio
c/o P.O. Box 343
136 R. Bank St.
New London, CT 06320 U.S.A.

Rural Southern Voice for Peace
c/o Social Concerns Dept.
Arthur Morgan School
Rt. 5
Burnsville, NC 27814 U.S.A.

Scientists Against Nuclear Arms
  (SANA)
Barbara Pearce, 11 Chapel St.
Woburn Sands
Milton Keynes MK 178 PG
U.K.

Southern California Alliance
  for Survival
Resource Center
1503 Hobart Boulevard
Hollywood, CA 90027 U.S.A.

Triangle Area Project on
  Military Spending and Human
  Needs
c/o War Resisters' League
604 W. Chapel Hill St.
Durham, NC 27701 U.S.A.

Triangle Chapter of Physicians
  for Social Responsibility
P.O. Box 3218
Chapel Hill, NC 27514 U.S.A.

Union of Concerned Scientists
1384 Massachusetts Ave.
Cambridge, MA 02138 U.S.A.

Union of Psychoanalysts and
  Psychotherapists for Nuclear
  Disarmament
Dr. Everett Angel
355 Riverdale Dr.
New York, NY 10025 U.S.A.

War Control Planners, Inc.
Box 19127
Washington, DC 20038 U.S.A.

World Association of World
  Federalists
43 Wallingford Ave.
London W10 6 PZ England

World Association of World
  Federalists
Leliegracht 21
Amsterdam
Netherlands 1016 GR

World Peace March
c/o Religious Task Force
Mobilization for Survival
85 S. Oxford St.
Brooklyn, NY 11217 U.S.A.

WORLD GOODWILL
3 Whitehall Court
Suite 51
London, England SW1A 2EF

BONNE VOLONTE MONDIALE
1 Rue de Varembe (3e)
Case Postale 31
1211 Geneva 20
Switzerland

WORLD GOODWILL
866 United Nations Plaza
Suite 566-7
New York, New York
U.S.A. 10017-1888

The Hidden Dangers of the Rainbow
*The New Age Movement and Our Coming Age of Barbarism**

I. The New Age Movement — What is it?

A. It is a worldwide coalition of networking organizations. It also includes individuals bound together by common mystical experiences. There are more than 10,000 "New Age" organizations (excluding branches) within the United States and Canada alone! Alphabetically, they range from Amnesty International through Zero Population Growth. (See *Networking: the First Report and Directory* by Jessica Lipnack and Jeffrey Stamps, Doubleday, 1982. See also *New Age Politics* by Mark Satin, Dell Books Division of E.P. Dutton, 1979.) New Age organizations include (but are not limited to) the following types:

   1. Religious cults, including the following prototypes:
      a. The Church Universal and Triumphant and its spawned organizations, Summit Lighthouse and Summit University headed by Elizabeth Clare Prophet (syncretistic mixture of exoteric "Christianity," Buddhism, Hinduism, Spiritualism, etc.);
      b. Children of God (labels itself as a New Age ashram) which is designed to appeal to young people who might otherwise be attracted to charismatic Christianity.
      c. Unity School of Christianity (headquartered in Unity Village, Missouri).
      d. 3HO (Buddhist/Hindu seekers).
      e. Ashram of Bhagwan Shree Rajneesh (syncretistic mixture of Hinduism, Buddhism, Tantric Sex (aka "free love"), holistic health, mind

*Copyright © 1983 by Constance E. Cumbey

control techniques, etc.).

2. Mind control classes and organizations such as Silva, EST (Erhard Seminars Training), New Age Thinking, TM (Transcendental Meditation), Lifespring, Arica, etc.).

3. Holistic health practitioners, many homeopathic physicians and many (but not all) nutritionists and health food stores and centers.

4. Many "appropriate technology," environmental, and ecological organizations (not all) such as Clamshell Alliance, Sierra Club, etc.

5. Political interest organizations such as the California New Age Caucus, New Organization for an American Revolution (N.O.A.R.), New World Alliance, World Federalists, SANE, Society of Emissaries (combines esotericism with political action), Friends of the Earth, Planetary Citizens, Planetary Initiative for the World We Choose, etc.

6. Intentional communities, such as Findhorn Foundation (probably the Vatican City of the New Age Movement), Stelle Community (Illinois), The Farm (Tennessee), etc.

7. Esoteric philosophy and religious groups such as Lucis Trust (probably the "brains" of the New Age Movement), Theosophical Society, Rosicrucians, etc.

8. Some organizations purporting to fight world hunger such as The Hunger Project.

9. Although not officially a part, the New Age Movement's adherents have infiltrated orthodox medical, religious, governmental, business, and other organizations.

B. It is known by many other names, including, but not limited to the following:

1. The Aquarian Conspiracy;
2. The Age of Aquarius;
3. Humanistic Psychology;
4. Networking Movement;
5. New Thought Religion;
6. The New Church;
7. The Third Wave;
8. The Third Force;
9. New Consciousness;
10. Transcendental Movement;
11. Human Potential Movement;
12. The New Spirituality;
13. Secular Humanism;
14. Humanism.

C. The principle aims of the New Age Movement include:

1. A New World Order;
2. A New World Religion;
3. A New Age Christ (who is neither Jesus nor "Christ").

D. Much New Age doctrine is found in the following sources:

1. Writings of Helena Petrovna Blavatsky (1836-91), including:
   a. *Isis Unveiled;*
   b. *The Secret Doctrine.*

2. Books of Alice A. Bailey (1880-1949), including:
   a. *The Externalisation of the Hierarchy;*
   b. *The Rays and the Initiations;*
   c. *Initiation: Human and Solar;*
   d. *The Reappearance of the Christ;*
   e. *The Destiny of the Nations;*
   f. *The Unfinished Autobiography;*
   g. *Discipleship in the New Age* (2 volumes);
   h. *Esoteric Psychology* (2 volumes).

3. Writings of Nicholas Roerich (1874-1947), including:
   a. *Maitreya* (Roerich Museum Press, 1932);
   b. *Shambhala, the Resplendent;*
   c. *The Agni Yoga* series.

4. Letters of Helena Roerich (Nicholas' wife).

5. Writings of George Gurdjieff (1872-1949).

6. Writings of H.G. Wells (1866-1946), including:
   a. *An Open Conspiracy: Blueprints for a World Revolution;*
   b. *An Outline of History* (2 volumes).

7. Writings of David Spangler (1945-   ), including:
   a. *Revelation: the Birth of a New Age* (treated as a bible within the New Age Movement);
   b. *Reflections on the Christ* (calls for Luciferic initiations on pages 44-45);
   c. *Links With Space;*
   d. *Relationship and Identity;*
   e. *The Laws of Manifestation;*
   f. *New Age Rhythms;*
   g. *Conversations With John;*
   h. *Towards a Planetary Vision.*

8. Writings of Marilyn Ferguson, including her best selling, Book of the Month Club selection, *The Aquarian Conspiracy.*

II. Roots of the New Age Movement are found in some of the world's earliest recorded traditions:

A. Many New Age esoteric historians claim their traditions originated in Atlantis.

   1. It is probable that Atlantis existed, but as the world prior to the Noachian flood — a world that God judged and condemned.

   2. New Age literature supportive of the Atlantis tradition include (but is not limited to) the following:
      a. *Isis Unveiled* by H.P. Blavatsky;
      b. *The Golden Thread* by Natalie Banks.

B. New Agers then claim that at the time of the cataclysmic destruction of Atlantis that their "White Lodge" of "Ascended Masters" then withdrew from the earth and left the earth temporarily in the control of the "Black Lodge."

A clear reading of New Age literature reveals that they define "Black Lodge" as the source of Judeo-Christian tradition and "White Lodge" as the source of their occult teachings.

C. The claim is then made that the teachings were preserved in the ancient land of Babylon and surrounding Plains of Shinar and from there disseminated throughout the earth, including Taoist doctrines of China, Mayan-Aztec teachings of Mexico and Central/South America; Great Spirit teachings of the American Indians, Hindu/Buddhist teachings of Asia, etc.

1. This clearly correlates with the biblical teachings of the building of the Tower of Babel and God's work in scattering these builders throughout the globe after confusing their language.

2. Other evidence of the probability of the truth of the biblical teaching include the following:
   a. The extreme similarity of the alphabet of the Aztecs to the Egyptian hieroglyphs;
   b. The similarity of South American pyramids to Egyptian pyramids and Babylonian ziggurats;
   c. Common legends about such things as a worldwide flood, the building of a great tower, the scattering of mankind, and the confusion of languages:
      1) It is improbable that this much could be explained away as mere "coincidence."
      2) New Age literature corroborates it — much as a negative displays a photograph.
      3) The doctrinal similarities between pagan religions of the world and the sharp doctrinal disagreement with the Judeo/Christian traditions.

         The only religion which may truly be

called a "hybrid" is that of the Muslims.

D. The biblical story of the Garden of Eden is fully borne out in the negative in the pagan religions of the world.

1. The lies of the Serpent in the Garden of Eden are preserved as doctrinal points in the pagan religions of the world:
    a. "You shall not surely die."
    b. "You shall be as gods."

2. These points are also the central theological theme of the New Age Movement, of the "New Theology" and of the so-called "Cosmic Gospels" of "UFO" visitors.

3. These points are also the doctrine of nearly every religious cult in the world today.

4. Further evidence for this may be found in the prevalence of snake worship throughout nearly every pagan religion of the world — ranging from Eskimoes to Chinese and from Aztecs to Hinduism.

E. The New Age Movement includes full-fledged worship of Lucifer.

This corroborates the biblical teaching that Lucifer was expelled from heaven for the sin of pride — for wanting to be worshipped as God — exalting himself above God.

III. Make no mistake about it, the New Age Movement *is* a religion which closely parallels all the pagan traditions of the world. It is a counterfeit — albeit a poor one — of Christian doctrine:

A. The New Age Movement has its own bibles: *Oahspe; The Aquarian Gospel of Jesus the Christ; My Truth, the Lord Himself; My Peace, the Lord Himself; The Book of Urantia; The Secret Doctrine; The Keys of Enoch: the Book of Knowledge; Revelation: the Birth of a New Age*, etc.

B. The New Age Movement has a comprehensive body of doctrine which includes the following tenets:

1. Belief in a central spiritual being known as "The Source," or "The God of Force," which is to them "God Transcendent." (Sometimes they also say that our God is something or someone known as "Sanat Kumara" — probably a scrambling of the name "Satan"!)

2. Belief in a "God Immanent" which means "god within";

3. Belief in the divinity of man as a necessary part of belief in "God Immanent" (see II. D. 1., *supra*).

4. Belief in "The Law of Rebirth" which is also known as reincarnation.

5. Belief that God is inferior to something known as "The Solar Logos."

6. Belief that Jesus and the Christ are two separate entities and that the Christ is an office rather than a man. (Note scripture 1 John 2:22 which states that the antichrist will deny that Jesus is the Christ and 1 John 4:3 which states that he will deny that Jesus Christ is come in the flesh.)

7. Belief in evolution.

8. Belief in the perfectability of man as a corollary belief to that of evolution.

9. Belief in the Law of Avatars — a teaching that at the start of every "New Age" the Solar Logos or Sanat Kumara sends "The Christ" who overshadows a human being, imparting through that possessed individual to the world "new revelation" to help them through the coming "New Age." (Christians and Jews should easily recognize this process as good old-fashioned demonic possession.)

10. Belief in salvation by initiation and works rather than by atonement and grace.

11. Belief in the interconnectedness of all things — the Doctrine of Wholeness (sometimes called holistic

thinking or in Eastern mystical terms "Atman"). This is also known as the Doctrine of At-One-Ment, a deliberate occult perversion of the Judeo/Christian word "atonement."

12. Deep and abiding hatred for Judaism, orthodox Catholicism, and Fundamentalist Christianity in particular and all Christians in general.

13. Hatred for God the Father which expresses itself to hatred for Moslems who refuse to renounce their faith in Him.

14. Belief in the existence of "masters" and of an occult hierarchy.

15. Belief in an "inner government" of the planet which is administered by this so-called hierarchy of "masters" originating from a mythical "Shamballa."

16. Belief in the perfectability of Aryan man in a path evolutionary progress towards becoming "masters."

C. The New Age Movement is identical in basic cosmology and beliefs to *both* Nazism and the Ku Klux Klan which taught all of the above.

IV. The New Age Movement poses a real and present danger to both Jews and Christians.

A. The New Age Movement has announced through many of its leaders plans to try to launch a New World Order in the near future.

1. A major such effort, the Planetary Initiative for the World We Choose, is headed by Donald Keys who openly dedicated his book to Max Heindel (Rosicrucianism — identical to KKK and Nazi racial theories) and Djwal Khul (another name for the Alice Bailey teachings).

2. The same effort also features David Spangler (the man who said we must take a Luciferic initiation to enter the New Age) on the board of its secretariat organization — Planetary Citizens of New York City.

3. The same effort also features — believe it or not — a "World Council of Wise Persons" headed by Norman Cousins! Buckminster Fuller and Dr. Carlos Romulo of the Philippines are also to serve on this "distinguished" panel.

4. According to the Alice Bailey writings, which the Planetary Initiative folks are openly following, present religious practices of orthodox Christians, Jews and Moslems are to be outlawed and will be replaced by those of the "New World Religion."

5. Another facet of their scheme to take over the world which they call "The Plan" is to bring forth a New Age "Messiah" — a so-called "Maitreya the Christ."

6. They further make the claim in the Alice Bailey writings Benjamin Creme endorses that other "masters" posing as religious "messiahs" will appear to adherents of all the major world religions to persuade them of the "truths" of the New World Religion and its "new revelations."
   a. It is claimed that the "Imam Mahdi" will appear to the Moslems to inform them they are to accept "Maitreya the Christ."
   b. It is further claimed that the "Buddha" will appear to world Buddhists to convince them their better fate lies with "Maitreya the Christ."
   c. It is further claimed that "angels" (probably demons) will appear with this so-called "Christ" to convince people that he should be followed by all men.
   d. It is even claimed that the "Master Jesus" will appear to Christians so as to settle the controversy as to whether Jesus and the Christ are one and the same and to attempt to persuade Christians that they are not. (Note 1 John 2:22. This is a distinct test of antichrist!)

7. Spokesmen for the New Age Movement (Alice Bailey, David Spangler, Nicholas Roerich, etc.), have threatened a world war in the field of world

religions and even extermination of Christians, Jews and Moslems, and others who refuse to accept Maitreya as "The Christ."

8. A similar fate awaits those who refuse to convert to the "New World Religion."

B. The New Age Movement through its seminal writings (Alice Bailey, Helena Petrovna Blavatsky, etc.) maintains the traditional occult doctrines of Aryanism and a blood taint resting on individuals of Jewish extraction.

The Movement is profoundly antisemitic all the way to its esoteric core, although many of its lesser initiates are blissfully unaware of this sordid fact.

C. These seminal teachings and writings of certain New Age leaders (Foster Bailey of Lucis Trust and Gregory Bateson) call for the ending of separation between church and state immediately.

D. The Alice Bailey writings openly followed by the leadership of the Planetary Initiative even call for using the atomic bomb for such "creative" purposes as using it on the Church of Rome and other religious groups who "don't know how to leave politics along." (See pages 191, 584 of *The Externalisation of the Hierarchy* by Alice A. Bailey!)

E. The New Age Movement's leadership is proposing to implement all the systems set forth in Revelation, chapter 13:

1. They have called for the abolishment of a cash monetary system.

2. They propose instead to institute a "more rational means of exchange" such as an economy based on a computerized barter system.

3. The openly propose to give every world resident a number and require the usage of this number in all financial transcations of any sort.

The motive here is probably not efficient feeding of folks as they claim will be done by their proposed "World Food Authority," etc. Instead it probably is that stated by R. Buckminster Fuller, a New Age leader who states that for an organization to control the world it must first control the world's supply routes. (See *The Critical Path*, St. Martin's Press, 1981, p. xx.)

4. In the interests of giving the peasants a "new mythology" to shape their necessary new world view, they plan to make their New World Religion compulsory for all.

5. They plan to institute a "New World Order" which will be a synthesis between the U.S.S.R. ("feet like a bear"), Great Britain ("spoke like a lion") and the United States ("like unto a leopard"), also featuring the ten nation Common Market nations of Europe (ten horns), and a worldwide government or "planetary guidance system."

6. The system they propose to implement is *identical* in belief systems and cosmology to the Nazi system of Adolfus Hitler (the beast that was dead and came back to life — Nazism)?!

V. The New Age Movement has characteristics of a well-thought out military operation patterned after Hitler's organization of his "Third Reich":

A. They openly call their scheme to take the world for the antichrist "The Plan."

1. Probably the main vehicle for implementation of "The Plan" at present is the Planetary Initiative for the World We Choose which is sponsored by hundreds of cooperating New Age, older, more well-established organizations, and even banks and distinguished business and university professors and presidents.

2. Planetary Citizens of New York City serves as the secretariat for the Planetary Initiative. David Spangler (the man who said we must take the Luciferic initiation to enter the New Age) serves also

on the Board of Directors of Planetary Citizens and his Lorian Association is one of the sponsoring organizations of the Planetary Initiative.

3. The Planetary Initiative went public on February 8, after an obviously well-financed and prominently supported kick-off press conference and cocktail party at the Cathedral Church of St. John the Divine, Episcopal, New York City.

B. Those inside the Movement communicate between themselves with code words and signals. Some of the code or buzz-words include:
   1. Holistic;
   2. Transformation;
   3. Spaceship Earth;
   4. Global village;
   5. Interdependent or interdependence;
   6. Manifestation or manifest;
   7. Initiation or Initiate;
   8. Crowded planet;
   9. Transcendent;
   10. Consciousness-raising;
   11. Paradigm or "new paradigm";
   12. Vision of "new vision";
   13. Global thread;
   14. New Consciousness;
   15. Planetary vision;
   16. Global vision;
   17. Transpersonal.

C. The Movement claims, according to New Age writer Mark Satin, to have something for everybody (see *New Age Politics.*).

D. According to the Alice Bailey writings and Marilyn Ferguson, author of *The Aquarian Conspiracy*, the Movement has infiltrated every aspect of modern society. According to these writers, it has also infiltrated every organization and institution.

D. Similarly to Hitler's Brownshirts, many youth are organized into the paramilitary Guardian Angels. The

Guardian Angels were the cover story on November 1981 *New Age* Magazine — an organization (the magazine) being described by the Findhorn Foundation (Findhorn serves as a type of Vatican City/Washington, D.C., for the New Age Movement) as a "light center" whose role is to help spread the New Age Movement. David Spangler serves as contributing editor of the *New Age* Magazine.

E. Hitler had a prisoner reach-out effort. So do the New Agers. Prisoners are reached by such programs as the New Age adopt-a-prisoner program, encounter programs, New Age thinking programs, Prison Ashrams, Project Start (for ex-prisoners), Silva Mind Control, TM (Transcendental Meditation), EST (Erhard Seminars Training), etc.

In *Signs of Christ* by Harold Balyoz (Altai Publishers, Agoura, California 91301: 1979) it was written of the New Age society to come that:

> "It is astounding how the world is going to ruin! The destroyers and the destroyed will be swept away. The new ones approach. From pure clean places will appear new ones: nomads and ploughmen, orphans and vagabonds, monks and convicts, scientists and singers — in short, all those strong in spirit. A legion of its own kind with understanding of spirit. . . . Accept everyone who comes to you and says a word about the spirit. Even in the hardened eyes of a brigand at times a thought of achievement gleams. And even a convict understands self-sacrifice when on watch.
>
> "I want to see your cohorts real abodes for strong spirits. Remember that Christ prayed among thieves and that Buddha revealed the sacrament to a brigand. . . ."

F. The Nazis featured a pagan style battalion known as the SS. Similarly, there is a United States Military/private hybrid equivalent to this: The First Earth Battalion headed by Lt. Colonel Jim Channon. This outfit which claims to computer linked military wide and worldwide, with influence even extending behind the Iron Curtain openly bills itself as "New Age" and states it is working to build an "army of light." Its Evolutionary Tactics manual is complete with flow and time charts. Members are initiated rather than sworn into the battalion.

G. There is a carefully planned propaganda effort which sets the tone and rationales for future persecution and violence towards Christians, Jews, and others who refuse to go forward with their New Age "Christ."

   1. Dick Sutphen's war on Fundamentalism;
   2. Norman Lear's People for the American Way;
   3. *Humanist Magazine's* ridicule of fundamentalism, etc.

H. The New Age Movement has placed a high premium on survivalism and self-reliance. Many New Agers practice "voluntary simplicity."

   1. The rationale for this is to increase susceptibility to hypnosis and "The Spirit." (See Alice Bailey books for details.)

   2. In Donald Keys' book *Earth at Omega*, he boasted that this would keep the public from becoming wise to strength of the New Age Movement:

      "We mentioned earlier how the dominant straight' society has apparently not recognized the strength and pervasiveness of the new consciousness culture. Perhaps this is just as well, as so far a polarization between the old culture and the new one has been avoided. If the New Age Movement does become a target of alarmed forces and defenders of the *status quo ante*, however, it will offer a widely dispersed and decentralized target, very hard to identify and dissuade or subvert from its life-serving values. Indeed, the expression of these values emphasizes the good old pioneering American virtues of self-reliance, thrift, self-discipline and good neighborliness, qualities tending to nullify in advance charges of deviation from desirable norms."

I. The New Age Movement went public in 1975 with an exquisitely planned and executed propaganda campaign. This campaign had been mapped out well in advance within the Alice Bailey, Angi Yoga, and H.G. Wells writings. The propaganda campaign psychologically conditions the world to accept the New Age Movement and the New Age "Christ" as well as his accompanying "hierarchy," including the following:

1. Emphasize evolution together with a corollary belief man is ultimately perfectible.

2. Teach the interconnectedness of all souls and all life and matter.

3. Teach that the "kingdom of God" is merely the appearance of "soul-controlled" men on earth in everyday life.

4. Teach that some men on earth have already reached the goal of soul-control or perfection.

5. Teach that although all men and races, etc., are equal, that they are at "varying stages of evolutionary development." (We are all equal, but some are more equal than others!)

6. Teach that there has always been a plan (The Plan) and that this plan has always been present and at varying stages of evolution throughout history.

7. Color therapy, holistic health, mind control, and iridology.

J. The New Age Movement has several important symbols for identification and mystical (hypnotic) use. They are not all used simultaneously, but all are in current use within the Movement:

1. The Rainbow (also called the Antahkarana or Rainbow Bridge). This is used as a hypnotic device. They also call it an "International Sign of Peace." They claim they are building a rainbow bridge between the personality (you) and the over-soul or Great Universal Mind (literally Sanat Kumara, i.e.,

Lucifer!). See Isaiah 24:5 which states that one reason the Lord is destroying the earth in the latter days is for breaking the everlasting covenant. The rainbow is the sign of the everlasting covenant according to Genesis, chapter nine!

2. The Triangle.

3. The Centering Symbol: a series of progressively smaller circles within a larger circle leading to a dark and distant (or light and distant) center.

4. Rays of light: to represent the seven rays they believe exist in nature and in the rainbow.

5. A cross with diagonals placed against it.

6. The Circle.

7. The circle with a point in the center (see also Centering Symbol, *supra*).

8. The circle divided into two.

9. The circle divided into four.

10. The Swastika. See pages 161, 172 of Alice Bailey's *A Treatise on Cosmic Fire* and also *Esoteric Astrology*. This is also used widely within the Theosophical Society.

11. 666: That's correct! Even the logo on *The Aquarian Conspiracy* by Marilyn Ferguson distinctly resembles a 666. Page 79 of *The Rays and the Initiations* by Alice discusses some of the meaning and "sacred qualities" of the 666. *A Treatise on Cosmic Fire* states on page 306 that 666 is the number of one of the three "heavenly" men. *The Keys of Enoch: the Book of Knowledge*, another important New Age "bible" tells initiates to use the numerical sequence as frequently as possible to hasten the coming of the so-called "New Age." This instruction is found on page 391 of that book.

12. Pegasus (the winged horse) and the Unicorn.

Selected Bibliography

This book was researched by the reading of hundreds of books and the close analysis without a full reading of many hundreds more. A full bibliography would require a volume in itself. Nevertheless, the following bibliography should be of value for anyone who wishes to gain a greater understanding of the subject.

NEW AGE DIRECTORIES AND CATALOGS:

Brand, Stewart: Editor. *The Next Whole Earth Catalog*, Access to Tools. New York, Point/Random House, 1981.

Circle Network. *Circle Guide to Wicca & Pagan Resources*. 1982-1983 Edition. Madison, Wisconsin: Circle Publications. 1981.

Circle Network. *Magickal Contacts:* An Updated Supplement to the 1981 Circle Guide to Wicca and Pagan Resources. Madison, Wisconsin: Circle Publications. 1981.

Cousteau, Jacques-Yves. *The Cousteau Almanac: An Inventory of Life on Our Water Planet.* Garden City, New York: Doubleday & Company, Inc. 1981.

Henderson, C. William. *Awakening: Ways to Psycho-Spiritual Growth.* New Jersey: Prentice-Hall, Inc. 1975.

Holzer, Hans. *The Directory of the Occult.* Chicago, Illinois 60601: Henry Regnery Company. 1974.

International Cooperation Council. *Directory for a New World: A Planetary Guide of Cooperating Organizations.* Los Angeles: International Cooperation Council. 1979. Unbelievable. A *must* for the serious New Age researcher.

Kidron, Michael & Segan, Ronald. *The State of the World Atlas.* New York: Simon & Schuster. 1981.

Kulvinskas, Viktoras, M.S. *The New Age Directory: Holistic Health Guide.* 1981 Revised and Updated Edition. Woodstock Valley, Connecticut 06282. 1981. (Includes over 3700 entries in 45 categories.)

Lipnack, Jessica & Stamps, Jeffrey. *Networking: The First Report and Directory.* Garden City, New York: A Dolphin Book, Doubleday & Company, Inc. 1982. (A must for the serious New Age researcher. This lists 1500 key networks and organizations sharing New Age values.)

Lucis Trust. *The Master Index of the Tibetan and Alice A. Bailey Books.* Agoura, California: Aquarian Educational Group. 1974. (Again, if you are contemplating serious research, this is a must!)

Paratma Singh Khalsa, Editor. *The New Consciousness Sourcebook: Spiritual Community Guide #5.* Introductions by Daniel Ellsberg and Marilyn Ferguson. Berkeley, California: Spiritual Community/NAM. 1982. (The most current directory available, but limited in scope. The same publisher makes a 10,000+ organizational directory available by special order, but I personally have been unsuccessful in securing same to date.)

Peterson, Severin. *A Catalog of the Ways People Grow.* New York: Ballantine Books. 1971.

Regush, Nicholas & June. *The New Consciousness Catalogue: A Comprehensive Guide to the Dimensions of Psychic and Spiritual Development.* New York: G.P. Putnam's Sons. 1979.

Regush, June & Nicholas. *PSI — The Other World Catalogue: The Comprehensive Guide to the Dimensions of Psychic Phenomena.* New York: G.P. Putnam's Sons. 1974.

Satin, Mark. *New Age Politics: Healing Self and Society.* New York: Dell Publishing Co., Inc., 1978, 1979. (An absolute must for gaining familiarity with the aims and euphemisms of the New Age Movement. He has an excellent list of resources compiled from the perspective of his extreme pro-New Age bias which will help you learn more of what this Movement is all about. Do not venture in the water without an excellent Bible basis, however. Unless you know the real, the counterfeit could be seductive.)

Spiritual Community Publications. *A Pilgrim's Guide to Planet Earth: A Traveler's Handbook and New Age Directory*. Introduction by Edgar D. Mitchell, Apollo Astronaut. San Rafael, California: Spiritual Community Publications. 1981.

CHRISTIAN BOOKS WITH SOME NEW AGE THEMES:

Bryant, David. *In the Gap: What it Means to Be a World Christian*. Madison, Wisconsin, Inter-Varsity Missions, Inter-Varsity Christian Fellowship. 1979, 1981.

Camara, Archbishop Dom Helder. *Race Against Time*. Denville, New Jersey: Dimension Books. 1971. (Helder is the archbishop of Brazil and leans heavily towards Pierre Teilhard de Chardin. Benjamin Creme has endorsed Camara's efforts and claimed them as evidence that Maitreya is on his way almost any day now.)

Cox, Dr. Harvey. *Turning East*. New York: Simon & Schuster. 1977.

Fontinell, Eugene. *Toward a Reconstruction of Religion*. West Nyack, New York: Cross Currents. 1979.

Fox, Matthew, O.P. *Breakthrough: Meister Eckhart's Creation Spirituality in New Transition*. Garden City, New York: Image Books Division of Doubleday & Company, 1980.

Fox, Matthew. *A Spirituality Named Compassion and the Healing of the Global Village, Humpty Dumpty and Us*. Minneapolis: Winston Press, Inc., 1979.

Fox, Matthew, O.P. *On Becoming a Musical, Mystical Bear: Spirituality American Style*. New York: Paulist Press. 1972, 1976.

Fox, Matthew, O.P. (Editor). *Western Spirituality: Historical Roots, Ecumenical Routes*. Sante Fe, New Mexico: Bear & Company, Inc. 1981.

Fox, Matthew. *Whee! We, Wee All the Way Home . . . A Guide to a Sensual, Prophetic Spirituality*. Santa Fe, New Mexico: Bear & Company, Inc., 1981.

Hesburgh, Theodore M. *The Humane Imperative: A Challenge for the Year 2000*. New Haven, Connecticut: Yale University Press. 1974.

Mooneyham, W. Stanley. *China: A New Day*. Plainfield, New Jersey: Logos International. 1979.

Mooneyham, W. Stanley. *What Do You Say to a Hungry World?* Waco, Texas: Word Books, Word, Inc., 1975.

Romney, Dr. Rodney R. *Journey to Inner Space: Finding God in Us*. Nashville, Tennessee: Abingdon Press. 1980.

Samartha, S.J. *Courage for Dialogue*. Maryknoll, New York: Orbis Books, 1982.

Sider, Ronald J. *Rich Christians in an Age of Hunger*. Downers Grove, Illinois: Inter-Varsity Press. 1977.

Sine, Tom. *The Mustard Seed Conspiracy*. Waco, Texas: Word, Incorporated. 1981.

Weaver, Dr. Horace R. *Getting Straight About the Bible*. Nashville, Tennessee: Abingdon Press. 1975 (4th Printing, 1980)

Wilkinson, Loren (Editor). *Earthkeeping: Christian Stewardship of Natural Resources* (By the Fellows of Calvin College). Grand Rapids, Michigan: William B. Eerdmans Publishing Co., 1980.

NEW AGE STRUCTURE:

Bailey, Alice A. *The Destiny of the Nations*. New York: Lucis Publishing Company. 1949. (5th Printing, 1974).

Bailey, Alice A. *Education in the New Age*. New York: Lucis Publishing Company, 1954.

Bailey, Alice A. *The Externalisation of the Hierarchy*. New York: Lucis Publishing Company, 1957.

Bailey, Alice A. *Problems of Humanity*. New York: Lucis Publishing Company. 1964 (5th Edition, 1972).

Bailey, Alice A. *The Reappearance of the Christ*. New York: Lucis Publishing Company, 1948, 1976. (9th Printing, 1979).

Creme, Benjamin. *The Reappearance of the Christ and the Masters of Wisdom*. North Hollywood, California: Tara Center, 1980.

Ferguson, Marilyn. *The Aquarian Conspiracy*. Los Angeles: J.P. Tarcher, Inc., 1980. (See credits also.)

Keys, Donald. *Earth at Omega: Passage to Planetization.* Introduction by Norman Cousins. Brookline Village, Massachusetts: Branden Press. 1982.

Fuller, Buckminster. *The Critical Path.* New York: St. Martin's Press. 1981.

Spangler, David. *Explorations: Emerging Aspects of the New Culture.* Scotland: Findhorn Publications. 1980.

Spangler, David. *Festivals in the New Age.* Scotland: The Findhorn Foundation. 1975.

Spangler, David. *Revelation: The Birth of a New Age.* Introduction by William Irwin Thompson. Elgin, Illinois: The Lorian Association. 1976.

Spangler, David. *Reflections on the Christ.* Scotland: Findhorn Foundation. 1978.

CRITIQUE OF NEW AGE CONCEPTS:

Hunt, Dave. *The Cult Explosion: An Exposé of Today's Cults and Why They Prosper.* Eugene, Oregon: Harvest House Publishers. 1980.

Hunt, Dave. *A Study Guide to the Cult Explosion.* Eugene, Oregon: Harvest House Publishers, 1981.

Wilson, Clifford, Ph.D. and John Weldon. *Occult Shock and Psychic Forces.* San Diego: Master Books, a Division of CLP. 1980.

Lemius, Rev. J.B., O.M.I., *A Catechism on Modernism,* founded on the Encyclical *Pascendi Dominici Gregis* (On Modernism) by Pope Pius X. Although founded on the writings of the Catholic Pope at the turn of the century, this is still one of the best descriptions of present-day apostasy and methods of apostasy.

Martin, Ralph, *A Crisis of Truth: The Attack on Faith, Morality and Mission in the Catholic Church,* Servant Books, 1982, Box 8617, Ann Arbor, Michigan 48107. Although this book deals primarily with apostasy within the Roman Catholic Church, everything stated applies equally to Protestant apostasy discovered in the course of my own research.

Miceli, Vincent P., *The Antichrist,* Christopher Publishing House, West Hanover, Massachusetts 23339. Although I disagree with some of the theology contained in this book, the scriptural analysis concerning the man of sin and the analysis of the dangers of occultism makes the book valuable reading for one who wants background information on the New Age Movement.

MORE GOOD BOOKS FROM HUNTINGTON HOUSE

Inside the New Age Nightmare *by Randall Baer*
Now, for the first time, one of the most powerful and influential leaders of the New Age movement has come out to expose the deceptions of the organization he once led. New Age magazines and articles have for many years hailed Randall Baer as their most "radically original" and "Advanced" thinker ... "light years ahead of others" says leading New Age magazine *East-West Journal*. His best-selling books on quartz crystals, self-transformation, and planetary ascension have won world-wide acclaim and been extolled by New Agers from all walks of life.

Hear, from A New Age insider, the secret plans they have spawned to take over our public, private, and political institutions. Have these plans already been implemented in your church, business, or organization? Discover the seduction of the Demonic forces at work — turned from darkness to light, Randall Baer reveals the methods of the New Age movement as no one else can. Find out what you can do to stop the New Age movement from destroying our way of life.
ISBN 0-910311-58-7 $7.95

The Devil's Web *by Pat Pulling with Kathy Cawthon*
This explosive exposé presents the first comprehensive guide to childhood and adolescent occult involvement. Written by a nationally recognized occult crime expert, the author explains how the violent occult underworld operates and how they stalk and recruit our children, teenagers and young adults for their evil purposes.

The author leaves no stone unturned in her investigation and absolves no one of the responsibility of protecting our children. She dispels myths and raises new questions examining the very real possibility of the existence of major occult networks which may include members of law enforcement, government officials and other powerful individuals.
ISBN 0-910311-59-5 $ 8.95 Trade paper
ISBN 0-910311-63-3 $16.95 Hardcover

From Rock to Rock *by Eric Barger*
Over three years in the making, the pages of this book represent thousands of hours of detailed research as well as over twenty-six years of personal experience and study.

The author presents a detailed exposé on: many current Rock entertainers, Rock concerts, videos, lyrics and occult symbols used within the industry. He also presents a rating system for over 1,500 past and present Rock groups and artists.
ISBN 0-910311-61-7 $7.95

The Deadly Deception: Freemasonry Exposed By One Of Its Top Leaders *by Tom McKenney*
Presents a frank look at Freemasonry and its origin. Learn of the "secrets" and "deceptions" that are practiced daily around the world. Find out why Masonry teaches that it is the true religion, that all other religions are but corrupted and perverted forms of Masonry.
ISBN 0-910311-54-4 $7.95

Lord! Why Is My Child a Rebel? *by Jacob Aranza*
This book offers an analysis of the root causes of teenage rebellion and offers practical solutions for disoriented parents. Aranza focuses on the turbulent teenage years, and how to survive those years — both you and the child!

Must reading for parents — especially for those with strong-willed children. This book will help you avoid the traps in which many parents are caught and put you on the road to recovery with your rebel.
ISBN 0-910311-62-5 $6.95

Seduction of the Innocent Revisited *by John Fulce*
You honestly can't judge a book by its cover — especially a comic book! Comic books of yesteryear bring to mind cute cartoon characters, super-heroes battling the forces of evil or a sleuth tracking down the bad guy clue-by-clue. But that was a long, long time ago. Today's comic books aren't innocent at all! Author John Fulce asserts the "super-heroes" are constantly found in the nude engaging in promiscuity, and satanic symbols are abundant throughout the pages. Fulce says most parents aren't aware of the contents of today's comic books — of what their children are absorbing from these seemingly innocent forms of entertainment. As a comic book collector for many years, Fulce opened his own comic book store in 1980, only to sell the business a few short years later due to the

steady influx of morally unacceptable material. What's happening in the comic book industry? Fulce outlines the moral, biblical, and legal aspects, and proves his assertions with page after page of illustrations. We need to pay attention to what our children are reading, Fulce claims. Comic books are not as innocent as they used to be.

ISBN 0-910311-66-8 $8.95

New World Order: The Ancient Plan of Secret Societies *by William Still*

Secret societies such as Freemasons have been alive since before the advent of Christ, yet most of us don't realize what they are or the impact they've had on many historical events. For example, did you know secret societies played a direct role in the French Revolutions of the 18th and 19th centuries and the Russian Revolution of the 20th century? Author William Still brings into focus the actual manipulative work of the societies, and the "Great Plan" they follow, much to the ignorance of many of those who are blindly led into the society's organizations. Their ultimate goal is simple: world dictatorship and unification of all mankind into a world confederation. Most Masons are good, decent men who join for fellowship but they are deceived, pulled away from their religious heritage. Only those who reach the highest level of the Masons know its true intentions. Masons and Marxists alike follow the same master. Ultimately it is a struggle between two foes — the forces of religion versus the forces of anti-religion. Still asserts that although the final battle is near-at-hand, the average person has the power to thwart the efforts of secret societies. Startling and daring, this is the first successful attempt by an author to unveil the designs of secret societies from the beginning, up to the present and into the future; and to educate the community on how to recognize the signals and to take the necessary steps to impede their progress.

ISBN 0-910311-64-1 $7.95

Hidden Dangers of the Rainbow *by Constance Cumbey*

The first to uncover and expose the New Age Movement, this national #1 bestseller paved the way for all other books on the subject. It has become a literary giant in its category. This book provides a vivid expose' of the New Age Movement, which the author contends is dedicated to wiping out Christianity and establishing a one world order. This movement, a vast network of occult and pagan organizations, meets the test of prophecy concerning the Antichrist.

ISBN 0-910311-03-X $7.95

Order These Books From Huntington House!

_____America Betrayed/*Marlin Maddoux* ....$6.95 _____
_____Backward Masking Unmasked/*Jacob Aranza* .... 6.95 _____
_____Backward Masking Unmasked Audiotapes/*Jacob Aranza* .... 6.95 _____
_____Deadly Deception: Freemasonry/*Tom McKenney* .... 7.95 _____
_____*Delicate Balance/*John Zajac*.. 7.95 _____
_____Devil Take the Youngest/*Winkie Pratney*... 7.95 _____
_____*The Devil's Web/*Pat Pulling with Kathy Cawthon*Trade paper .... 8.95 _____
                                                                   Hard cover .... 16.95 _____
_____Exposing The Aids Scandal/*Dr. Paul Cameron* .... 7.95 _____
_____*From Rock to Rock/*Eric Barger* .... 7.95 _____
_____Great Falling Away Today/*Milton Green* .... 6.95 _____
_____Hidden Dangers of the Rainbow/*Constance Cumbey* .... 7.95 _____
_____*Inside the New Age Nightmare/*Randall Baer* .... 7.95 _____
_____Jubilee on Wall Street/*David Knox Barker* .... 7.95 _____
_____Last Days Collection/*Last Days Ministries* .... 8.95 _____
_____*Lord! Why is My Child a Rebel?/*Jacob Aranza* .... 6.95 _____
_____Lucifer Connection/*Joseph Carr* .... 7.95 _____
_____Pat Robertson: A Biography/*Neil Eskelin* .... 6.95 _____
_____*New World Order/*William Still* .... 7.95 _____
_____Personalities in Power/*Florence Littauer* .... 8.95 _____
_____A Reasonable Reason To Wait/*Jacob Aranza* .... 5.95 _____
_____*Seduction of the Innocent Revisited/*John Fulce*............................... 8.95 _____
_____*To Grow By Readers/*Janet Friend / Marie Le Doux* .... 64.95 _____
_____Twisted Cross/*Joseph Carr* .... 7.95 _____

                                                 Shipping and Handling_____
                                                                     TOTAL_____

* New Titles

AVAILABLE AT BOOKSTORES EVERYWHERE or order direct from:
Huntington House, Inc., P.O. Box 53788,Lafayette, LA 70505.
Send check / money order. **For faster service use**
VISA/MASTERCARD, call toll-free 1-800-572-8213.
Add: Shipping and Handling, $2.00 for the first book ordered,
and $.50 for each additional book.

Enclosed is $_____including Shipping and Handling.

Card type: VISA/MASTERCARD #_____ Expiration date _____

NAME _____

ADDRESS _____

CITY/STATE/ZIP _____

118364